HOLLYWOOD JEWELS

HOLLYWOOD

JEWELS

MOVIES
JEWELRY
STARS

PENNY PRODDO
DEBRA HEALY,
MARION FASEL

Photography by David Be

Harry N. Abrams, Inc., Publishers

Editor: Robert Morton

Designers: Carol Robson and Amy Gottlieb

Photo Editor: Susan Sherman

Library of Congress Cataloging-in-Publication Data

Proddow, Penny.
    Hollywood jewels : movies, jewelry, stars / Penny Proddow, Debra
Healy, and Marion Fasel ; photography by David Behl.
        p.   cm.
    Includes bibliographical references and index.
    ISBN 0–8109–3412–4
    1. Jewelry—United States—History—20th century.   2. Jewelry—
History—20th century.   3. Costume jewelry—United States—
History—20th century.   4. Costume jewelry—History—20th century.
5. Motion picture actors and actresses—United States—Anecdotes.
6. Motion picture industry—United States—History.   I. Healy,
Debra.   II. Fasel, Marion.   III. Title.
NK7312.P77   1992
739.27′0973′0904—dc20   92–7769
                                                          CIP

Published in 1992 by Harry N. Abrams, Incorporated, New York
A Times Mirror Company

Printed and bound in Italy

Contents

1. The Silent Movie Era   7

2. The Talkies:
   Alluring Women,
   Jewel Thieves, Gangsters,
   and Musicals   31

3. Historical Revivals   65

4. The Glamour Years   81

5. World War II Movies   123

6. Alfred Hitchcock   139

7. Dark Themes and
   Color Extravaganzas   151

8. Elizabeth Taylor   171

Afterword   185

Acknowledgments   192

Bibliography   193

Index   195

Illustration Credits   200

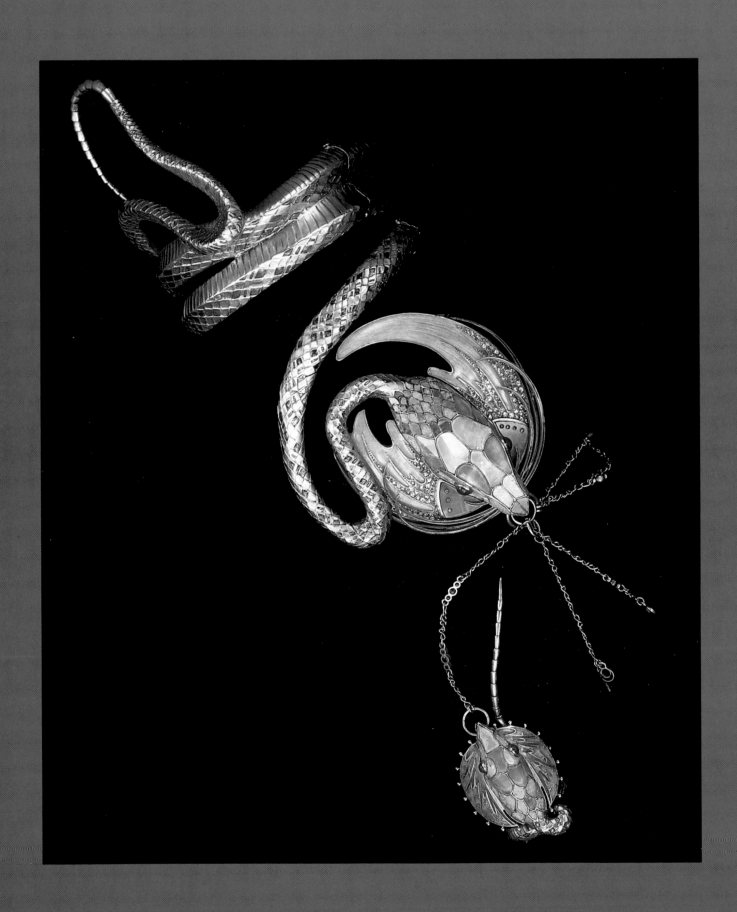

The Silent Movie Era

The humble origins of film gave no inkling whatever of the glamour that would one day be associated with the movies and movie stars. The first film strips were viewed through the peepholes of Thomas Edison's Kinetoscopes at the cost of a penny. Even after films moved out of the penny arcade to be projected onto screens in makeshift storefront theaters or in vaudeville shows, they remained very simple. Running anywhere from five to ninety seconds, they reproduced such slices of life as Edison's first film, *Fred Ott's Sneeze* (1891), or the hurtling surge of the sea in *The Beach at Dover* (1896). The most famous Edison short, the *John Rice–May Irwin Kiss* (1896), lifted from the actors' Broadway show *The Widow Jones*, gave the first hint of screen romance.

By the end of their second decade, the movies had settled into entertainment palaces, where they spun stories that held their audiences spellbound. Whether comedies, romances, or adventures, these silent movies depended heavily on costume for their success. The first wave of costume designers, most notably Paul Iribe, Natasha Rambova, and Adrian, made sophisticated statements onscreen with period, contemporary, and fantasy dress. Offscreen, the beneficiaries of an evolving star system, led by Gloria Swanson and Pola Negri, were dressing with equal flamboyance in slim beaded frocks, rich furs, bewitching hats, and increasingly lavish jewelry, as they began to attain the reputation and celebrity status of international opera singers and actresses of the legitimate stage. Initially, the stage and opera stars remained aloof from the movies, seeing them as a low form of entertainment. A few realized the importance of the new medium—among them Italian-born opera star Lina Cavalieri and Edna Goodrich—but the star who led the way and championed moviemaking was perhaps the most famous and distinguished of them all: Sarah Bernhardt.

Americans, particularly, adored the Divine Sarah, the Parisian tragedienne who commanded record appearance fees on her tours to the United States. Not at all averse to publicity, she fed the American appetite for information about her way of life with copious newspaper accounts and many photographs, and she was received in every city as an ambassador of style. At home in Paris, Bernhardt presided over a gifted coterie of playwrights, poets, novelists, actors, costumiers, and jewelers, who worked with her on various productions and directed their talents to enhancing her larger-than-life image.

Sarah Bernhardt saw in film her "one chance for immortality." Seeking to preserve her theatrical performances for future generations, she began making movies in 1900. In her first film, the famous duel scene in Shakespeare's *Hamlet,* she recreated her controversial stage role as the prince of Denmark. In the film her movements, which appeared agitated, appalled her, but she persisted in making movies, determined to conquer the new art form. For her second film, *La Tosca* (1908), of a play she had made famous, Bernhardt assembled a superb cast

Opposite: Sarah Bernhardt's 18K gold serpent forearm cuff joined to a reptile ring by a gold and enamel link chain was designed by Alphonse Mucha and executed by Georges Fouquet. Both beasts have enamel scales, opal heads, and red enamel eyes. The serpent's head rests on a crescent with diamond rays and has an articulated tail. The cuff's painterly setting of colored stones and the sculptured, textured effect of the gold serpent mount present a stunning example of the Art Nouveau style.

Sarah Bernhardt appeared as Melissinde, princess of the Orient and countess of Tripoli, in *La Princesse Lointaine.*

and crew. The results were so disappointing that the film was never released, and Bernhardt begged to have the negative destroyed so that no one would ever see it.

In 1911 she was paid $30,000 to recreate on screen her role of Marguerite Gautier in *La Dame aux camélias,* the play by Alexandre Dumas *fils* that had grossed $3 million on American tours alone. This time Bernhardt studied the medium with industry experts, and she finally succeeded. After its first screening, which generated positive reviews, American newspapers heralded the preservation of a Bernhardt play with headlines like "Canned Bernhardt Drama" from the *Indianapolis News* (March 1, 1912). Bernhardt herself proclaimed, "I have conquered a new world—that of the photoplay." The Société du Film d'Art, whose goal was to commit classical theatrical works to film, distributed *La Dame aux camélias.* One year later it asked Bernhardt, then sixty-seven years old, to make a screen adaptation of *Queen Elizabeth,* her most recent hit in Paris.

Filmed directly from the stage by a camera stationed in the audience, *Queen Elizabeth* was a static piece with excessive footage focused on immobile players simply moving their lips. However, critics on both sides of the Atlantic found much to recommend the production and studied the costumes and sets. Bernhardt's long, brocaded robes were designed by Paul Poiret, the couturier responsible for banishing the corset and, with it, the hourglass figure. Her jewelry presented a modification of contemporary styles, with ropes of pearls and beads festooned from the sleeves and ruffs of her costume. Commenting on Bernhardt's penchant for theatrical jewelry, the *Boston Transcript* (April 25, 1912) singled out the

In *Queen Elizabeth* (1912) Bernhardt asserts her regal bearing before the kneeling earl of Essex (Lou Tellegen). Costing more than $250,000 this was the first feature-length movie ever made. From the Poiret gowns and precious jewelry to historic documents on loan from the British government, nothing was spared on the production and it became a world hit.

diamonds and pearls of her yellow silk brocade gown and the highly visible baroque pearl displayed in her reddish wig. To add authenticity, producer Daniel Frohmen persuaded the British government to loan several important documents of English history—including the decree by the queen making Essex lord lieutenant of Ireland and Essex's death warrant.

After the international success of *Queen Elizabeth,* Bernhardt went on to make more films of plays. In 1912 a documentary, titled *Sarah Bernhardt at Home,* was shot at her chateau on the Brittany coast. In it, the public was treated to a view of Bernhardt's personal life, which included family meals, tennis matches, and glimpses of her menagerie—a cheetah, a python, and a pack of dogs. The actress was also shown painting and making sculpture, arts she pursued along with her theatrical work.

In the course of Bernhardt's long career, she built up a substantial jewelry collection. She bought pieces in Paris and also collected objects on her international tours. At Tiffany & Co. in New York, for example, Bernhardt acquired a toilet set with a silver bowl large enough to bathe in.

Bernhardt also received special jeweled gifts from her admirers. Poet Victor Hugo gave her a pear-shaped diamond, which he called a tear after she appeared in his plays *Ruy Blas* and *Hernani.* As a gift to her as his leading lady in 1895, Edmond Rostand had a script of his play *La Princesse Lointaine* bound and studded with jewels.

Though her vast jewelry collection encompassed a wide range of styles, Bernhardt is chiefly remembered today for her influence on Art Nouveau jewelry. Eye-catching, thought-provoking, and even slightly sinister, this jewelry delighted the demimonde, a group of actresses, dancers, and "kept" women for whom colorful, enamel Art Nouveau jewels, with their unexpected subject matter, were an appealing alternative to the traditional gem-set jewelry worn on formal occasions.

The Art Nouveau jewelers of Paris were inspired by the major scientific and artistic currents of the second half of the nineteenth century. Charles Darwin's *Origin of the Species* (1859) had provided a shocking view of the natural world, and heated controversy surrounding Darwin's theories of evolution challenged the accepted Christian theology of Creation, making nature one of the foremost issues of the period. Also, in the 1880s Impressionist painters held exhibitions of their new paintings, which broke with the rigid, formulaic, academic style of the time. These paintings presented images as groupings of fragmented tones and hues, astonishing the public and changing the direction of Western art. Simultaneously, photographs and Japanese prints were being exhibited showing unusual angles and cropped corners.

Artist jewelers reacted to the ferment of such influences with new subjects and unique forms, colors, and materials: New landscapes of shaded forests and swan-filled lakes became subjects for brooches and pendants. Numerous varieties of reptiles, bees, insects, and even trilobites (prehistoric creatures found only in paleontology textbooks) began to appear in jewelry. Serpents gaped with open jaws, and swarms of bees lit with spread wings. To approximate the fluidity of nature, oval and circular pendant frames were discarded, as were the predictable symmetries of necklace and bracelet forms.

Edmond Rostand, author of *La Princesse Lointaine*, gave Sarah Bernhardt a copy of the text bound in beige leather with a diamond and citrine lily on the cover. The lily echoed the crown she wore in the play. The binding has a scrolling clasp of hessonite garnets, peridots, tourmalines, rose-cut diamonds, and a cabochon amethyst. These unusual stones were chosen for their muted colors, popular in the late nineteenth century. Bernhardt's motto, "Quand Même" ("In Spite Of"), encloses her entwined initials in gold letters on the back. Whether Rostand and Bernhardt had an affair is disputed, but he showed his devotion to her in a dedicatory poem, handwritten on the front page of the book. Dimensions: $7\frac{5}{8} \times 5\frac{3}{4} \times \frac{5}{8}$ in.

Art Nouveau jewelry was distinguished by its use of enamel, a powdered glass that was colored with metallic oxides and fused onto metal in a kiln. Several different enamel techniques created a variety of effects. The plique-à-jour technique produced a backless enamel fused within metallic cells, giving the effect of stained glass; it was used for the transparent wings of insects and butterflies. En ronde bosse, an overall surface technique, was employed on such three-dimensional areas as the body of an insect or a tree trunk. Champlevé enamel, loosely packed in engraved areas or metallic cells and fired repeatedly until the enamel was flush with the jewel's surface, served for highlighted details—the individual feathers of a swan or the scales of a fish.

The most famous Art Nouveau jeweler, René Lalique, began his career as an apprentice to the Parisian jeweler Aucoc, whom Dumas had chosen to be his heroine Marguerite Gautier's special jeweler. In turn, Lalique, with his feel for dramatic jewelry, attracted the attention of Bernhardt, who later played Marguerite. For the 1894 production of *Theodora*, Lalique made Bernhardt a magnificent crown with snakes, griffins, and shoulder-length hanging beads. For *La Princesse Lointaine*, in 1895, Lalique is believed to have made Bernhardt's crown and a sapphire ring. She later gave the ring to Edmond Rostand's son, Maurice, who wore it all his life in her memory. And, to celebrate Bernhardt's twenty-nine years in the theater, Lalique designed a gold commemorative medal that depicted her profile in high relief. Lalique was also so inspired by Bernhardt's own skills as a sculptor that he based some of his designs for a jewelry collection shown at the Paris Exposition of 1900 on her studies of animals, flowers, and flowing-haired maidens.

Another Art Nouveau jeweler whom Sarah Bernhardt favored was Georges Fouquet. Fouquet took over his father's firm in 1895 and made the transition from his father's sculptural Renaissance style to Art Nouveau. The change was not at first applauded. In 1898 at the Salon de la Société des Arts Français, his first jewelry exhibited was criticized as heavy. One critic complained that the gold work resembled that of a bronze worker rather than that of a jeweler. The next year Fouquet enlisted Sarah Bernhardt's theatrical manager and artistic director, Alphonse Mucha, to improve the design of the firm's jewelry. Mucha had overseen Bernhardt's productions for six years and had designed the Art Nouveau posters that featured her image.

Mucha and Fouquet together created a linked forearm cuff and ring with a serpent motif, a jewel in keeping with Bernhardt's exotic image. The jewel marked the beginning of a two-year collaboration between Fouquet and Mucha during which the designer not only conceived imaginative Art Nouveau jewelry but also restyled the interior and exterior of Fouquet's salon. Mucha's efforts brought Fouquet into the ranks of the leading Art Nouveau jewelers. Though Fouquet probably sold Bernhardt other jewels in the intervening years, the only piece recorded is a modest sapphire and white enamel friendship ring, which the actress gave to Suzanne Seylor in 1910.

Although Art Nouveau jewelry never fully caught on in the United States, Americans were fascinated by the European sensibility that produced it. Bernhardt's breathtaking collection of jewelry made for her by the best artist-jewelers highlighted her sultry demeanor and embodied the sensuous life-style of the avant-garde of the 1900s.

Film exhibitor Adolph Zukor, perceiving the box-office potential of Bernhardt, paid $35,000 for the American distribution rights to *Queen Elizabeth*. He elevated her American movie debut, on July 12, 1912, to an evening of theater, completely remodeling the Lyceum Theatre in New York into a plush movie palace for the occasion, and inviting a more sophisticated audience than had ever before been seen at the movies.

Continental glamour paid off magnificently. Bernhardt's international star stature and dramatic performance made Zukor's reputation and gave him a hit, providing him with the funds to finance his own movie company. The company, called Famous Players Film Company, was to fulfill his vision, "famous players in famous plays"—an idea he had once scribbled on the back of an envelope. (Famous Players evolved into Famous Players–Lasky Corporation and, eventually, Paramount Pictures Corporation.) Bernhardt reinforced the point: A star could sell a movie.

At this time Thomas Edison's film companies, collectively known as the Edison Trust, controlled both the making and the distribution of all movies. In an effort to keep costs and salaries down, the Edison Trust limited the length of movies to one- or two-reelers and denied screen credit to actors, directors, and writers. Carl Laemmle, head of Independent Motion Picture Company of America (IMP) and a rabid and outspoken opponent of the trust, realized the value of two players for one of the trust companies, Biograph, who were known anonymously as The Biograph Girl and Little Mary to the public that avidly followed them on screen. He schemed to get them for his own company, secretly signing a contract with "Biograph Girl" Florence Lawrence in 1910 and then planting a newspaper story saying that she had been killed by a streetcar. Later Laemmle said that Biograph had issued this story to keep the truth from getting out—that Lawrence was

An Art Nouveau pendant of a woman's profile by René Lalique bears a striking resemblance to Bernhardt as she was depicted in posters by Mucha. The face is of pale enamel and the hair of purple plique-á-jour enamel crowned with orange, yellow, green, black, and pale blue plique-á-jour enamel flowers on leafy stems, accented with a circular-cut peridot and hessonite garnet, mounted in gold. Dimensions: 3⅜ × 3¼ in.

moving to IMP. Soon afterward, with less melodrama but equal fanfare, "Little Mary" Pickford defected from Biograph to IMP to begin a new career under her own name.

Pickford was one of the first major stars of the Hollywood star system. She enchanted the public with her little-girl looks and roles. In the United States she was known as America's Sweetheart and abroad as the World's Sweetheart. Movie audiences could not get enough of her naïveté and innocence on screen, and, at twenty-seven, in *Pollyanna* (1920), she was still playing a twelve-year-old. Her publicity campaigns were in keeping with her screen personality; during the height of her fame as a silent star, she was rarely photographed in any jewel more elaborate than a pearl necklace, although she shopped at Cartier in Paris and New York for jeweled items that she wore at private parties. In the late twenties and early thirties, her collection of Art Deco jewelry, consisting of wide diamond bracelets, chokers, and necklaces, set predominantly with rubies, was commensurate with her position as a leading star and pioneer of American film.

Where business was concerned, Little Mary Pickford was a seasoned professional second to none. She brilliantly orchestrated her career, moving from studio to studio and upgrading her contracts with every move. By 1916 Adolph Zukor was paying Pickford $10,000 a week, with a $300,000 bonus, and he formed the Mary Pickford Company, a subsidiary studio devoted solely to her films for Famous Players. Still dissatisfied with her contract and income, Pickford moved to First National, where she received $350,000 a picture.

In 1919, with D. W. Griffith, who began his career directing movies for Biograph, Mary Pickford, Douglas Fairbanks, and Charlie Chaplin formed their own studio, United Artists Corporation, which removed them from studio interference and gave them control over their careers, movies, financing, and salaries. The formation of the studio prompted an industry wag to make the now-famous remark, "The lunatics have taken over the asylum." The following year Mary Pickford and Douglas Fairbanks married, an alliance that further increased their fame and power. Moviegoers all over the country wanted to hear about their every activity together.

The age of the movie star was in ascendance. Fans developed an insatiable appetite for information about the stars' lives, from the details of their wardrobes to the scandals in their private affairs and the machinations of their dealings with studios, and the magazines that had once devoted pages to movie plots switched to personal-interest stories about the stars. One of the first fan magazines, established in 1911, was *Photoplay*, a splashy journal that grabbed the attention of its readers through titillating headlines, a constant flow of gossip, innuendo, movie trivia, fashion, and a few hard facts. In a more civilized tone, the elite magazine *Vanity Fair* also reviewed actresses and charted their careers.

Ironically, the prestigious women's fashion magazines, *Vogue* and *Harper's Bazaar*, which would eventually make a regular practice of using movie actresses as models, rarely mentioned movie stars in the formative years of Hollywood. The most fashionable actresses presented in *Vanity Fair*, or any other fashion or movie magazine, were opera stars, who were making the transition from the stage to the screen. Their jewelry had been itemized by the press since the nineteenth century, when they began making highly publicized world tours, and just a glimpse or description of their treasures during performances and public appearances made headlines. Not for another twenty-five years would the jewelry of movie stars be reviewed with such enthusiasm, detail, and accuracy.

On November 24, 1906, the *St. Louis Star* announced, "The most beautiful woman in the world has arrived in the United States." The subject of the piece was the European opera singer Lina Cavalieri. One day later, the newspaper reflected that Broadway beauties might be considered as beautiful as Cavalieri, "if only they had her luck in clothes and diamonds." Cavalieri's jewelry was estimated to be worth half a million dollars. Among her many gifts from admirers were a string of pearls that had belonged to Italy's Queen Margherita, an emerald necklace, once the property of Queen Marie Leszczynska, wife of Louis XV, and an emerald collaret that had been in the possession of Lady Emma Hamilton. Over the years, a general jewelry list for Cavalieri swelled to include: a thirty-inch rope of diamonds, seven yards of pearls, a two-inch wide, one-yard-long ribbon of woven diamonds and pearls, as well as numerous coronas, collarets, tiaras, necklaces, bow brooches, rings, and individual diamonds ranging in size from acorns to walnuts. When her marriage to an American fortune hunter fell through, Cavalieri explained it to the press by revealing that his wedding present to her had been a mere platinum ring—with no diamond.

Lina Cavalieri was one of a small group of international opera stars, which included Dame Nellie Melba, Mary Garden, and Anna Case (wife of silver magnate Clarence MacKay and future mother-in-law of songwriter Irving Berlin), who mingled with royalty, dressed in equal splendor, and collected important jewelry, which, more often than not, came from Cartier.

With roots in Paris and a flourishing branch in New York, Cartier catered to a wide range of women, all of whom wanted the rarest pearls and the finest gems.

Jacques Cartier sails on a pearl ship to Maharrek on the coast of Bahrain in the Persian Gulf in 1911. Uniquely among jewelers, he often traveled to the sources of pearls and gems to ensure that the family firm kept its supremacy in world markets.

On June 20, 1920, newlyweds Mary Pickford and Douglas Fairbanks set sail for Europe. Pickford's sautoir can be seen through her fur collar.

The firm was established in 1847 by Louis-François Cartier. It began a steady rise to prominence during the Second Empire and the reign of Napoleon III, when styles were arbitrated by Princess Mathilde and Empress Eugénie, his first important clients. After the Franco-Prussian War, Cartier's son Alfred transformed the enterprise into an emporium, with jewelry, works of art, porcelain, fans, and small sculptures to entice a new clientele of bankers and industrialists. In 1902 Cartier created twenty-seven diamond tiaras for the coronation of Edward VII of England, after which a branch was opened in London. Cartier's reputation was assured throughout Europe as the finest court jewelers, with seventeen royal appointments.

The Cartier tradition of quality and artistry was further enhanced in the teens by Alfred Cartier's three sons, Louis, Alfred, and Jacques. When Jacques Cartier came of age, he traveled to form alliances with the merchants, sheiks, and princes who controlled the trade and supply of precious gems. This guaranteed a flow of materials for precious jewelry to Paris through channels that no other retailing firm had managed to discover.

A principal of the family firm, Jacques Cartier maintained close contact with merchants in the East to make sure that Cartier kept its supremacy in world markets of pearls and gems. Cartier's biographer Hans Nadelhoffer wrote of this period, "Whenever a perfect pearl was found in the Persian Gulf, the whole of the European pearl trade was put on a state of alert." To assemble necklaces of pearls that were perfectly matched in color and graduated in size, women waited as long as ten years.

Jacques Cartier was the first French jeweler to realize the potential of the American market. He opened an office at 712 Fifth Avenue in New York in 1909. By 1915 he had expanded his business considerably and cleverly swapped a necklace with two rows of pearls for a mansion at 633 Fifth Avenue.

The firm's association with actresses began early in the century. First came opera singers, whose collections consisted of pearl necklaces, intricate diamond and platinum chains, and tiaras in grand European court styles. Lina Cavalieri and Queen Elizabeth of Belgium each purchased a Cartier kokoshnik tiara in the Louis XV style. (A kokoshnik is a flaring, oversized headdress whose design was inspired by a cock's comb.) One of the wickedest jewelry stories involving Cartier jewelry was initiated by Cavalieri when she bested the famous Spanish dancer La Belle Otero at the Monte Carlo Casino. After several days in an unofficial competition to outshine each other, La Belle Otero put on her Cartier bolero—a network of diamonds set with emeralds—her diamond shoe buckles, necklaces, bracelets, and rings and waited to confront Cavalieri in the casino. When Cavalieri stepped over the threshold, it was clear to observers, and to at least one American reporter, that the diva had devilishly outwitted her rival. Cavalieri had given her priceless jewelry collection to her maid to carry on a cushion while she herself entered in a simple gown.

Cavalieri started a second career as a film star in 1914. Her first film, for the Playgoers Film Company, was *Manon Lescaut* (1914), in which she starred opposite her third husband, tenor Lucian Muratore. Despite the lack of sound, the production was termed a film opera. Two years later, the couple made another successful silent film opera, *Shadow of Her Past*, for Pathé Exchange, the American branch of the French company. Signing with Paramount Pictures, Cavalieri started to make films in earnest, beginning with *The Eternal Temptress* (1917). Opening with a triumvirate of temptresses—Persephone, Aspasia, and Cleopatra—the film traces the effect of such exotic females on men and nations. As a major star at Paramount, with her screen successes mounting, Cavalieri was confirmed as a Hollywood star when she made the cover of *Photoplay* in 1918.

During a press conference for *The Eternal Temptress*, a reporter asked Cavalieri if her pearls were real. Deeply offended, she retorted for the benefit of the *New York Telegraph* (November 4, 1917), "Of course they are real. I never wear imitation." The intense demand for pearls made the artificially cultivated pearls patented by Japanese scientist Mikimoto widely available in the late teens. The lack of distinction between the two types of pearls caused a furor among the jewelers in Paris, who took their case to the Chambres Syndicales de la Bijouterie-Joaillerie, where it was ruled that the artificially cultivated pearls must be called cultured. The presence of cultured and imitation pearls lifted the price and reputation of real pearls, and it became a point of honor for a woman like Cavalieri to possess only natural pearls.

Movie studios took advantage of the coverage fan magazines offered to push forward their candidates for stardom. A little-remembered silent-film actress, Edna Goodrich, was publicized in *Photoplay* for her film from Mutual, *Reputation* (1917). Goodrich had made her debut in 1900 at the New York Casino Theater as one of the original members of the Florodora Sextet, an auspicious start. She won further publicity as one of the highest-paid show girls in America when she toured with Anna Held's company. Her first starring role was in a Napoleonic drama. By 1905 Goodrich was buying the rights for and producing

Dressed in a frock by couturiere Jeanne Lanvin, Mary Pickford was "America's sweetheart." She wears a valuable pearl and diamond sautoir, a type of necklace traditionally composed of a seed pearl chain terminating in diamond-capped tassels.

Pickford's forty-inch sautoir comprises two strands of three-millimeter pearls. The necklace was her favorite daytime accessory.

16

and starring in her own plays. Around this time she married an equally well-known actor and producer, Nat C. Goodwin. Both made the transition from the New York stage to Hollywood movies on the strength of their national following.

Goodrich wore a king's ransom of precious jewels in *Reputation*—a diamond tiara, crowns, necklaces, and rings of pearls, sapphires, and diamonds. At this time studios were experimenting with different ways of enticing the public to go to the movies, and the appearance of lavish jewels in *Reputation* was its prime attraction. The actress's personality, her life history, and even the plot of the movie were subsidiary to the jewelry coverage.

In their search for stars, some studios looked beyond opera and the stage and created screen originals. Of these, few were more original than Theda Bara. William Fox, longtime adversary of the Edison Trust and head of Fox Studios (eventually Twentieth Century–Fox), transformed Theodosia Goodman, born in Cincinnati, Ohio, into an exotic star. The Fox publicity department announced that her (new) name was an anagram for Arab Death, her astrological signs were those of Cleopatra, and her parentage was French and Egyptian. Bara traveled to press conferences in a white limousine attended by male Nubian slaves. She addressed reporters while fondling serpents in a darkened room redolent with incense. The public thrilled.

Bara's jewels were in keeping with her image. "The sparkle of diamonds fascinates me. But only through the [shop] window," she wrote in her nationally syndicated newspaper column for May 22, 1916. "I do not care for diamonds as a personal decoration." More to her taste was an unusual emerald ring reportedly given to her by a blind sheik, the last of his line, who encouraged her to pray to the jewel—engraved with a camel and a dog—whenever the need arose. She also owned a jade Mandarin necklace, whose chain contained exactly 108 beads. And in all her movies, she wore an oval turquoise ring she called her talisman, either on her finger or concealed in her clothing.

In forty pictures made over a period of four years Bara played a series of women who lead men to disaster and ruin. In her first film, *A Fool There Was* (1915), the word *vampire* was shortened to *vamp* to describe her character, thus creating a new noun which also doubled as a verb, as well as a new movie type for actresses. In the same film, Bara's command to a doomed lover on the title card, "Kiss me, you fool," was quickly assimilated as a popular saying.

An ideal vamp in looks and temperament, Pola Negri took up where Theda Bara left off. The Polish-born Negri became a star in two German films, *The Eyes of a Mummy* (1918) and *Gypsy Blood* (1918), both directed by Ernst Lubitsch. In 1923 Adolph Zukor brought Negri from Europe to Famous Players–Lasky to groom her for even greater glory. She personified the sleek European look with her stark white-powder makeup, rouged lips, and a *garçonne* haircut—short and shaved in the back—that which emphasized her chin line and long neck. She wore deftly chosen precious jewelry.

Touring the Lasky studios with Jesse L. Lasky in 1922 before she signed her contract, she wore her long diamond pearl-studded bar pin with a bold plaid suit. Another jewel from her collection, the openwork medallion with diamond spokes centering on a button pearl, accessorizes her period costume in *Forbidden Paradise* (1924). This sophisticated comedy, directed by Lubitsch, stars Negri as

New York stage actress, theatrical producer, and silent movie star Edna Goodrich wears a diamond bow in the Garland style, descriptive of the wreaths, bows, and tassels that characterized late-nineteenth- and early-twentieth-century diamond jewelry. Goodrich also wears two long necklaces of diamonds in round platinum mounts called collets. The small diamonds in her bow and collet necklaces were readily available: the discovery of the Kimberley diamond mines in South Africa in the nineteenth century provided jewelers with a virtually limitless supply of stones.

Inset: Lina Cavalieri was photographed by Victor Georg for a *Vanity Fair* profile in 1918 to announce her first film for Paramount, *The Eternal Temptress.* She wears a double emerald drop bead and diamond necklace with a diamond pendant, diamond earrings, and a Louis XV-style diamond diadem from Cartier.

In *Cleopatra* (1917) Theda Bara wore a costume that oozed sensuality. Her diadem is pharaoh's cobra symbol, the Uraeus, and her serpent bra is composed of coiled metal snakes with synthetic jeweled heads and heavy, rectangular link straps. The whole costume echoes the sinuous, avant-garde Art Nouveau gold jewelry made by such European artist-jewelers as Lalique and Fouquet.

Right: Theda Bara displays the turquoise ring that she was never without. She called the delicate nineteenth-century jewel her talisman.

Opposite: Pola Negri wears the diamond necklace, suspending a medallion with circular-cut diamond spokes and a button pearl center, that she wore in *Forbidden Paradise* (1924). She combines it with three matching strands of round diamonds in square mounts and a diamond and gem-set bracelet. Her tiered, diamond girandole earrings took their name from similar earrings worn by eighteenth-century Spanish nobility.

Queen Katherine, an all-powerful ruler whose jilted lover Alexei (Rod La Rocque) joins a revolutionary plot against her. Negri's medallion gleams regally against the dark fur ruff of her tight-fitting beaded gown.

A star from the moment she arrived, Negri told the studio personnel to address her only as Madame Negri. One of the first actresses to smoke cigarettes in a movie, she was popular on screen for her passionate and exotic personality. Offscreen, her affair with Rudolph Valentino made headlines in the fan magazines.

Pola Negri's grand entrance in Hollywood ignited a legendary feud with another star in Zukor's firmament, Gloria Swanson. Fan magazines observed that Negri's European fame, sultry looks, wardrobe, and jewelry threatened American Swanson's supremacy and declared them enemies from the start, reporting on their career moves as if they were military maneuvers. When Swanson went to make her movies at the Famous Players–Lasky Studios in Astoria, Queens, the magazines claimed that Zukor had to distance her from Negri's animosity.

The director-general of Famous Players–Lasky, Cecil B. DeMille, was primarily responsible for Swanson's reign of glory. After Mary Pickford's defection,

Pola Negri's ring reveals an appreciation for late-nineteenth-century Continental styles. A small rose-cut diamond flower pot is the centerpiece on a royal blue enamel background in a frame of even smaller rose-cut diamonds set in a gold mount. Dimensions: $3/4 \times 1/2$ in.

A publicity still of Pola Negri's jewelry reveals that by the early 1920s Hollywood stars were beginning not only to assemble, but to flaunt their personal collections. Her selection includes: a gold mesh evening purse with a diamond frame, c. 1919; a diamond bracelet, c. 1923; a medallion necklace, c. 1918; a string of pearls; a pearl and diamond bar pin; two single stone diamond rings; and a black pearl ring.

DeMille persuaded Zukor to let the studio create its own stars rather than pay top dollar to established players. And DeMille saw star quality in the Mack Sennett comedienne Gloria Swanson, whose looks had the exoticism that DeMille wanted for his extravagant productions. Together DeMille and Swanson made *Male and Female* (1919), *Don't Change Your Husband* (1919), *Why Change Your Wife?* (1920), *Forbidden Fruit* (1921), and *The Affairs of Anatol* (1921).

Swanson sailed through these DeMille films in costumes that echoed couture but were actually exaggerated creations accessorized with more jewels, feathers, and furs than even the most profligate woman would consider donning in real life. With Swanson, DeMille took the movie viewer into the most intimate parts of the home—the boudoir and the bathroom—previously unexplored in the cinema. When Swanson disrobed and stepped into her sunken, pool-size marble bath in *Male and Female*, all viewers were transfixed—and some were shocked. DeMille's combination of graphic and suggestive staging was one of the reasons Hollywood created the censorial Motion Picture Producers and Distributors of America, with former postmaster general Will Hays as moral arbiter.

To play her part as star, Famous Players–Lasky wanted Swanson to exude glamour offscreen as well as on. Two special clauses were written into her contract demanding that she watch her weight and appear publicly dressed only in the latest fashions. Swanson spent a fortune on her clothes. In 1924 *Photoplay* reported the annual figures for her wardrobe: shoes, $5,000; silk stockings, $9,600; perfume, $6,000; headdresses, $5,000; purses, $5,000; lingerie, $10,000; wraps, $10,000; furs, $25,000; gowns, $50,000. Jewelry was the most expensive item, and to provide the amount of precious jewelry that was necessary to accessorize an already elaborate wardrobe, Swanson rented her jewelry at ten percent of its cost. One year she ran up a rental bill of $500,000—meaning she wore $5 million worth of jewelry. Fan magazines dubbed Swanson a clotheshorse, and women all over America tried to emulate her style. When Eddie Cantor chided Swanson about the epithet, she quipped, "I don't mind, Eddie, it happens to be true. I have to work like a horse to have these clothes."*

Ironically, by 1924 Swanson had become such a big star that Famous Players–Lasky, the studio that had created her, was forced to pay her a million dollars a year to keep her. Around Hollywood it was often said that Swanson was "the second actress to make a million and the first to spend it." Unlike the adroit businesswoman Mary Pickford, Swanson quickly spent her money—on mansions, husbands, furs, and jewelry. In 1925 Swanson married into an old French family and further enhanced her star status by becoming the Marquise de la Falaise de la Coudraye. She was the darling of every echelon of society and epitomized the free-spirited, wealthy American woman of the Roaring Twenties.

After her final film for Famous Players–Lasky, *Fine Manners* (1926), Swanson left DeMille and the studio to be the producer-star of her own movie company, financed by her close friend and admirer Joseph Kennedy (President John F. Kennedy's father). Partly as a result of her support of director Eric von Stroheim and his extravagant film *Queen Kelly* (1928), in which she starred, and partly because of her inability to choose the right vehicles for a continuing career in talking pictures, Swanson's company began to lose money, and in 1934 she retired from the movies.

* Eddie Cantor, *As I Remember Them* (New York: Duell, Sloan and Pearce, 1963), 88.

In her final film for Famous Players–Lasky, *Fine Manners* (1926), Swanson portrays a feisty small-time Irish actress named Orchid Murphy, who is swept away to Park Avenue by her wealthy young fiancé. At his Aunt Agatha's apartment she is taught fine manners—and the connoisseurship of pearls. The long pearl necklace worn by Swanson in *Fine Manners* represents one of the most widespread pearl styles of the Roaring Twenties, one that spelled wealth as well as chic. Because the three- to four-millimeter pearls that made up these necklaces were very costly to assemble, women added imitation pearls to authentic necklaces to achieve the desired length. (Courtesy Paramount Pictures)

Above: Gloria Swanson removes a miniature powder puff from a pearl tassel vanity suspended from a woven seed-pearl ribbon necklace. Although vanities and tassels were common in the 1920s, a powder or rouge compartment hidden in a tassel was unusual.

Above, left: Swanson wears a pearl choker with graduated pearls intersected by emerald beads suspending an emerald and pearl tassel.

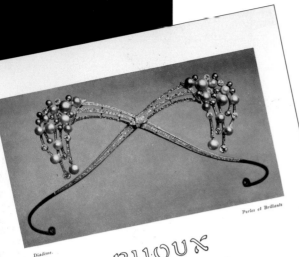

Perles et Brillants

Diadème.

BIJOUX
dessinés par IRIBE

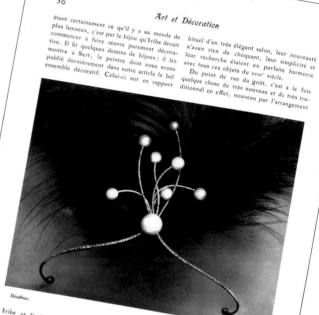

Diadème.

étant certainement ce qu'il y a au monde de plus luxueux, c'est par le bijou qu'Iribe devait commencer à faire œuvre purement décorative. Il fit quelques dessins de bijoux; il les montra à Sert, le peintre dont nous avons publié dernièrement dans notre article le bel ensemble décoratif. Celui-ci mit en rapport

bituel d'un très élégant salon, leur nouveauté n'avait rien de choquant, leur simplicité et leur recherche étaient en parfaite harmonie avec tous ces objets du XVIII° siècle.

Du point de vue du goût, c'est à la fois quelque chose de très nouveau et de très traditionnel en effet, nouveau par l'arrangement

Iribe et l'orfèvre Robert Linzeler, et les dessins furent ainsi réalisés.

Les bijoux ont été exposés récemment et comme encore on ne l'avait pas fait. Suspendus sur de longues tiges de métal, posés sur des turbans, devant des aigrettes, sur des coussins de soie, à l'angle de commodes, de guéridons, de consoles anciennes, entourés de tapisseries, de tableaux, devant des sièges de damas ou de Beauvais, dans le décor ha-

des couleurs, le mélange du vert et du violet, l'émeraude et l'améthyste, le blanc mat des perles entourant l'améthyste, le blanc mat des par le choix des pierres de couleurs employées seules sans le secours de l'émeraude, ce qu'on ne pouvait admettre dans un bijou de grand prix et vraiment somptueux; nouveau aussi par la disposition des pierres, perles suspendues à des fils de brillants, emploi de pierres calibrées non plus pour des entourages

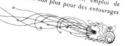

EPUIS quelque temps, on voyait dans la conception du bijou se former une tendance nouvelle. Des gens de goût, extrêmement rares, avaient

ratif dont la matière est le plus opulente. Mais on voulait s'affranchir des deux tendances d'après lesquelles depuis vingt ans les joailliers avaient travaillé, la première celle de Lalique, la seconde celle de Cartier, réaction déjà contre la première. Le bijou exécuté d'après la conception de Lalique, était le plus souvent un bijou charmant de couleur. Des pendentifs en pierre et en émail ont pu rappeler quelques délicieux tableaux et certaines teintes d'émail faisaient songer à des reflets de lumière dans des paysages de Claude Monet ou de Sisley. Il y avait là une recherche de la couleur, un goût pour l'éclat des pierres qui était très original à ce moment et qui heureusement devait se conserver sans qu'on ait pu cependant en tirer tout le parti qu'il pouvait fournir. Trop souvent les pierres employées étaient de qualité médiocre; elles

donné l'idée de bijoux très simples, anneaux de pierre calibrés, gros cabochons ou pierres taillées posées sur un fil de platine, ou au centre d'une barrette de

On recherchait une on combinait des lignes et on arrivait ainsi à tinguée, mais aussi très fâcheuse da

dans la composition du bijou qu'une

Bijoux d'Iribe

ou des lignes droites, mais pour un rayonnement par exemple et comme un prolongé d'une pierre dont on a voulu augmenter l'effet; nouveau surtout par le dessin d'une si grande simplicité, si naturelle souvent qu'on s'étonne de n'y avoir pas songé. Rien n'est aussi simple que soi-même épingle de jabot, éclatement lumineux d'une

du modern style cond esprits. C'est aussi quelq ditionnel par le goût l'adaptation exacte à la r le grand devant de cors Toqué ne se conçoit pa brocart de Marie Leczinsk

Du point de vue techni

Diadème.

fusée, où les perles de grosseur inégale, très rondes et très belles, pendues à des lignes très minces de brillants, tremblent comme de petits globes de feu qui vont s'éteindre dans la nuit. Et les lignes sont souples et pleines, ces formes sont très bien proportionnées, sans maigreur et sans sécheresse, sans la pauvreté des dessins géométriques, losanges, cercles ou lignes droites ou l'aversion des styles ou

en œuvre des procédés les plus simples et les plus délicats. L'alliage du platine avec l'iridium permet de réaliser des montures d'une finesse extrême. Le serti dressé aminci en core la ligne de métal en donnant l'impression du tranchant d'un rasoir. Le joaillier a pu accomplir ainsi ce qu'avait désiré le dessinateur et rendu à peine plus visible qu'un trait de plume le métal sertissant la pierre.

As Swanson was beginning her ascent at Famous Players–Lasky, Zukor and DeMille brought Parisian jewelry designer Paul Iribe to Hollywood to design sets and costumes for *Male and Female* (1919). Responsible for the most daring new pearl designs, Iribe had begun his career sketching serpent jewels for René Lalique and went on to conceive imaginative items for the pearl dealers Juclier and Maxima. An article in *Art et Decoration* (1911) was devoted entirely to Iribe's jewels and pearl diadems for fine jeweler Robert Linzeler. Iribe's creations, while airy fripperies, looked imposing when worn with the Oriental-style dress that was the rage of Paris and required garb at couturier Paul Poiret's celebrated party of the year, "The Thousand and Second Night."

For *Male and Female,* Iribe strung a dress entirely of imitation pearls. The designer's knowledge and experience in the field of couture and jewelry brought an unprecedented refinement to the Hollywood wardrobe departments. In *The Affairs of Anatol* (1920), Gloria Swanson wore an important Iribe jewel, an emerald, amethyst, and gold pendant necklace, which had previously belonged to Poiret's wife and model, Denise. Its bold color scheme of green, purple, and gold was reminiscent of the sets and costumes of Diaghilev's Ballets Russes as well as the work of Poiret, with whom Iribe had collaborated on an album of fashion.

Iribe worked with DeMille on three other films: *The Ten Commandments* (1923), *The Road to Yesterday* (1925), and *Madame Satan* (1930), and contributed greatly to his vision of a grand and artistic epic design with an attention to jewelry details that forever distinguished DeMille's style. Iribe, in turn, left his mark on costume design in Hollywood; his pearl dress, for example, was imitated by costume designers throughout the 1920s.

One designer who adopted Iribe's use of pearls was Natasha Rambova. An American heiress née Winifred Shaunessy Hudnut, Rambova was selected by actress Alla Nazimova—a Russian emigrée who had studied with Stanislavsky—as art director, costume, and set designer for her film *Salome* (1922). Rambova and Nazimova were both melodramatic, highly stylized, and self-consciously artistic in their approach to moviemaking, lacing their work with literary and art-historical references. *Salome* was described in the opening credits as "A Pantomime after the Play by Oscar Wilde." The association with the English poet was further emphasized by a second credit, "Titles from Oscar Wilde." Rambova envisioned the movie heroine Salome as "a living pearl, precious, but cold, her veins throbbing with quicksilver instead of blood," and created an extravagant costume for Nazimova inspired by Iribe.*

Alla Nazimova, who gave her name to a Shubert theater in 1910, was a highly respected stage actress in America, famous for her interpretations of Henrik Ibsen's heroines. As reported in the press, her taste in jewelry was studied and contained references to mythical figures and artworks of antiquity: a ring of carved silver ascribed to Cellini, a necklace with skull charms said to have been excavated from the tomb of Scipio on the Appian Way in Rome, and a hair ornament modeled after the Great Sphinx of Giza. She owned a ring with a ruby hollowed out to hold poison that had belonged to the Borgias. In *Salome,* when the title card reads that something has fallen to the ground (it is the head of John the Baptist), the camera pans to Herod's skull-and-bones ring—a jewel from Nazimova's very individual collection.

Opposite, top: Designed by Paul Iribe, this pearl, diamond, and platinum crossover diadem, with hanging sprays of pearls and diamonds, was illustrated in *Art et Decoration* in 1911. A graceful abstract arrangement of pearl and platinum rods, it is based on the traditional wheat sheaf motif.

Opposite, center: A pearl, diamond, and platinum aigrette by Iribe with a circular-cut diamond spray, pearl tips, and an egret feather was based on a naturalistic pattern of plant tendrils.

Opposite, below: A dramatic skullcap arrangement of pearls and pearl strands by Iribe echoed ancient helmet designs.

23

* W. Robert La Vine, *In a Glamorous Fashion, The Fabulous Years of Hollywood Costume Design* (New York: Charles Scribner's Sons, 1980), 10.

On the set of *Camille* (1921) Nazimova brought together Natasha Rambova and Rudolph Valentino, the premier lover of the screen. Rambova found even greater scope as an art director after she married Valentino on May 13, 1922. In his first major film, *The Four Horsemen of the Apocalypse* (1921), based on a novel by Vicente Blasco Ibáñez, Valentino had played a Latin lover so seductively that he went on to play lovers of different nationalities in every film he made, the change in nationality represented by a change of costume and jewelry. After he appeared in *The Sheik* (1921), American girls called their boyfriends sheiks, called flirting sheiking, and went crazy over Eastern styles and fashion.

Valentino held undisputed sway over fashion in America. A simple circlet of oval links worn by Valentino offscreen became a nationally best-selling jewelry item exotically called a slave bracelet. The wristwatch owed much of its success to Valentino. Its appearance on the star's wrist triggered a run on the new male accessory, which soon became an indispensable part of every man's wardrobe.

In 1922 Valentino repeated his role as a Latin lover in the screen adaptation of another Blasco Ibáñez novel, *Blood and Sand*. As the Spanish toreador Juan Gallardo, Valentino forsakes his childhood sweetheart and wife, Carmen (Lila Lee), for the villainous Doña Sol (Nita Naldi), who gives him Cleopatra's serpent ring after seeing him perform in the bullring. The transfer of the ring from her finger to his is reported by the newspapers for everyone to read, including Carmen. Juan's betrayal of his wife leads him to recklessness and despair, and, in the final scene, a bullfight—in which he and the bull die simultaneously. With his last breath, Juan reconciles with Carmen, but not before he has removed the serpent ring from his finger.

Throughout the movie Doña Sol wears pearls, necklaces, bracelets, and hair ornaments, but in this scene she outdoes herself with a five-foot-long bead necklace. The serpent ring, her gift to Gallardo, flashes on his finger when he takes his first cigarette and later, as he draws closer to her. A diamond tie tack holds his tie, a watch chain appears at his vest, and his wedding ring is also visible.

Valentino's popularity began to flag after he married Rambova. She took

NAZIMOVA
in *Salomé*

Opposite: In order to film the lion's bride scene from *Male and Female* (1919), Gloria Swanson, playing a Babylonian princess, entered a real lion's den. After learning that the lion mauled someone two weeks later, Swanson was shocked to hear a member of the audience exclaim at the premiere, "I wonder which one is stuffed." During this perilous sequence in the film, Swanson wears an Iribe masterpiece of costume design in imitation pearls: a pearl dress, a peacock aigrette made of egret feathers with pearl trim, a pair of armlets, and rings with pearl medallions.

In dreaming up the sets and costumes for *Salome* (1922), art director Natasha Rambova was influenced by Aubrey Beardsley's erotic black and white illustrations for Oscar Wilde's original poem-drama. In a lobby card for the movie, Alla Nazimova is shown in a drawing wearing a cape inspired by Beardsley and in a photograph clad in a voluminous imitation-pearl stole and headdress, which she wears briefly in a scene with Herod.

Opposite, at top: In *Blood and Sand* (1922), the torcador Juan Gallardo (Rudolph Valentino) gazes longingly at Doña Sol (Nita Naldi), who has lured him to her home, ostensibly for dinner with her family. As the hour grows late and they are alone, she moves to the harp to soften his resolve to remain faithful to his wife. Throughout the movie Doña Sol wears pearls, necklaces, bracelets, and hair ornaments, but in this scene she outdoes herself with a five-foot-long bead necklace. He is adorned with a serpent ring that she had given him, a diamond tie tack, a watch chain, and a wedding ring. (Courtesy Paramount Pictures)

Opposite, center: In *Monsieur Beaucaire* (1924), Rudolph Valentino as the duke of Chartres (alias Monsieur Beaucaire) wears a gem-set dome brooch of the nineteenth century. Princess Henrietta of Bourbon (Bebe Daniels) has a diamond floral spray in her hair. Her earrings are a waterfall of diamonds and silver collets. Both stars wear authentic period jewelry throughout the movie.

Opposite, below: Natasha Rambova's flamboyant use of extravagant materials and yards of imitation pearls contributed to the box-office disaster of *The Young Rajah* (1922). Audiences howled with laughter at scenes like this, where Valentino (playing the Hindu god-prince Krishna) fights a stuffed tiger threatening a young beauty. She wears a pearl-encrusted diadem—ancient symbol of a temple prostitute—a pearl bra, pearl necklaces, and a swirling skirt of jet and imitation-pearl beads.

absolute control of his career, disrupted productions, issued artistic diktats, and went over budget assembling her husband's costumes and accessories. At Rambova's instigation, Valentino threatened to leave Paramount unless he was allowed to make *The Young Rajah* (1922) and play the Hindu god/prince Krishna, famous for romancing mortal women. Krishna, raised in New England as Amos Judd, falls in love with Molly Cabot (Wanda Hawley) and proves his ability to prophesy by foretelling their marriage. When Rambova art-directed *The Young Rajah,* she again followed Iribe, using imitation pearls to portray the exoticism of the East. This film generated terrible reviews and barely recouped the original investment.

Disgusted by what she viewed as an indifferent studio attitude, Rambova set her sights on a seventeen-week tour of public appearances, each show culminating in her re-creation with Valentino of the famous tango from *The Four Horsemen of the Apocalypse.* After this, the couple went on a shopping binge in Europe, buying Poiret gowns for Rambova (later published in *Photoplay*), and a touring car with vermilion upholstery for Valentino, as well as paintings, silver, and furniture for their apartment in New York and home in California.

To replenish their funds, Valentino and Rambova repaired to Hollywood to make *Monsieur Beaucaire* (1924), a historical romance about a French noble, Louis-Philippe of Orléans, duke of Chartres (Valentino), who flees Louis XV's court to avoid an arranged marriage to an unwilling beauty, Princess Henrietta of Bourbon (Bebe Daniels). Disguising himself as Monsieur Beaucaire to avoid execution, the duke takes up residence in Bath, England, until pardoned by Louis XV and Madame de Pompadour, who write from France that they are bored without him. Rambova wished the sets and costumes to be true to the eighteenth century as depicted by painter Antoine Watteau. Along with fountains, statues, and marble love seats, to say nothing of parasols, gowns, and other period touches including a small pet monkey, Rambova spent $85,000 on French antique jewels for Valentino and his leading lady—an extraordinary amount for 1924. In one scene Valentino's hand reveals rings on every finger. For her parting and final reconciliation with Valentino, Daniels wears different diamond floral hair ornaments. Unfortunately, this film was too laden with artistic devices to make a favorable impression on the public. They wanted a quicker-paced adventure story from Valentino, who came across here as effete, with his heart-shaped beauty mark, rings, gem-set and cameo brooches, and brocades.

Rambova's domineering presence behind the scenes prompted Adolph Zukor to rewrite Valentino's contract to include a clause barring her from the sets of his productions. Instead of signing the contract, Valentino left Paramount in 1925 at his wife's insistence. The following year Valentino and Rambova were divorced, and he signed a contract with United Artists.

In his comeback film, *The Eagle* (1925), Valentino portrays the Cossack lieutenant Vladimir Dubrovsky, who spurns the love of the czarina (Louise Dresser) and then flees the court for this offense and, more important, to take revenge on the brute who stole his father's estates. Unwittingly, he falls in love with the beautiful Mascha Troekoureff (Vilma Banky), who turns out to be the villain's daughter.

Every aspect of this production was successful. Director Clarence Brown refined the traveling shot, by which the movie camera was able to sweep down the center of a banquet table in one take. Hans Krawly's scenario was praised by *The New York Times*. And it was the general consensus that Valentino had given his best performance yet. His portrayal of the Cossack lieutenant was enhanced by the up-and-coming studio designer Adrian, whose dashing yet rugged costumes for the star brilliantly blended manliness and sophistication.

With this film Adrian established himself as a designer who, rather than

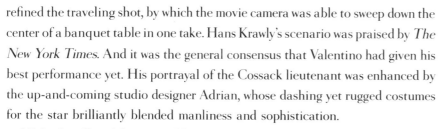

burdening his audience with fussy, historical detail, instead enchanted them with breathtaking costumes, blending the old and the new. Banky's slim gowns could be presented in any twenties fashion circular. One of her loveliest accessories is a light-colored hat with imitation pearls strung from side to side, framing her face during the famous banquet scene, when she realizes that her French tutor, Monsieur Le Blanc, alias Vladimir Dubrovsky, is the Eagle—there to kill her father.

Valentino's next film with United Artists, *The Son of the Sheik* (1926), was made to capture some of the glory of the original desert adventure, *The Sheik*

In *The Son of the Sheik* (1926) Valentino plays a desert chieftain with a love of Western accessories. Although Jacques Cartier observed in his travel diaries that Eastern potentates were fascinated by Cartier pocket watches, Valentino wore his signature timepiece, the Cartier Tank wristwatch, in the film.

(1921), which was the tale of the kidnapping and seduction of a young English girl by an Arab chieftain (Valentino). The sequel was an expensive production with an inventory of decorative objects that included some of the reigning male accessories—a Cartier tank watch, a cigarette case, a patented cigarette lighter, and a man's platinum sapphire ring—as well as those of a romantic Eastern hero, who would not be without a revolver, antique belt, knife, and sword. At the

Left: Cartier Tank watches, whose lines were inspired by the shapes of World War I tanks, achieved great popularity in the twenties. Worn by sportsmen and aviators as well as Valentino, they went a long way toward replacing the cumbersome pocket watch. The watch in the foreground, of platinum and 18K gold, features a cabochon sapphire wind-stem and an alligator strap; the other is of 18K gold with a lizard strap.

Cecil B. De Mille's 18K gold pocket watch by Tiffany & Co. was acquired when the director and Gloria Swanson were making some of the most acclaimed films of the silent era. Tiffany had been founded in 1837 and quickly became one of the biggest New York jewelers, laying the foundation for the American jewelry industry.

premiere, Pola Negri, Valentino's new flame, appeared at his side in a diamond tiara, pearl necklace, and silver gown.

The reviews were overwhelmingly favorable. One industry sage told him that the audience would now pay to see any film with his name on the marquee, but *The Son of the Sheik* was the last movie Valentino would make.

Despite Valentino's change from the foppish image at United Artists, Natasha Rambova's costuming came back to haunt him when the *Chicago Tribune* in 1926 ran an editorial titled "Pink Powder Puff" lamenting his effect on American manhood. This review, coming at the time of his traumatic divorce from Rambova and the debts incurred by his spending sprees, compounded Valentino's misery and mounting depression. Later that year, at age thirty-one, he died of a perforated ulcer. His funerals, one in New York and one in Hollywood, were theatrical pageants. Pola Negri made dramatic appearances at both, grief-stricken and attended by nurses. Fans all over the world were stunned by his death; a few of the very dedicated were said to have committed suicide.

In *Expensive Women* (1931) Dolores Costello (dining with Warren William) wears a pearl necklace and an Art Deco jewelry suite: multiple-cut diamond pendant earrings, an emerald and diamond bracelet, and an emerald bead and diamond brooch. All are mounted in platinum. With the Art Deco style, the brooch came into its own. There were brooches for every time of day. The carved emerald and diamond brooch in *Expensive Women* served as an evening jewel because of its visual grandeur.

The Talkies:
Alluring Women,
Jewel Thieves,
Gangsters, and
Musicals

B y the mid-1920s the novelty of going to the movies had worn off. Radio had arrived in the home with up-to-the-minute newscasts, live sports coverage, and upbeat comedy and talk shows—all for free. Desperate for a gimmick to bring the public back to the movie theaters, the struggling family film studio Warner Bros. invested in Vitaphone, a device for adding sound to moving pictures. (Harry Warner had dismissed it—"Who the hell wants to hear actors talk?" But his brother Sam prevailed in getting what the rest of the family derisively called Sam's toy phonograph.)

Warner's first experiment in sound, *Don Juan* (1926), an action film starring John Barrymore, boasted recorded musical accompaniment and sound effects. The critics derided the sound, calling it a cheap form of live music. But, one year later, when Al Jolson sang three songs and uttered a snatch of dialogue in *The Jazz Singer*, everyone sat up and took notice. Talking pictures rekindled the excitement of the first moving pictures, and audiences returned to the movie theaters in droves.

Hollywood worked frantically to switch over to the new system—which involved restructuring the entire industry. The path forward was strewn with obstacles, large and small. Clarity in recording did not come easily. Highly elaborate costumes—pearl gowns, metallic cloths, and bead fringes—thundered and clanked in the recording devices, completely drowning out the actors' speech. For a brief moment, it appeared that rubber jewels would be the accessories of the future. Le Marie, costumer for the Marx brothers' film *The Coconuts* (1929), was more optimistic when he told *Photoplay* (July 1929) that the talkies would precipitate a new style of jewelry, "wide bands of gold and silver, beautifully engraved, or studded with brilliants, made to fit the arm perfectly, and tight-fitting necklaces of the same type."

The brouhaha over jewelry and costumes proved short-lived, however, as better sound equipment was developed, around 1930. The studios emerged from their ordeal more technically oriented in every aspect of moviemaking, with additional departments being organized and staffed to systematize what was successful and

When "The Boy Wonder" of MGM, Irving Thalberg, proposed to Norma Shearer in his office, he brought out of his desk drawer a selection of engagement rings. She chose a very fashionable, slender, platinum band set with a large marquise-cut diamond. The ring was prominently featured in Shearer's movie *The Divorcee* (1930).

Norma Shearer appears perfectly poised, wearing a long necklace called a lavalliere, which derives its name from Louise de la Valliére, a mistress of Louis XV.

An ink and gouache drawing from the archives of a leading American jewelry manufacturer, William Scheer, illustrates a diamond lavalliere, with a cushion-cut diamond mounted in platinum. The term lavalliere was used loosely for a scrolled necklace of small diamonds suspending one or more pendants in a delicate mount. Originally associated with the Garland style, lavallieres continued to be popular in the 1920s in abbreviated and geometric forms with trimmer chains, their lightness and length pleasantly enhancing the importance of one stone, usually a diamond. Americans once thought the term referred to Eve Lavalliere, Parisian light opera singer and comedienne of the mid-nineteenth century, but in fact she had been named for her love of lavallieres by an adoring French press.

generate it over and over again, giving rise to assembly-line filmmaking.

The change to talkies also caused a shakedown of the star system. Established actors virtually had to audition to keep their contracts; those with thick accents, such as Pola Negri, were quickly discarded; their voices were unintelligible through the primitive sound equipment. Actresses who had been minor players in silent films, such as Joan Crawford and Norma Shearer, began their ascent to stardom.

The actress of the talkies was a greater financial asset to her studio than ever before, and the manipulation of her life reflected the marketing skills of a maturing industry. As soon as a movie mogul thought he detected a potential star, hairdressers, makeup artists, designers, fitters, wardrobe mistresses, and personal maids descended from all corners of the studio complex to transform her. Simultaneously, a backup team was assembled to manage her social life, from purchasing a suitable house and hiring domestic help to carefully selecting an offscreen wardrobe, a circle of friends, and even escorts. With so much money tied up in a star, decking her out with precious jewelry was considered not an extravagance but a part of the investment. So commonplace was beautiful jewelry in publicity stills and movies, that it was rarely described or documented by the press. And, as one style is pervasive, it is difficult to determine exactly where it had come from — Paris or New York.

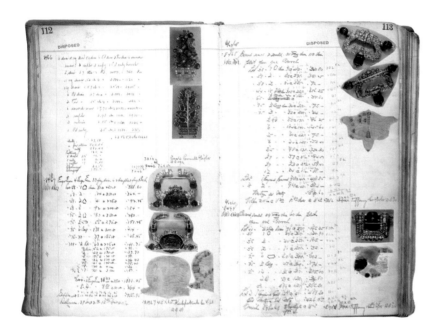

A selection of carved emerald, circular, baguette, and fancy-cut diamond and platinum openwork gallery brooch designs from a 1925 ledger of William Scheer, Inc., manufacturers whose jewels were retailed by Black, Starr & Frost, Tiffany & Co., as well as Cartier and Van Cleef & Arpels.

Jewelry had gone through a revolution equal to that of the movies. Thirty Parisian jewelry firms, among them Cartier, Van Cleef & Arpels, Lacloche Frères and Mauboussin, spent more than 500 million francs in an extraordinary effort to create a collection for the 1925 Exposition Internationale des Arts Décoratifs et Industriels Modernes that would "astonish the world," as Georges Fouquet, president of the jury, put it in the catalogue. Their designs, in a style later termed Art Deco, burst on fairgoers like fireworks and rendered nineteenth-century jewelry and the Garland style immediately obsolete. The new style presented at the 1925 exposition continued to prevail, with modifications, through the Depression.

Acting as an ambassador for the Art Deco style, Pierre-Yves Mauboussin opened a branch at 330 Park Avenue in New York, and with personal appearances backed by illustrated single- and double-page advertisements in *Vogue*, *Vanity Fair*, and *Town & Country*, he educated his clients on the finer points of precious jewelry. Although critics and industry experts credit Cartier with the finest examples of the new style, compared to Mauboussin, Cartier had a relatively low profile in the American media. The two most popular items that Mauboussin advertised at its exhibits were the flower-basket brooch, filled with carved precious gems, and the ubiquitous wide diamond bracelet.

Hollywood stars were greatly taken with these bracelets, packed with fancy-cut diamonds in all manner of mosaic and openwork arrangements and containing more diamonds per millimeter than any other jewel. European gem cutters had been steadily advancing technically since the early years of the century, honing their skills on the quantity of small- to medium-size diamonds coming from the South African mines. By the mid-1920s they were routinely cutting diamonds in rectangular, baguette, emerald, triangular, bullet, epaulette, half-moon, hexagon, and other fancy shapes, as well as in the traditional pear, marquise (navette), circular, and cushion shapes, which jewelers applied to wide bracelets. The actresses flaunted their collections ostentatiously, wearing at least two or three wide bracelets at a time. The wide bracelet became a symbol of Hollywood glamour and to this day is used to conjure it up. A variation made during the Depression retained the diamond clasp while substituting precious beads for the wide panels of diamonds.

For a casual daytime Art Deco jewel, the favorite among Hollywood stars was the flower-basket brooch. The design is sometimes credited to Paul Iribe for

Left: Actress Claire Luce wears a white satin Lucien Lelong gown and a dazzling array of jewelry by the French jeweler Mauboussin: a diamond and platinum scrolled necklace suspending a huge emerald-cut emerald; a wide diamond bracelet accented with emerald cabochons; a wide diamond bracelet with a swirl design; three-stone diamond and platinum girandole earrings; and a cushion-cut diamond ring. Mauboussin received a credit on all of Luce's publicity photographs, which was unusual for the period.

A page from the catalogue of the 1925 Exposition des Arts Decoratifs in Paris, where the Art Deco style was first widely exhibited, illustrates some of the Mauboussin jewelry that won the Grand Prix. Art Deco jewelry broke new ground, the extraordinary skills of European gem cutters having led to an infusion of masterfully cut, geometrically shaped stones that mark the style.

In 1932, Claire Luce modeled Art Deco jewelry by Mauboussin: a pendant diamond and emerald-cut emerald choker, two openwork diamond bracelets, and a tapered emerald and diamond bracelet threaded through the sash of her Lelong crepe gown.

Luce's Mauboussin necklace consists of a pavé-set, circular and baguette-cut diamond choker with a fluted emerald bead blossom and buff-top emerald leaves, accented by cabochon emerald three-stone motifs and mounted in platinum. In 1931 *Photoplay* magazine illustrated her choker and discussed the jewelry Mauboussin had created for Luce's film *Painted Woman*.

A diamond, mother-of-pearl, black onyx and enamel vanity by Mauboussin, mounted in platinum and gold, was influenced by René Lalique's design for the magnificent fifty-foot-high crystal fountain at the center of the exposition pavilions. The vanity was owned by French actress Yvonne Printemps, a leading musical-comedy star who made the popular *La Dame aux Camélias* among other films. Dimensions: $3\frac{1}{2} \times 2 \times \frac{1}{2}$ in.

Above: Mauboussin used its success at the 1925 exposition as a springboard to stimulate jewelry sales abroad. These two pages from the catalogue *Las Joyas de Arte* for the 1927 exhibition at the Mauboussin salon in Buenos Aires feature a drawing of the fountain vanity and a selection of rings and wide bracelets.

A double-page Mauboussin advertisement from *Vanity Fair* (1927) shows wide bracelets and flower basket brooches among other jewels.

Cartier and other times to Mauboussin, but every jeweler made a variation of it. The dainty little motif was composed of rubies, sapphires, emeralds, and diamonds in fancy cuts and small carved bud and leaf shapes, the latter coming from India. Cabochons, unfaceted stones with a curved surface, were used as accents in flower-basket brooches or for the bodies of urns. During the Depression, the little cabochon gems began to assume prominence as central stones, since they were less expensive than faceted gems and were readily available.

American jewelers, who did not exhibit at the 1925 Paris exhibition, had to

A desperate Monroe Owsley grasps Clara Bow's wide bracelets, which represent cash and his only means of escape from the sanitarium in *Call Her Savage* (1932). (Courtesy Paramount Pictures)

watch the success of French jewelers from the sidelines. Since the Americans could not hope to emulate the Europeans' facility in gem cutting, they were forced to buy stones and purchase (or pirate) new designs in Paris.

Along with Tiffany, Black, Starr & Frost was one of the most venerable of the American jewelers. In the nineteenth century, Harriet Beecher Stowe wrote that the prince of Wales visited New York, danced, supped, and bought pearls at Black, Starr & Frost. The Vanderbilts, Guggenheims, and Carnegies had all shopped there. Then, in the 1920s, the new clientele was represented by such women as Peggy Hopkins-Joyce, a Ziegfeld girl turned socialite who generated the publicity of a movie star. Like other American firms, it had started to change its displays to champion the more fashionable look presented at the Paris exposition, and its promotion of Art Deco served as a stamp of approval in the United States.

Opposite: To publicize her new movie with Gary Cooper, *Fighting Caravans* (1931), Lily Damita wears several diamond openwork bracelets, a line bracelet, and a slave bracelet in a fashion portrait by George Hoyningen-Heune for *Vanity Fair.* A chorus girl from the Casino de Paris Revue who acted in German, Austrian, and British films, Damita was brought to Hollywood by Samuel Goldwyn in 1931 to make two films. Her biggest hit with the public was her marriage to Errol Flynn.

The precious sapphire bead bracelets that Jean Harlow wears here were a variation on the diamond openwork bracelet; the beads replace the band and links. Only a platinum geometric clasp remains, representing a considerable financial saving.

Two ink and gouache drawings from the archives of William Scheer show multiple sapphire bead bracelets with diamond and platinum openwork clasps.

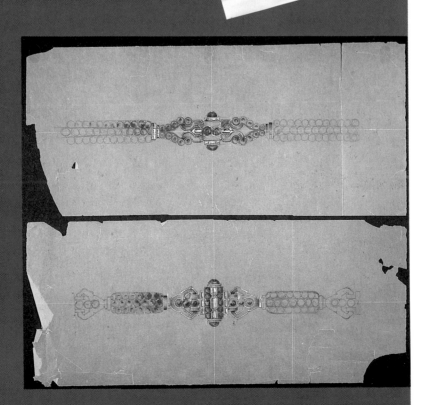

Two Art Deco geometrical bracelets: the one at left is composed of three panels of circular, epaulette, rectangular, octagonal, and navette-shaped diamonds, enhanced with small fancy-cut emerald triangles, with diamond links, mounted in platinum; at right, the bracelet is composed of three panels of circular-cut diamonds, accented with marquise and baguette-cut diamonds, calibré and fancy-cut emeralds, mounted in platinum.

Jean Harlow's clip brooch shines on the strap of her gown. Fancy-cut diamonds surround an enormous cabochon gem, most probably a sapphire, a stone that Harlow is said to have collected.

Cabochon gems were not very popular or particularly expensive, even in large sizes, until movie stars, who recognized their photogenic qualities, made them jewelry best-sellers of the late 1930s.

Joan Crawford wears a flower basket brooch for an MGM publicity still.

ALLURING WOMEN

With breathlessness and a wide-eyed innocence, Peggy Hopkins-Joyce published an autobiography in 1930, *Men, Marriage and Me,* in which she told of the ups and downs of her life from child bride to Ziegfeld girl to socialite to film actress toiling on a movie. While married to Chicago millionaire Stanley Joyce, she received quantities of jewels as gifts, bought jewelry herself, and built up one of the best-publicized jewelry collections in the world. Ever dreaming of new ways to increase her jewelry collection, Hopkins-Joyce fantasized rapturously about Mr. Black of Black, Starr & Frost: "Mr. Black is a distinguished man and a great jeweler. I wonder how it would feel to be married to a big jeweler like Mr. Black? I should think it would be wonderful, because then a person could wear all the jewels she wanted and they would not cost her anything."

Life stories like Peggy Hopkins-Joyce's were among the most frequently replayed themes in Hollywood—a poor, struggling working girl of extraordinary charm and beauty is swept off her feet by a rich man. Whether she was a shop girl, show girl, or call girl, she quickly adjusted to a life of beautiful clothes and jewelry. This theme became even more popular after the stock market crash of 1929 and the beginning of the Great Depression, when actual riches and true-life success

Five Art Deco flower basket brooches: at center is a pavé-set diamond basket brooch with black onyx trim, containing an arrangement of sapphire leaves, an emerald bead bud, a heart-shaped diamond bud with cabochon ruby, sapphire and onyx buds, and moveable gem sprigs on the sides. On the reverse is a watch. The basket is suspended by twin baguette and round diamond chains from a geometrical diamond motif with a small half-moon cut diamond bowl with black onyx and millegrain trim and gem-set fruit mounted in platinum. By Lacloche, Paris. At lower right is a carved emerald and fancy-cut diamond basket with round and baguette-cut diamond blossoms, carved ruby, emerald, and sapphire buds and leaves, with navette-shaped diamond drops mounted in platinum, by an unknown jeweler. At upper right, is a pavé-set and baguette-cut diamond urn of flowers, sprinkled with ruby and emerald cabochon buds, mounted in platinum. By Lacloche, Paris. At lower left, two pavé-set doves alight on a pavé-set diamond and calibré-cut ruby openwork basket with twin circular-cut ruby and emerald flowers and a diamond navette accent, mounted in platinum and yellow gold. At upper left, is a flower pot pendant watch suspended from a scrolled brooch pendant, set with an epaulette-cut ruby, filled with carved ruby, emerald, and sapphire foliage, accented with fancy-cut diamonds and black enamel trim and mounted in platinum. The watch is on the other side. By Mauboussin.

stories, once commonplace, grew scarce. To escape from their economic woes, people flocked to movies that played to their longing for glamour with sumptuous fashions, precious jewelry in the Art Deco style—which they associated with pre-Depression prosperity—and actresses chosen as much for their ability to model clothes and jewelry as for their talent in acting.

Dolores Costello was a New York beauty from a theatrical family, a famous matinee idol's daughter who, after modeling for top illustrator James Montgomery Flagg and dancing in George White's Scandals in New York, won a contract at Warner Bros. and established herself as an actress in *The Sea Beast* (1926), a romantic silent-screen adaptation of *Moby Dick,* which costarred her future husband, John Barrymore.

In *Expensive Women* (1931), Costello played a call girl named Connie whose dramatic clothes and important jewelry provide a wealth of detail about extravagant wardrobes. Unlike the wife of her client, whose gowns are conservative but beautiful, Connie's clothes are suggestive, with beaded boleros, embroidered designs, and silk ribbons that trail to the floor and accentuate her slender form. Connie's Art Deco jewelry is very much in evidence: a large cushion-cut diamond ring, an even bigger sapphire ring in a diamond cluster platinum mount, a few wide bracelets, a wide geometrical diamond bar pin centering on a small cabochon gem, and diamond pendant earrings. Two fine jewels enhance these standard items and are reserved for the important first and last scenes.

In the first scene, when dining with talented musician Neil (Warren William), Connie wears a pale evening dress accented with an Art Deco carved emerald bead brooch. Emeralds have special properties with unique possibilities for jewelry design—their crystals are larger than those of rubies and sapphires, and their softness allows them to be cut into fluted beads and carved melon shapes. In contrast to diamonds, which twinkle brightly on the black and white screen, carved emeralds add mass and texture and increase the drama of jewelry.

During the movie Connie falls in love with millionaire Art Raymond (Anthony Bushell), who wants to leave his wife for her until she is banished from his life by his domineering father. At a New Year's Eve party where they accidentally meet again, Connie appears in a sleeveless black tank gown with a beaded and fringed short bodice made more impressive by a diamond lariat necklace terminating in a tassel. In a moment of passion Art kills one of her previous escorts, after which—to save his good name—Connie claims that it was she who fired the gun. In the

Peggy Hopkins-Joyce wears her twin baguette-cut diamond and platinum necklace, centering on an octagonal emerald-cut diamond weighing 127 carats. The diamond was bought in Paris by Black, Starr & Frost: American jewelers at the time did not have the workshops or skilled labor to cut such large stones.

46

end she is acquitted and freed and goes back to her first love, Neil.

The scenario in which a call girl finds true love was repeated in *Girls About Town* (1931). The film stars the brunette and blond duo of Kay Francis and Lilyan Tashman as Wanda and Marie, ladies of the evening who are paired at a yachting party with two businessmen from Lansing, Michigan, Jim Butler (Joel McCrea) and Benjamin Thomas (Eugene Palette). Wanda falls in love with Jim, but Marie finds her escort, Benjy, so stingy that she opts to side with his wife, and she takes the couple on a spending spree that includes shopping for jewelry at Cartier. Meanwhile, Wanda's ex-husband finds out about her romance with Jim and threatens to expose them unless he receives $10,000 in blackmail. To repay Jim, who thinks that Wanda and her ex are in collusion, the girls sell their beautiful clothes. In addition, Marie returns the jewelry to Benjy's wife. Overcome by gratitude, Benjy's wife gives Marie an emerald worth exactly $10,000, which settles the debt and leaves Wanda and Jim free to marry.

In *Girls About Town* everyone shops for jewelry at Cartier. But in fact, the emerald necklace that Kay Francis wears came from another leading jeweler in Paris, Lacloche Frères. Hollywood stars were ranging far afield to find the very best of Art Deco jewelry.

Although Paramount billed *Girls About Town* as a movie starring two of its best-dressed actresses, Lilyan Tashman held the official media title of the best-dressed woman on the screen. A Ziegfeld Follies girl who had made her film debut in 1921, she was in the chorus line with none other than Peggy Hopkins-Joyce. In a 1917 routine, "The Ladies of Fashion," Hopkins-Joyce played The Terrible Temptation and Tashman, A Symbol of Change and Emotion. (Several years later, when Hopkins-Joyce collapsed on the set of Walter Winchell's *Thru a Keyhole* (1933), Tashman, fresh from *Girls About Town,* took Hopkins-Joyce's place.) Married to actor Edmund Lowe, Tashman was a social leader and hostess of legendary parties at their home in Hollywood, "Lilowe," and their beach house in Malibu. She died at thirty-four in 1934, and Eddie Cantor delivered the eulogy at the funeral.

Tashman's estate was contested by her sisters, who sued Lowe for $121,750 worth of furs and jewelry that they considered their rightful legacy. The controversy made headlines for weeks, and ultimately, Lowe's claim was vindicated.

The jewelry under dispute was never detailed, but, from publicity stills, Tashman's collection can be assessed as dramatic, unusual, and in perfect taste. In addition to the prescribed wide bracelets, clips, and flower-basket brooches, she had two single stone rings, a star ruby and star sapphire, which she invariably wore together on the same finger. Her two double-strand twelve-millimeter pearl necklaces were a combination of black and white pearls in alternating sections. Tashman deftly mixed precious and semiprecious pieces, wearing her emerald, ruby, and diamond openwork bead bracelet on one wrist and her five-inch coil of red coral beads on the other. Hearst syndicated columnist Louella Parsons honored Tashman posthumously: "When Lilyan Tashman was alive, there was never any question of who was Hollywood's best-dressed woman. Everyone conceded that distinction to Lil, who made a business of wearing dashing clothes and affecting styles that few women could or would wear."

A good friend of Lilyan Tashman and her costar in *Girls About Town,* Kay

A Black, Starr & Frost advertisement from *Vanity Fair* (1927) features a choker in an Art Deco design that no French jeweler would have showcased. Black, Starr & Frost's American clients preferred large gems over elaborate mounts.

For a profile in *Vanity Fair* (1931) Peggy Hopkins-Joyce was photographed by Edward Steichen to drum up publicity for *Men, Marriage, and Me.* She conspicuously displays some magnificent jewelry, including diamond and gem-set rings, a wide diamond bracelet, three gem-set line bracelets, and her well-publicized Black, Starr & Frost necklace.

Francis was one of the most popular, not to mention most highly paid, stars of the 1930s. Called an aristocrat of the screen, she was sharp and intelligent, the product of a convent education, and she played to the hilt the wisecracking glamour girl of the early 1930s whom nothing could faze but love. Francis's private life remained very private. Even though she was married four times, her separations were amicable and her remarriages were sometimes undisclosed in the press. The greatest controversy concerning this most silent of great stars was her proposed marriage to a German baron rumored to have Nazi connections.

Francis shopped for her Art Deco jewelry at the Italian firm Bulgari in Rome. She was also a habitué of the rue de la Paix, the street of exclusive shops in Paris where both Cartier and Lacloche Frères were located.

Another popular glamorous star of the Depression years, Joan Crawford emerged as one of the most-valued players at Metro-Goldwyn-Mayer Corporation (MGM), helping to establish that studio's claim that it purveyed "Beautiful Pictures for Beautiful People." Crawford (Texas-born Lucille Fay Le Sueur) had been plucked out of a New York chorus line in 1925 by an MGM talent scout. In her first starring role in *Our Dancing Daughters* (1928) as the flapper Diana, who loved fast cars and dancing, she performed a Charleston on a table — a scene that became a legend in movie history. A year later, she greatly increased her value to the studio by marrying the scion of Hollywood's first family, Douglas Fairbanks, Jr. They joined together professionally as well, starring in *Our Modern Maidens* (1929). Their alliance, like that of Fairbanks's father and Mary Pickford a generation earlier, made excellent copy and kept the pair uppermost in the headlines of the fan magazines. In her publicity shots from the twenties and early thirties, Crawford wears Art Deco multiple wide bracelets and flower-basket brooches, and in each decade she updated her jewels to blend with the fashions.

Possessed (1931) was a better-than-average rags-to-riches saga starring Crawford. She plays Marian, who works in the local paper-box factory until she gets fed up with small-town life and leaves for the big city. There she falls in love with millionaire lawyer Mark Whitney, played by MGM's dashing leading man Clark Gable, who sets her up in an apartment and keeps her generously. However, when he enters politics, the affair is used by his enemies to discredit him. In the finale, Marian's public defense of his character saves his political career and leads to their marriage.

Possessed was enhanced by some of MGM's best talent. Besides the actors,

Six Art Deco line bracelets similar to those worn by Peggy Hopkins-Joyce: two with calibré-cut sapphires and rubies respectively; one with tapered calibré-cut emeralds; and three with alternating circular-cut diamonds and calibré-cut rubies, sapphires, and emeralds. All are mounted in platinum. American jewelers were considered brilliant mechanics if not fine cutters and designers, and they were able to close the gap with their European competitors by creating and patenting flexible mountings for line bracelets, sometimes going to court to protect mechanisms. The line bracelets were a simple way of showing off a row of calibré-cut gems perfectly matched in color and size, and in the United States they were nicknamed "Service Stripes" after the chevrons worn on military sleeves; as gifts to wives they denoted successful marital "tours of duty."

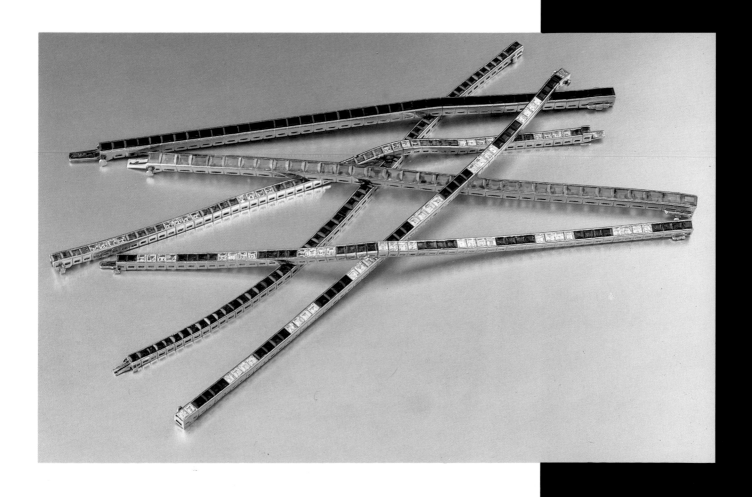

The Lacloche sautoir Kay Francis wore in *Girls About Town* was shortened later by an unknown jeweler to make a pair of earrings; an openwork diamond bell-shaped pendant was added. The chain is composed of carved emerald beads intersecting pavé-set diamond navette-shaped links. Length of sautoir: 24 in.; earrings: 2¼ in.

there was Cedric Gibbons, who went on to establish himself as one of the greatest art directors of American cinema. Gibbons was responsible for the film's deft sets, which conveyed a refinement unrivaled in movies by other studios, and an attention to detail that extended down to a cut-glass brandy decanter. Crawford's gowns, designed by Adrian, transcended the usual fashion parade; each was appropriate to its occasion, fittingly tasteful as well as strikingly glamorous.

In one very romantic scene, Marian and Whitney stand in front of a mirror as she puts on her jewelry, each piece celebrating an anniversary, which prompts them to reminisce about their relationship. Their first year together is represented by a pair of large, fancy-cut diamond girandole earrings, the second by a big diamond ring, and the third by a string of pearls. As she lifts the necklace Marian comments, "I seem to grow more valuable to you each year." Then she slips on the ring from Tiffany that Whitney gave her the day he decided she should pretend to be a divorcée living on alimony, so the outside world would not know he was paying her bills.

The romance between Crawford and Gable, so convincing on screen, was not feigned: they were madly in love. Their affair was not good news for MGM, which preferred the positive publicity that the Crawford-Fairbanks marriage brought. All the studio's attempts to save the marriage proved futile. Nothing MGM devised, not even sending Fairbanks and Crawford on an extended publicity tour, could extinguish the rumors — or the stars' passion, which outlived studio interference and Crawford's marriage. On and off for the rest of their lives they alternated as close friends and lovers. Still, when asked about a possible marriage, Crawford replied that Gable preferred the chase to the prize.

Below left: In *Girls About Town* (1931), Kay Francis and Lilyan Tashman wear diamond and emerald wide bracelets of open-work geometric design. Francis also wears a sautoir by Lacloche Frères of carved emerald beads, diamonds, and platinum.

An entry from the William Scheer ledger of 1928–1937, "Mounted Miscellaneous and Scarf Pins," shows a flexible emerald bead necklace thirty-six-and-a-half inches long.

JEWEL THIEVES

In 1932 Hollywood studios added the spice of adventure to their glamour stories with a run of sophisticated jewel thief movies. The winner of the Academy Award for Best Picture this year was *Grand Hotel,* not exactly a jewel thief movie but one whose leading man was a jewel thief. *Trouble in Paradise* and *Jewel Robbery* were among the capers focused on dapper thieves whose route to success involved the seduction of women whose jewels shone like beacons. These movies featured not so much the wearing of jewelry as banter about practically every conceivable aspect of it—the presence and pursuit of jewelry illuminating character and keeping the pace scintillating. Only one film from this era, *15 Maiden Lane* (1936), relates with any seriousness to an actual gem.

Ernst Lubitsch directed the classic film in this genre, *Trouble in Paradise,* which tells the story of the romantic travails of a thief named Lily (Miriam Hopkins) who falls in love with an internationally known jewel thief named Gaston Monescu (Herbert Marshall). Together they try to con the wealthy widow Madame Colet (Kay Francis), but Gaston's charm has an unexpected side effect, producing a romantic triangle. When Madame Colet finds herself alone with Gaston late at night, she coquettishly removes her jewelry and quips, "When a lady takes her jewels off in a gentleman's room, where does she put them?" In the end, however, Gaston returns to his partner in crime with a peace offering— Madame Colet's double-strand pearl necklace, which Lily had coveted from the moment she laid eyes on it.

Miriam Hopkins received top billing for *Trouble in Paradise,* and as one of Lubitsch's favorite actresses she was a star equal to Kay Francis and Lilyan

At a garden party in *Trouble in Paradise* (1932) a wealthy cosmetics heiress (Kay Francis) flirts with her new secretary (Herbert Marshall), who is actually an international jewel thief. Her displaced suitor (Charles Ruggles) frowns his disapproval. She wears a gem-set ring of approximately thirty carats, a wide diamond openwork bracelet, and a diamond clip brooch on her waistband.

In *Possessed* (1931) Joan Crawford, playing opposite Clark Gable, wears six bracelets—three wide diamond bracelets and three precious bead bracelets—as well as diamond pendant earrings, a cushion-cut diamond ring, and a string of pearls.

Tashman at Paramount. A graduate of Broadway and the Music Box Revue, Hopkins shunned ingenue parts, telling the *Los Angeles Times* (January 17, 1934) that she "lived in mortal dread of sweet, young things" and preferred "fallen women." As a successful leading lady, Hopkins had a significant jewelry collection, but it was never detailed in the press. It was, however, acknowledged to be important when it appeared on a list of thefts by the yet-to-be-apprehended "phantom burglar of Bel Air."

In *Jewel Robbery* (1932), Kay Francis repeated as a millionairess, this time playing Baroness Terry. Bored with her husband and lovers, she confides to her friend, "I haven't found one to supplant my jewels." Then Terry meets a jewel thief (William Powell) when he is robbing one of the most exclusive jewelry stores in Vienna, where she happens to be shopping. His suave handling of the heist triggers their romance. Although the actors' performances may have convinced the audience that the jewelry in safes and trays was real, in fact it was paste—no jeweler would have lent the amount of stock necessary to create the entire inventory of a store on screen.

Set in an awesome, old-world institution of rank and privilege, the number-one hotel of Berlin and perhaps of all Europe, *Grand Hotel* was well designed to have a jewel thief in its cast of characters. Movie audiences are shown a teeming lobby swarming with bellhops and concierges and are then taken behind the scenes to

A montage in *Possessed* conveys the passing of time as well as the increasing sophistication of the character that Joan Crawford played. The sequence shows a woman's hand tearing yearly pages from a calendar as the wide diamond bracelets on her wrist grow in number.

These compacts that belonged to Hollywood stars show variety and reveal individual taste: at far right, Mary Pickford's gold and black enamel Islamic-style vanity case, made by Cartier-Paris, opens to reveal a powder compartment and a small tube of lipstick that had to be returned to the jeweler to be refilled. Pickford's initials are on the lid and her name is inscribed on the inside cover of the powder compartment. Dimensions: 1¾ × 2½ × ½ in. At lower left, Carole Lombard's engine-turned 14K gold compact has an applied monogram in calibré-cut sapphires, mounted in platinum. The twin panel top springs open to reveal her initials inscribed on the inner lid of the compact, which has a mirror on the reverse. Dimensions: 1¹³⁄₁₆ × 1¹¹⁄₁₆ × ⅜ in. At top is Sonja Henie's engine-turned 14K white and yellow gold compact. The cover is designed in a pattern of textured rays emanating from a rising sun of cabochon emeralds supporting a circular-cut diamond "S" and a baguette-cut diamond "H." Dimensions: 3 × 3 × ⅝ in.

view the nonstop activity of telephone operators switching calls to rooms all over the hotel. The guests reside in palatial suites, dance to jazz music, and drink cocktails like the "Louisiana Flip" in an American-style bar. However, behind this magnificent facade lurks unrest and tragedy, revealed in the life stories of the various characters, who are united only by the locale. The stenographer Flaemmchen (Joan Crawford) is desperately trying to work her way out of her menial, dead-end job, while at the other side of the social spectrum, Baron von Gaigern (John Barrymore) becomes a jewel thief to pay his debts. He attempts to steal the priceless pearl necklace owned by the most celebrated guest, the world-famous ballerina Grusinskaya (Greta Garbo). Grusinskaya is wearied by her fame, leading as it has to isolation and loneliness.

From the moment Greta Garbo appeared in American movies in 1924, her presence riveted audiences to the screen, and MGM adroitly staged her productions to make the most of her uncanny ability to speak with her eyes and gestures in silent films. In order not to lose its most valuable player, the studio continued to

Right: Miriam Hopkins holds a vanity case, an item that came into fashion in the twenties when women first put on makeup in public. Jewelers encouraged the new fad by producing luxury accessories for powder, lipstick, and rouge. The first Art Deco vanities were bright and color-ful, with semiprecious stones, mother-of-pearl, enamel, and small diamond highlights. As jewelry fashions changed and vanities became a necessity, they were made in durable 18K gold with the gems relegated to clasps and monograms. Vanities continued to be made and sold widely through the fifties.

In 1936 the industry magazine *Jewelers' Circular* published an article about the film *15 Maiden Lane,* a drama that borrowed from jewelry history. The magazine juxtaposed stills from the film with photographs of Maiden Lane, the street in the old downtown diamond district of New York where the action takes place.

cast Garbo in silent movies until her voice was properly trained; its caution paid off when Garbo went on to even greater fame in talkies with a rich and resonant voice that perfectly matched her acting ability. Her uniqueness as a Hollywood star stemmed from her mania for privacy in the face of the blitz of publicity MGM was accustomed to create around its foremost players. But since Garbo was playing highly beautiful, introspective, mysterious — and sometimes temperamental — women anyway, the public adapted themselves to her elusiveness and eventually fused her onscreen and offscreen personas, making the "Swedish Sphinx," the "Mysterious Stranger," and the "Divine" a legend in her own lifetime.

In *Grand Hotel* as well as *The Temptress* (1927) and *A Woman of Affairs* (1928), Garbo's jewels represent the burden of a life she has been forced into by beauty, circumstance, or talent, reversing the conventional symbolism of jewelry by turning it into a powerful prop representing malaise and a feeling of hopelessness. In *Grand Hotel* she equates her pearls with her lonely success, for example, lamenting, "The pearls don't break. They hold together and bring me bad luck. I hate them." Nevertheless, despite the freighted meaning of the rings or strings of pearls, Garbo wore a negligible amount of jewelry in her early movies.

In *15 Maiden Lane* (1936), Cesar Romero stars as jewel thief Frank Peyton and Claire Trevor as his heiress prey, Jane Martin, who steals her own jewelry to prove that she will make a good accomplice. Set in the New York diamond district, the film includes a reenactment of the cutting of jeweler Harry Winston's famous Jonker diamond.

In the 1920s Harry Winston acquired several famous estates including those of Rebecca Stoddard (1925) and Arabella Huntington (1926) and such celebrated gems as the "Lucky" Baldwin Ruby (1930). By the Depression era, Winston had a reputation, a knowledge of historical jewelry, a taste for the antique, and a passionate desire to buy and put away to sell at a higher cost. In 1932 Winston incorporated and opened at 527 Fifth Avenue. His motto was "Rare Jewels of the World."

Two years later he became an international figure with his purchase of the Jonker diamond, then the second-largest diamond in the world, weighing 726 carats uncut. The stone was featured in newsreels, exhibited at the American Museum of Natural History in New York City, and photographed with child movie star Shirley Temple. The best gem cutters of the international community submitted their plans for cutting the stone, but Winston surprised the world when he chose an American for the job. Lazare Kaplan carefully and masterfully cut the stone into twelve diamonds, the largest weighing 143 carats.

GANGSTERS

In stark contrast to the intelligent and bloodless thievery of jewels was the violent banditry depicted in gangster movies. Since Prohibition was an American phenomenon, movies about the gangsters of Prohibition became as American as Westerns. When journalist Cornelius Vanderbilt interviewed Mahatma Gandhi for the article "They Love Movies, Too" in *Photoplay* (1937), Gandhi asked, "To what class there, sire, do you belong?" Seeing Vanderbilt's surprise, he qualified his question, "Well, sire, are you a gangster, gentleman, or cowboy?"

Gangster movies and Westerns drew huge audiences through the physical excitement of their plots and the flouting of authority, but the equating of the two types of movies raised ethical questions. A cowboy movie was usually a good-versus-bad saga, whereas a gangster movie was often merely a picture of moral degradation. Gangster movies were made initially to expose the evils of the big cities, and many films carried with them the warning to the public that their characters were not fictionalized but true-to-life. Although these films were presented as public-interest productions and ultimately the mobsters they portrayed were brutally killed, a portion of the scenarios always glorified the underworld.

The toughs who supplied the cities with spirits during Prohibition became wealthy through their trade, and although their business was crime and they routinely handled machine guns, their off-hours were spent in lavish speakeasies where they indulged themselves and their molls in every luxury. The tough

In *The Public Enemy* (1931) Jean Harlow wears a diamond and platinum brooch clipped to the back of her dress, as well as a diamond gem-set and platinum bracelet and diamond, cabochon gem, and platinum cluster earrings. She uses a diamond and black onyx cigarette holder.

Opposite: During the Depression jewelers created less expensive accessories as well as less expensive jewelry. Cigarette lighters and holders, ashtrays, and matchboxes were often made of semiprecious materials and black onyx, sometimes enhanced with small diamonds. Over the years cigarette holders came to identify eccentric or attention-grabbing females in the movies—the long onyx holder, like a ring, drew the eye to the hands. At top is an Art Deco holder made by Cartier-Paris with a coral and diamond motif between a white onyx filter and black lacquer stem, mounted in platinum, yellow and white gold. Length: 5¼ in. At bottom, an Art Deco holder by Cartier features a gold and black lacquer motif between the crystal filter and black lacquer stem, mounted in white and yellow 18K gold. Length: 5¾ in.

59

attitude expressed by the hoodlums was also apparent in their molls, making them far more bold than their counterparts—the kept women, call girls, and society ladies of the movies. Even though all of these women wear Art Deco jewelry, the molls toss it onto gowns that are low-cut in the front, back, and sides, creating their own dégagé look of flesh and jewels.

The Public Enemy, one of fifty gangster movies made in 1931, traces the life history of two Irish kids, Tom Powers (James Cagney) and his friend Matt Doyle (Edward Woods), who start out with petty thievery and shoplifting and graduate to guns and bootlegging, emerging as the top henchmen of a Prohibition gang lord. Jean Harlow is introduced as the luscious, streetwise Gwen Allen, who becomes Tom's moll. For Gwen he leaves Kitty (Mae Clarke), who so enraged him that he jammed a grapefruit in her face.

In the big nightclub scene, when Tom and Matt show off their molls, Gwen

wears a clip brooch at the back of her low-slung gown and a wide bracelet. The anonymous moll on Matt's arm wears three wide diamond bracelets with large synthetic stone centers. Such bracelets, an unusual fashion of the Depression and Prohibition periods, stretched buyers' dollars yet created the impression of being important, valuable jewels.

The Public Enemy launched Jean Harlow's career. Harlow was a platinum blond comedienne and Hollywood sex kitten, who had paid her dues to the industry for several years, working in comedy shorts, including a Laurel and Hardy piece, *Double Whoopee* (1928). The critics had stereotyped Harlow as a tart, but her loose, savvy style came through in her portrayal of Gwen Allen. It won her a contract at MGM, where she made such American classics as *Bombshell* (1933) and *Dinner at Eight* (1934).

In *Saratoga* (1937), Harlow's last film appearance, she wore her 150-carat cabochon sapphire, the second engagement ring from her fiancé, leading man William Powell. The first ring he had given her—a traditional faceted diamond— was not in keeping with her flamboyant style, but the second ring was very much in evidence in her personal appearances and in publicity stills. Tragically, later in the same year of *Saratoga*'s release and before her wedding, Harlow died at the age of twenty-six.

Right: In *Scarface* (1932) the struggle between gang lords (Osgood Perkins and Paul Muni) simmers as they both reach to light the cigarette of a gangster moll (Karen Morley). She wears fancy-cut diamond girandole earrings, seen in profile, and a bracelet and ring.

Opposite, lower left: In *The Great Ziegfeld* (1936) Anna Held, played by Luise Rainer, holds the diamond necklace that Florenz Ziegfeld her to celebrate their first wedding anniversary. The wide diamond bracelet on her wrist is Art Deco in design, but the delicate diamond necklace harks back to the turn of the century, when frilly arrangements of small diamonds were every show girl's favorite.

Opposite, lower right: Among Florenz Ziegfeld's many beauties shone a plain girl from Brooklyn, Fanny Brice, whose comedic gifts and winsome femininity made her famous. She starred in all but two Follies from 1910 through 1923 and made screen appearances in two movies about Ziegfeld, *The Great Ziegfeld* (1936) and *Ziegfeld Follies* (1946). Brice's success brought wealth and a jewelry collection as grand as those of the New York Four Hundred, with whom she socialized. One night, while entertaining at home, Brice complimented Averill Harriman's wife on her diamond and emerald bracelet. A couple of weeks later, Harriman sent Brice a similar one. This 1921 fashion portrait by Abbe from *Vanity Fair* shows Brice with a pearl bracelet, a gem-set bracelet, and a diamond pinky ring.

Jean Harlow wore precious jewelry as she did clothes, in a bold, offhand, provocative manner that exuded sensuality. Large diamond clip brooches appeared where they were least expected: on the shoestring straps of her sleek dresses, at the small of her back, or on her hip, drawing attention to her curvaceous figure and undeniable sex appeal.

Men wore jewelry in gangster movies as a visible sign of success. An ambitious young hoodlum on his way to the top, Rico (Edward G. Robinson) in *Little Caesar* (1931) sizes up gang lord Diamond Pete Montana (Sidney Blackmer) by his diamond horseshoe tie tack and diamond ring. After Rico conquers Detroit by killing friends as well as enemies, he admires the jewelry of his adversary, Little Arnie Lorch (Maurice Black) before he runs him out of town. After studying Arnie's gaudy stickpin, which the camera shows in close-up, Rico fondles his own thick platinum and diamond ring and says, "Nothing phony about my jewelry."

Similarly, in *Scarface* (1932), when Tony Camonte (Paul Muni) begins his ascent to power, he, too, invests in jewelry—the same two items, tie tack and platinum ring—prompting moll Poppy (Karen Morley) to tell him, "I see you're going in for jewelry. It's kinda feminine, isn't it?" Tony is not put off. When he murders the mob's boss after a memorable evening that includes a nightclub sequence, a high-speed chase, and a shoot-out, he goes straight to Poppy's apartment and tells her to pack her bags.

MUSICALS

Along with the quick, snappy dialogue of dramas and narratives, talking pictures introduced the musical. The earliest film musicals imitated Broadway's theatrical-revue style of the Music Box Theatre, George White's Scandals, and the most famous of them all, the Ziegfeld Follies. Florenz Ziegfeld was the

A Ziegfeld Follies girl known as Dolores appeared as the White Peacock in *Vanity Fair* (1919). Her costume, designed by Pascaud of Paris, had a six-by-ten-foot peacock tail, which she spread with sequined ropes.

Jewels that Shine in 'The Midnight Sun'

Alice O'Neill shows the foreign designers some new tricks in these ballet costumes

The marquise ring might have been designed for Gloria Swanson. It's one of the unusual costumes worn in "The Midnight Sun" staged by Dimitri Buchowetski for Universal

"A pearl of great price" or why the lowly oyster breaks into society. One of the Fanchon and Marco dancers who take part in the ballet

The one jewel no woman likes to refuse—the diamond solitaire engagement ring. It's the cause of a lot of trouble in the world

The icicle of precious stones—the cold white diamond. However, it has been known to be successful in thawing out frozen hearts

A popular jewelry trend of the Gilded Age was the phrase jewel. Bracelets were composed of a sequence of gems, whose names began with the corresponding letters of the word "Dearest": diamond, emerald, amethyst, ruby, emerald, sapphire, topaz. Ziegfeld asked couturiere Lady Duff Gordon to create costumes representing each stone for a "Dearest" dance routine to be part of the "Midnight Frolics." This jewel pageant was later imitated by Hollywood in the Universal film *The Midnight Sun* (1925).

Right: Like Paul Iribe, the other French designer in Hollywood, Erté had worked early in his career for Paul Poiret and incorporated the pearl style into his sets and costumes for the "Tableau of Jewelry" from *The Hollywood Revue* (1929). The underwater nymphs held batons that resembled pearl-studded stickpins blown up to life-size dimensions. Erté's dictum that costumes should extend the lines of the body into decorative arabesques resulted in ornate, pearl-studded, curvy outfits.

patriarch of New York revues, having produced shows with glamorous women since the 1890s, when he imported Parisian dancer Anna Held to give glamour to his company. Diamond Jim (Brady), the railroad magnate, put up the money, and together Ziegfeld and Held stormed the entertainment scene, touring across the country on the vaudeville circuit. Ziegfeld was notorious for his publicity stunts, and on one occasion he ordered quantities of milk to be delivered to Held. Then he leaked to the press that Held had exorbitant milk bills because she took daily milk baths. Although she had never taken one in her life, after this, women everywhere took milk baths emulating her, hoping to achieve her beauty.

Ziegfeld made Held an American star. In turn she inspired him, according to one of Ziegfeld's biographers, the entertainer Eddie Cantor, when she said, "Your American girls are the most beautiful in the world, if you could only dress them up chic and charmant. You could do a much better review than the Folies Bergères in this country."[*] Bent on surpassing the French in every aspect of showmanship, Ziegfeld opened the follies in 1907, refining, glorifying, and ultimately transforming the light-opera singers and dancers of the Gilded Age into the long-legged, fresh, lively American show girl. He instituted the Follies's Mannequin Parade, a troupe of beauties strolling across the stage in the sexiest, most elaborate costumes ever seen in the American theater. Emphasizing the costumes of his chorines, Ziegfeld was the first vaudeville producer to enter into a close and well-publicized collaboration with couturiers.

When the movie industry became more remunerative, Ziegfeld's girls began to desert the Follies to make movies. To be a Ziegfeld Follies girl was to have passed the first audition into the world of film; Eddie Cantor gave one reason why: Ziegfeld "was the first to see girls through a camera eye—long before the movie people, who learned the trick from him—and he often accepted women from their photographs after actually rejecting them in person."[**] Consequently, the Ziegfeld chorus line produced some of Hollywood's great beauties, among them Mae Murray, Bebe Daniels, Marion Davies, Peggy Hopkins-Joyce, Lilyan Tashman, Paulette Goddard, and Barbara Stanwyck.

The first all-singing and all-dancing movie precipitating a mass westward migration of performers from New York was *The Hollywood Revue* (1929),

* Eddie Cantor and David Freedman, *Ziegfeld, The Great Glorifier* (New York: Alfred H. King, 1934), 41.   **Cantor, 10.

starring practically every member of MGM's stable: leading men John Gilbert and Lionel Barrymore, comedians Buster Keaton, Laurel and Hardy, and Jack Benny, and screen beauties Joan Crawford, Norma Shearer, Marion Davies, Marie Dressler, and Bessie Love.

Among the many skits in *The Hollywood Revue* was a Tableau of Jewelry. It had been designed by a famous designer who was also occasionally a jeweler, Russian-born Romain de Tirtoff, who went by the French pronunciation of his initials, Erté. As illustrator and commentator at *Harper's Bazaar* from 1915 to 1930, Erté wrote articles from Europe, mostly Paris and Monte Carlo, directed fashion layouts, and illustrated 240 out of 264 *Harper's Bazaar* covers. He was already an American celebrity when William Randolph Hearst, *Harper's Bazaar's* publisher and communications tycoon, brought him to Hollywood to be a designer for Cosmopolitan Films, a company formed to promote the career of Hearst's mistress, Marion Davies. In *The Restless Sex* (1920), Erté's sequence, "Bal des Arts," was a resounding success. For the Tableau of Jewelry, Erté used costume designs that had proved successful the previous year at the Folies Bergères.

Ziegfeld himself held a long-standing prejudice against the movies. Only after losing over a million dollars in the stock market crash and seeking to recoup his investments was he persuaded by Samuel Goldwyn to undertake a cinematic venture. The vehicle was *Whoopee!* (1930), a Broadway production starring one of Ziegfeld's best comedians, Eddie Cantor, as Henry Williams, a hypochondriac set down in the Wild West among cowgirls, cowboys, and Indians. Dedicated to a superb production, Goldwyn had the movie filmed in two-tone Technicolor, a rudimentary color process in which red and green were projected on the screen by two cameras simultaneously. Ziegfeld's extravagant taste was manifested in the girls, as scantily clad in movies as they had been on the Broadway stage. There was even a Mannequin Parade of Indian women.

Most significantly for the history of the Hollywood musical, Broadway choreographer Busby Berkeley cut his teeth on cinematic staging in *Whoopee!* He managed the challenge of capturing on screen the beauty, majesty, and color of the chorus line with one camera, which he moved around the set on a monorail. He even hoisted it overhead, inspiring the term *Berkeley top shot*. The chorus line was metamorphosed into bud and flowerlike designs, snowflakes, sunbursts, and other circular patterns resembling a kaleidoscope. With a cinematic eye on the Hollywood musical, dance numbers bloomed. Berkeley's awesome effects changed the presentation of dance routines in the movies, and with the mere chorus line outdated, every studio scrambled to imitate his style.

Shortly after the thunderous success of *Whoopee!* Florenz Ziegfeld died. Realizing his great contribution to theatrical entertainment throughout a career spent glorifying the American girl, Hollywood tipped its hat to the New Yorker in several films about his life, times, Follies, and stars. In 1936 William Powell starred as Ziegfeld in the film biography *The Great Ziegfeld,* a three-hour extravaganza that received the Academy Award for Best Picture. One of Ziegfeld's most endearing traits, emphasized in the film, was his penchant for bestowing jewelry on his show girls and wives. Although *The Great Ziegfeld* was set in the teens, both Anna Held and the show girl Audrey are portrayed wearing the wide Art Deco diamond bracelets of the 1920s.

During the twenties, when Erté went to Hollywood to create costumes and sets, he was also designing jewelry in colors reminiscent of Poiret's Eastern palette. This ink and gouache drawing by Erté for a jewelled comb combines green jade, turquoise, and round diamonds.

Historical Revivals

Historical revivals were nothing new to Hollywood, but in the 1930s, an explosion of films with period settings, costumes, and jewelry hit the screen. The genre received an electric shock from the voluptuous Mae West, who, with her Gilded Age re-creations, had audiences laughing in the aisles during the depths of the Depression. At mid-decade, the historical revival was elevated to drama with such ill-fated heroines as Camille, Marie Antoinette, Elizabeth I of England, Carlotta of Mexico, and Scarlett O'Hara played by the most respected actresses Hollywood could find, Greta Garbo and Bette Davis leading the way. These films gave costume designers an opportunity to provide a view of history that included lavish re-created jewelry. And sometimes costume designers did not have to rely on imitations, as they were able to obtain authentic historical pieces.

In the 1930s jewels with royal provenance changed hands with great fanfare. Diamond prices plummeted in 1929. Even crown jewels, which had been so popular with Americans of the Gilded Age, went up for sale, prompting a columnist in a trade magazine to observe that European royalty used America as its pawnshop. Coming from the collections of the actual counterparts of the celluloid heroines—Marie Antoinette, Empress Carlotta, and other noble families—these jewels went into the hands of new owners just as the nation's economic recovery began. Hollywood stars, along with other women, were able to acquire actual historical jewels intact as well as important stones that could be incorporated into modern settings.

Along with the fashion for jewels with a regal lineage, the revival movie heroines sparked nostalgic styles in jewelry. A few years earlier only dowagers, aging actresses, and maiden aunts wore historical jewelry. An article called "Jewels for the Return to Romance" in *The Jewelers' Circular* by June Hamilton Rhodes compared styles of 1938 to those in eighteenth- and nineteenth-century France. The differences between the old and new stemmed from technology and stone cuts. The historical jewels were not mounted in platinum but in silver, which tarnished and turned black over time, and they were set with smaller stones in old-fashioned cuts that reflected far less light than the modern cuts. With the use of platinum and the repertoire of stone cuts broadened and improved, the modern jeweler was free to create a new romantic style, mounting important stones in impressive settings, sometimes taking inspiration from court motifs—bows, lace, and flowers.

The star credited with bringing back historical styles when everyone else was wearing Art Deco was Mae West, who uttered the most original phrase about jewelry in her first film, *Night After Night* (1932). After a hat-check girl gushes, "Goodness, what beautiful diamonds," West replies, "Goodness had nothing to do with it." This phrase and West's diamond collection became part of her persona.

Nineteenth-century lace was the design inspiration for Greer Garson's diamond necklace and bow-knot bracelet by the Los Angeles jeweler Brock. She appears in a *Harper's Bazaar* (1940) fashion portrait by Louise Dahl-Wolfe to publicize her new film, *Pride and Prejudice*, co-starring Laurence Olivier.

Opposite: Metropolitan Opera singer and MGM film star Grace Moore wears a necklace by Parisian jeweler Arnold Ostertag at her debut concert with the General Motors Symphony Orchestra at Carnegie Hall on October 24, 1937. The necklace is composed of a rectangular and baguette-cut diamond chain suspending a rectangular diamond frame holding a baguette-cut diamond and a pear-shaped frame holding a shield-shaped diamond, mounted in platinum. The jewel includes a stone of royal lineage. According to *Photoplay* (1937), the baguette diamond was cut from the Cullinan diamond, which weighed 3,106 carats when it was found in South Africa in 1905. The two most famous stones from the Cullinan are set in the British Imperial state crown and Edward VII's sceptre.

Cartier designed and mounted the emerald and diamond necklace that Irving Berlin gave to his wife, Ellin Mackay, after their first year of marriage. She was an American heiress whose family fortune came from the Comstock Lode of silver in Nevada. During their marriage Berlin commissioned Cartier several times to mount emeralds from her family's famous collection. This necklace, with cluster motifs reminiscent of historical pieces, is composed of five graduated square-cut and two pear-shaped emeralds set in circular and cushion-cut diamonds suspending a 60-carat rectangular-cut emerald with four shield-shaped diamond accents, mounted in platinum. The intensity of the emeralds' yellow-green hue marks them as perfect examples of gems from the Muzo mine in Colombia, which produced the finest emeralds in the world. Another Mackay emerald of 168 carats was donated to the Smithsonian Institution in 1931.

Opposite: The baguette-cut diamonds along the border of this huge pavé-set diamond floral choker and its barrel-shaped clasp combine a rejuvenated romantic style with touches of Art Deco. The choker centers on two life-size, three-dimensional diamond roses, their diamond leaves articulated with long baguette-cut veins. Both roses can be worn as clip brooches. Two additional diamond roses with unfurling petals form earrings to match. The jewel was commissioned in about 1938 by Queen Nazli, queen of Egypt and mother of King Farouk.

A New York vaudeville veteran who often wrote her own material, Mae West went to Hollywood under contract to Paramount in 1932. Her second film, *She Done Him Wrong* (1933), was an adaptation of her Broadway hit play *Diamond Lil*. West plays Lady Lou, a vaudeville singer with a knockout diamond collection. Lou lives in a luxurious suite above a dance hall, where she receives an assortment of underworld types and one reformer, Captain Cummings (Cary Grant). In the end, as her chums are taken off in paddy wagons by the police, Captain Cummings, the undercover policeman, takes Lady Lou away in a hansom cab—and not to prison. As they ride off, he removes all her oversize diamond rings and places one small diamond engagement ring on the appropriate finger.

West's prototype was the shapely actress Lillian Russell, nicknamed Diamond Lil for her love of diamonds. Lillian Russell's career began in 1881 when she was eighteen years old. In a witty takeoff on Gilbert and Sullivan's *Patience*, produced by Tony Pastor, she was an overnight success, captivating critics with her operatic singing voice and stage presence and charming the public with her beautiful blond hair and voluptuous figure. Russell's fame rapidly spread beyond New York as she went on grand tours across America and to London, playing the leading roles in comic operas such as *Paul and Virginia, The Princess Ida,* and *Poor Jonathan.*

Throughout her life Russell was the center of controversy and scandal. Constantly in court over broken contracts, she accepted far-flung engagements to escape creditors and irate managers. A favorite of gossip columnists on both sides of the Atlantic, she caused an uproar by flirting from the London stage with a young Haitian prince and by making sexual overtures to her leading man on the New York stage—as she admitted later to the press.

Russell inspired her admirers not only to choose expensive jewelry but to be creative in how they presented it to her. One sent her a basket of flowers with a new diamond jewel every night after her performance at the Casino Theater in New York—but when rebuffed by Russell, he demanded all the jewels back. As reported in the *Jewelers' Circular* of 1893, Russell was unable to return them, because her jeweler had removed the diamonds—a standard practice in the 1890s. Russell doted on large, lavish, flashy diamond jewelry made from designs of her own devising. During a London tour, she appeared on stage wearing a conspicuous brooch with the name of her fiancé, Teddie Solomon, spelled in diamonds, a shocking display of bad taste that horrified the British public.

The only person who could outdo Diamond Lil in vulgarity was her close friend and admirer James Buchanan Brady, "Diamond Jim," one of the most famous financiers of the Gilded Age, who made diamonds his emblem. From his early days as a traveling salesman of railroad supplies, Brady paid calls on pawnbrokers—as well as clients—driving hard deals for diamonds. He learned that the flaunting of diamonds won him the finest suites in hotels, the best tables at restaurants, and the most beautiful girls. What's more, diamonds could be converted into cold cash. Brady carried them around in his pockets.

Casting around for a way to display more jewelry, Brady asked his jeweler to make him a dress suite—a matching set of accessories such as cufflinks, belt buckles, shirt studs, rings, and lapel pins—with different stones and themes for every day of the month. His jeweler was at first overwhelmed, as there were not

In her signature attire, a corset and diamond jewelry, Mae West was described by *Vogue* (1933) as single-handedly bringing back Gilded Age finery.

Mae West
REVEALS THE FOUNDATION OF THE 1900 MODE
by CECELIA AGER

OUT in Hollywood, Mae West smooths her ever-so-gently undulating hips, swells her bosom, and, jiggling easily on one knee, hearkens to the tales of a Paris gone Mae West with the quiet equanimity of your true zealot vindicated—a crusader now suddenly become prophet, who can take it. "So Paris is beginning to understand about the freedom of the knees—" she murmurs, smiling a little. "... silhouette—what is it but a ... the ladies' way of saying that the de... at the waist-line, and you have ... A little squeeze of the ... Miss West has al... alts fascinated at ... d. There is some... ds, that gets the rov... , seem to lead it else... s, "and so accentuate ... fundamental as Euclid. ... ed in fundamentals—hon... Nature. Always, she's ap... e's beacons. When, as a girl, ... enus de Milo (and she did it' ... he being fired with the ambition ... d measurements of a fine figure, a ... she says, "I would spread cocoa... which I wished to attain prominence." ... her. (Everybody does.) Maybe it was ... maybe it was plain wish-fulfilment; but, ... ss West was never one to stop at wishing. ... self says: "If they bring corsets back—they'll ... something to put into them." ... t surprise her that the world is coming around ... y of looking at things; sooner or later, it was sure ... en. "I didn't discover curves, after all," she ex... modestly. "I only uncovered them. From the days ... dam and Eve, woman has had breasts and hips. If it

weren't intended for her to have them, she never would have been created with them. Why is it you never see men turn around and look at a girl as she passes them on the streets, the way they used to when women were women? Why? Because there's nothing for them to look at any more." Fortunately, this grievous male disinterest may soon be replaced by the lively contemplation Miss West has fought to restore, if, as a result of her persuasive work in "She Done Him Wrong," it again becomes the fashion for girls to have something to look at.

The Mae West silhouette so unselfishly revealed in "She Done Him Wrong" is not, then, chance—but the ultimate triumph of a lifelong conviction. Miss West's childhood instincts, it turns out, have not betrayed her. Old-fashioned about a great many things, she believes in the Battle of the Sexes—and in being well equipped for the fray.

Foremost of her own weapons is a generous measure of what she delicately characterizes as "that certain element," but, nevertheless, she brings heart to her more scantily endowed sisters. Says she: "That certain element gives a fine foundation to start from, but it must be nurtured. The tiniest bit of it, properly tended and set off, blooms into a passion flower. What can be accomplished by the feminine figure, once it is nipped here and there, but allowed free rein elsewhere, would surprise you."

Her words ringing in your ears, be encouraged then to the best possible enhancement of fore and aft. She suggests corseting, but done (*Continued on page 86*)

(*Continued on page 86*)

Later a subject of films, Lillian Russell appears here as the Milkmaid in *Patience* (1881).

In *She Done Him Wrong* (1933) Mae West wears a combination of diamond jewelry styles of the 1890s and 1920s. Here, she scrutinizes a cabochon that has been stolen for her by Gilbert Roland.

enough precious stones, or even semiprecious stones, to fulfill such a request, but pressured by Diamond Jim, the jeweler creatively produced dress suites using different cuts of diamonds—marquises, half-moons, pear shapes—for which he scoured the diamond-cutting centers of Amsterdam and Calcutta. He also monitored international markets for "freak" stones—green diamonds and pink sapphires.

Diamond Jim's jewelry and character continued to fascinate the public long after his death in 1917. In 1934, when jeweler Parker Morell published his biography, the store where Diamond Jim was a legendary shopper, Black, Starr & Frost, honored the book with an exhibition of the Transportation Set. The following year, a film biography of Brady written by Preston Sturges was released.

Diamond Jim Brady showered many actresses with sparkling baubles, but the one who received the most lavish gifts was Lillian Russell. He started by giving her diamond jewels, which he called doodads, every time he saw her perform, and soon jewelry became the center of their ebullient relationship. Diamond Jim once bet Lil a diamond ring that he could eat more than she could at dinner. Rising to the

Movies Form Important Publicity Medium

"Lillian Russell" Film May be Start of New "Jewelry" Style Trend if Trade Pushes Hard Enough

● ON May 15, the day it played host to the World Premier of the 20th Century Fox picture "Lillian Russell", the Mississippi river city of Clin... ...was treated to the most forcef... ...wels it had seen in many

...the life and loves of ...lad singer and chief ...iamond Jim" Brady ...showered her with ...ls in the land. Of ...the dripped pearls ...eaks and platters ...re with feeling ... poker. Cigars ... $3,900 gold- ...was a sensa- ...icycle, trim- ...apphires".

...haps, unre- ...ble is, of ...however, ...st addi- ...ies will ...arefree ...portant ...appy, ...ther ...the ...ill ...it

PHOTOGRAPHS of Alice Faye as "Lillian Russell", in full costume and wearing her gorgeous jewels about which so many romantic, if unauthentic, stories have been written, are available from the Jewelry Industry Publicity Board, 366 Fifth avenue, New York. Ideal for display purposes, they should be exhibited simultaneously with showing of the picture in community theatres.

Since that time the film capital has produced an unbroken string of epical productions, both educationally and from the standpoint of e x c e l l e n t entertainment — an achievement that has resulted in millions of dollars at the box office and many more millions of patrons in the theatres of the nation.

Business men and business organizations were quick to appreciate the great amount of publicity that accrued to persons, places and objects appearing on the silver screen and many trades founded organizations such as the Jewelry Industry Publicity Board, one of the main objectives of which was to secure favorable reaction to their products on the part of Hollywood studios.

Once this was accomplished, and jewelry has received a cordial reception from producers because of its value as a "prop" to say nothing of the romance interwoven into its ancient background, it remained for re-

At right are 4 "stills" of Alice Faye, star of the 20th Century Fox, 10 million dollar version of the life of Lillian Russell. With her in the picture at top right is Don Ameche who plays the part of Composer Edward Solomon, one of her husbands. At lower left is Edward Arnold as Diamond Jim Brady.

National Jeweler, June 1940

"DIAMOND JIM'S" JEWELRY ITEMIZED

Morell's new biography of James Buchanan Brady, the picturesque capitalist and spender of the "nineties" gives details of his unusual gem collection, in connection with his history and characteristics.

JAMES BUCHANAN BRADY

Jewelers even more than ...most of its general readers will appreciate the new work "Diamond Jim" by Parker Morell which was issued last month by Simon & Schuster. This work chronicles the life and times of James Buchanan Brady... and one of the most esque figure of the "Gay Nineties" and period. "Diamond bold and shrewd capitalists in the social, theatrical and Jim" was known to everybody in the... he was known as one financial worlds. With the jewelers... gems and jewelry worth between a million and a half... to two million dollars. of the "big spenders" who had bought... life is a member of a Mr. Morell who sketched Brady's... Alfred N Morell of 608 Fifth family of jewelers. He son of... interested in "Diamond Ave, New York. He first became... this interest that this biography "Jim" for professional reasons but... halftone illus- and it is due to this interest that... sections of the The 273 pages are filled with... much of trations of "Diamond Jim", his friends,... Especially inter- city of his time and particularly illustrations... his esting are the pictures of his house, his furniture and his ornaments. "Diamond Jim" spent a "million a year" ... and in all spent more than a million for his own personal large and specially made gem jewelry for his business use, and intimate friends, men and especially women. The In addition he bought fine jewelry for his business author claims that as a climax of this orgy of spending he

(Turn to page 57)

HIS BEAUTIFUL CAR WHEEL RING

The Transportation Set centered more diamonds than all the others. Brady car wheel ring. The center ring carried a 10 carats and had 42 smaller diamonds sur rounding it.

THE BICYCLE SHIRT STUD

Every appliance con nected with the han dling and carrying was represented on the set. The bicycle was pictured with 119 flashing gems while this enhanced this exhibit ion of transportation

THE STEAMSHIP PENCIL

AN EYEGLASS CASE DECORATION

THE JEWELERS' CIRCULAR
for November, 1934

55

DIAMOND JIM'S JEWELRY

(From page 55)

conceived the startling idea of owning a different set of jewelry for every day of the month. To quote from Mr. Morell's story:

"Let's see," he said to his amazed jeweler. "I've got six sets now—the diamond, the emerald, the turquoise, the ruby, and the sapphire. Round up twenty-four more different stones and let me know how much it'll cost to have sets made."

"But Mr. Brady—" the jeweler was startled. "There aren't twenty-four other different kinds of precious stones. It would be hard to get a collection of even twenty-four different semi-precious varieties."

"Is that so?" Jim boomed, sticking out his jaw. "Listen! I'm gonna have a different set for every day in the month. If you want to go on bein' my jeweler, you'd better see about gettin' 'em."

With much argument the jeweler convinced Jim that it would take years to assemble such a collection. Stones of a size and quality to catch the Brady fancy were not easily found in jewel markets. They had to be sought after and watched for. They had to be snapped up whenever news of their existence trickled in from great distributing centres such as Amsterdam and Calcutta. Moreover there were only three other precious gems from which sets could be formed—the pearl, the cat's-eye and the star sapphire.

"However," the jeweler continued, "as you know, there are other forms of diamonds—marquise, half-moons, and pear shapes. We could combine those into sets. And we could find freak stones like green diamonds, red sapphires and blue rubies, if you wanted."

"Sure," Jim told him. "I don't care much what they are, as long as I get 30 different sets. Say, as a starter I think I'll have you make me a 'Transportation Set.' I've been in the railroad business almost 40 years, and it's time I celebrated it."

This Transportation Set was the one which was destined to cause more comment than all the other Brady

(Turn to page 58)

POCKETBOOK CLASP . . . TIE CLIP

Desert transportation represented by t h e camel tie clip (above) was a prominent part of the set—the pocket book clasp at the left was greatly admired.

THE RAILROAD CAR CUFF LINKS

The four cuff links in the transportation set were a tank car, a hopper car, a gondola car and a coal car. One set is shown at the left

BIRDSEYE OF THE CAR WHEEL RING

THE AIRPLANE LAPEL BUTTON

THE JEWELERS' CIRCULAR
for November, 1934

57

A *Jewelers' Circular* (1934) review of a biography of Diamond Jim Brady illustrated the most famous of the gambler's jewelry: the Transportation Suite included a locomotive engine eyeglass case, studded with 210 diamonds, and a car wheel ring, with a 10-carat diamond center in a 42-diamond surround.

Right: The lavish period-style costume jewelry of *Lillian Russell* inspired an article in the trade magazine *National Jeweler* (1940) on how movies influence jewelry styles.

Right: Alice Faye played the title figure and Edward Arnold repeated as Diamond Jim in *Lillian Russell* (1940). One of the film's props was a recreated gem-set bicycle. Brady had, in fact, given Russell a solid silver bicycle from Tiffany, and another bicycle with her monogram in diamonds and emeralds on the handlebars.

challenge with gusto, Russell went to the ladies' room, took off her corset, and came back to win the bet. Brady's gifts to Russell reveal Gilded Age spending at its most profligate, since he ordered everything he could for her in precious materials from Tiffany. A chamber pot, with an eye mischievously engraved on the interior, was reproduced in gold. The garters he gave her were not simply circlets of diamonds and lace but spiders with emerald bodies and diamond and ruby legs. He also commissioned an anklet with the racy phrase "Heaven's Above" in diamonds.

Toward the end of Lillian Russell's career in 1914, Louis J. Selznick persuaded her to make a movie. Selznick, like Adolph Zukor before him, felt that a stage star would enhance a movie and generate box-office returns. He purchased the movie rights to *Wildfire*, a play that Russell had made famous internationally, and cast dramatic actor Lionel Barrymore as her leading man. Barrymore and Russell were a combustible combination. His sense of humor on the movie set reduced her to paroxysms of giggles in which she broke character and wasted valuable footage. Since the production was silent, Barrymore could say anything he liked to Russell; on one occasion, refusing to let go of her hand as directed in the script, he stared at her emerald ring, saying, "What a beautiful piece of green glass. Was it made from a beer bottle?" Russell burst into laughter, losing time and film.*

For the film biography *Diamond Jim* (1935), Binnie Barnes as Lillian Russell wears a modest cameo suite and Diamond Jim (Edward Arnold) sports a car-wheel ring recreated for the movie.

* Parker Morell, *Lillian Russell, The Era of Plush* (New York: Random House, 1940), 244.

Despite the high spirits of the leads, *Wildfire* turned out to be labored and wooden. It was panned by the critics and unpopular with the public, and it almost destroyed Selznick's company, the World Film Corporation. Although Lillian Russell never made another movie, *Lillian Russell* (1940), starring Alice Faye and Edward Arnold, told the story of her life. A wittier, livelier, and more enduring legacy was Mae West's play *Diamond Lil* and its movie adaptation, *She Done Him Wrong.*

Mae West went beyond simply writing about Lillian Russell; she put on a corset to cinch her waist, pushed up her bosom, and became Diamond Lil onstage and off. West's style brought back the fashions of the Gilded Age—the corset, the long, tight-fitting, trailing dress, the huge hat trimmed with feathers, and diamonds galore.

She Done Him Wrong catapulted West to international stardom and popularized her style abroad. French critics proclaimed that her acting had surpassed that of Greta Garbo and Marlene Dietrich; in Paris "Mae West" parties were organized, giving Parisians the opportunity to parade their new clothes and heirloom diamonds. The French couturiere Elsa Schiaparelli used West's hourglass figure as the inspiration for the bottle of her perfume Shocking.

By 1935 West was the highest-paid woman in America. She wrote in her autobiography, *Goodness Had Nothing to Do with It,* "With this kind of income, I was even paying for my own jewels—sometimes. I have always felt a gift diamond shines better than one you buy for yourself." Mae West collected jewelry in every style, combining frilly diamond necklaces of the Gilded Age with wide geometric diamond bracelets of the 1920s and flashing a diamond ring on every finger.

While Mae West was inspiring Paris with her turn-of-the-century American look, Hollywood was diving into European history for inspiration, coming up with looks that would influence the world's fashion. *Photoplay* (1936) reported, "It has often happened that Paris has been inspired by the clothes in a major film and has developed this inspiration. The trends, in turn, are reflected in New York, and so we have the Hollywood, Paris, American tie-up." When Adrian undertook the costuming of Marguerite Gautier in *Camille,* he was dealing with a character of proven ability to win audiences on both sides of the Atlantic; the casting of Greta Garbo in the leading role was an additional guarantee of the movie's drawing power.

In *Camille,* Greta Garbo's décolletage sparkles with necklaces from scene one, when she wears a large rectangular-cut gem in a tiered mount worthy of a courtesan known for extravagance. In precarious health and in love with Armand Duval (Robert Taylor), a worthy man of small means, Marguerite is forced in the course of the movie to sell her valuables, and this same necklace, bought from her for a song, later appears around the neck of her rival.

As reported in *Photoplay* (1936), Adrian supplied the precious jewelry Garbo wore in this film. He intuitively understood the relationship between her performance and precious jewelry. "At first, they hung bangles and glass beads on her," Adrian said. "I saw that she was like a tree with deep roots—deep in the earth. Never put an artificial jewel or imitation lace on Garbo. It would do something to Garbo and her performance."* Adrian reserved the most magnificent necklace, which he designed with real emeralds and pearls, for the most passionate—and

* La Vine, 164.

In a box at the opera in *Camille* (1936), the courtesan Olympe (Lenore Ulric, left), and her friends Prudence (Laura Hope Crews, center), and Marguerite (Greta Garbo) study the crowd. Prudence wears an imitation jet and diamond necklace designed by Joseff of Hollywood and Marguerite an imitation emerald and diamond necklace by Adrian.

tragic—scene of *Camille*. Marguerite wears the square-cut emerald and pearl cluster necklace when she visits Armand in his apartments, persuades him not to leave France, and sets in motion the decisions that ultimately cause her to forsake her old way of life and move to the country with him. Later, moved by the remonstrances of his father (Lionel Barrymore), she gives up Armand and returns to the wealthy baron who had paid her bills in the past.

Although it was Adrian who philosophized about Garbo and jewelry and took all the glory for the pearl and emerald necklace in *Camille,* it was the costume jewelry supplier Eugene Joseff who created her gold rope twist necklace. Garbo's perfectionism was in evidence when she turned down the first version, but Joseff's ability was proven when the second one passed her scrutiny. Joseff was first inspired to make costume jewelry for historical films after he saw Constance Bennett as the duchess of Florence wearing a contemporary necklace in *The Affairs of Cellini* (1934). Some time later, he advertised a rhinestone bracelet for rent to the studios, and he followed this policy for the rest of his career, creating a rental library of approximately three million jewels. He supplied jewelry for hundreds of films but never received an on-screen credit.

Eugene Joseff became Joseff of Hollywood, working with the studios as a member of the wardrobe team, creating jewelry to fit the specifications of the costume designers, making jewelry in bulk for extras, adding colorful, individual pieces in Czechoslovakian crystals—and occasionally semiprecious stones—and reproducing a real jewel when a fine jeweler refused to lend it indefinitely to a production. Paying careful attention to details, setting every piece by hand as though it were precious, and analyzing the impact of his work on screen, Joseff achieved authentic period effects as well as praise from the leading ladies, who commissioned him to make jewelry for their private collections. Becoming the most famous costume jeweler in Hollywood through his success with the studios, Joseff sold copies of his screen gems to department stores.

Garbo's screen jewelry did not all come from Joseff. An actual parure dating from the Napoleonic period, and not a costume copy, her suite of jewelry in

Actress Merle Oberon's Napoleonic necklace is composed of oval and rectangular-cut emeralds set in an old-mine–cut diamond, gold, and silver Garland style mounting. Along with a matching bracelet, the necklace had been given by Napoleon III to Baroness Haussmann, the wife of the city planner responsible for the reorganization of Paris during the Second Empire.

Conquest (1937) was the most important and valuable of all the pieces utilized in historical dramas. In *Conquest* Garbo portrayed Maria Walewska, a Polish countess who forsakes her elderly husband to become Napoleon's mistress and the mother of his illegitimate son. Unlike the rest of the female characters, who drip with jewels, Garbo does not wear a single earring, bracelet, or necklace until the climactic scene, when she plans to tell Napoleon (Charles Boyer) she is pregnant. He does not give her a chance to break her news, so intent is he on his own decision to marry the Habsburg princess Marie-Louise for the sake of peace and a royal dynasty. On this tragic evening Garbo wears a parure that Napoleon gave Marie-Louise at the birth of their son. An American firm pulled off a coup by obtaining the jewelry through its European offices from the Archduchess Immaculata of Vienna. The suite received a special credit in the movie: "Napoleon Jewels through courtesy of Trabert & Hoeffer Inc., Mauboussin." Trabert and Hoeffer had bought the name and inventory of the French firm Mauboussin when it was forced to close in New York after the stock market crash of 1929.

Wanting to keep important royal jewelry at the forefront of his repertoire of costume accessories, Adrian announced to *Photoplay* (1938) that he went to Paris in search of jewelry for *Marie Antoinette* (1938) and found jewels that once belonged to the French queen and her ladies-in-waiting for the production. The aura of authenticity surrounding the jewels was theatrical sleight of hand, as were the jewels themselves. One of the spurious jewels is a ring given by Marie Antoinette (Norma Shearer) to her Swedish lover (Tyrone Power) and used to verify their communications with each other. The romance, as well as the ring—inscribed in English and made by Joseff—are Hollywood history, not French.

However, *Marie Antoinette* did include an interesting reenactment of an authentic jewelry history scenario involving a diamond necklace, the "girdle of Marie Antoinette," which the queen was accused of buying with 1,600,000 livres from the royal treasury. The scandal that erupted implicated the queen, her personal secretary, and the cardinal, and it did indeed hasten the coming of the French Revolution. But the scandal was not based on a real purchase: The queen never considered buying the necklace and was quoted as saying that France needed a ship more than another jewel.

Historicism if not history also played a part in *Juarez* (1939). In the film Bette Davis portrays the wife of Emperor Maximilian of Mexico (Brian Aherne), who is betrayed by Napoleon III. He dies in front of the firing squad of a Mexican rebel army led by Benito Juarez (Paul Muni). The earrings that had belonged to Empress Carlotta advertised by Black, Starr & Frost in 1927 were not used in the production. But Bette Davis is accurately dressed by the head designer at Warner Bros., Orry-Kelly. The most historically proficient designer in all of Hollywood, his obsession with correct detail is evident in all his films. In *Juarez*, Carlotta wears a different suite of jewelry in each scene. Some of the pieces are antique, coming from Europe and Mexico City, and some are carefully styled costume pieces used to complete her attire.

Orry-Kelly reveled in jewels that were an extension of his costumes, and he oversaw their production and their integration. No film exemplifies this better than *The Private Lives of Elizabeth and Essex* (1939). Bette Davis as Queen Elizabeth and Errol Flynn as Essex were covered in Renaissance-style jewelry.

In the *Jewelers' Circular* (1929), R.J. Trabert of Trabert & Hoeffer, wrote an essay about a pair of diamond earrings that had belonged to Russian empress Catherine the Great. His firm was responsible for obtaining a Napoleonic necklace that Greta Garbo wore in *Conquest* (1937).

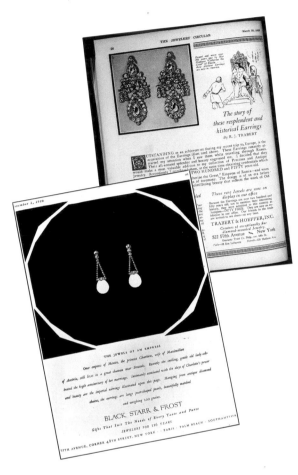

In 1926 Black, Starr & Frost advertised one of its acquisitions in *Vogue*—a pair of pear-shaped pearl and diamond earrings that had belonged to Empress Carlotta. The earrings did not sell at the time, probably because of the ascendancy of the Art Deco style. In 1937, during a revival of romantic styles, they found a buyer.

Charles Boyer as Napoleon embraces Garbo as Maria Walewska in *Conquest* (1937). Garbo wears an antique necklace and matching bracelets composed of rubies, emeralds, sapphires, amethyst, topaz, and black and white enamel mounted in gold. Trabert & Hoeffer-Mauboussin received a film credit for obtaining this historical suite of jewelry.

In *Juarez* (1939) Brian Aherne plays Emperor Maximilian and Bette Davis is his empress, Carlotta. She wears a portrait miniature. Small enamel portraits like these, worn as lockets on necklaces or bracelets or simply kept nearby as mementos, were called souvenir jewels in the nineteenth century. Miniatures were exchanged among members of royal families and others as tokens of affection or gifts of state. Later in *Juarez* the emperor lovingly handles a miniature of the absent Carlotta.

Right: Ricarde of Hollywood, a costume jeweler, capitalized on the popularity of *Juarez* by creating a line of replicated antique jewelry called "Maximilian" so that every woman could be a Carlotta. Photographs of Ricarde's garnet and imitation-pearl jewelry were reproduced in newspapers throughout the country.

Below: When Rhett Butler (Clark Gable) finally marries Scarlett O'Hara (Vivien Leigh) in *Gone with the Wind* (1939), he showers her with luxuries to make up for the deprivations of the Civil War. Here, her earrings are in the archaeological style of jewelry made famous by the Italian jeweler Castellani at the 1862 Paris Exposition.

Orry-Kelly's period creations exemplified the queen's taste, which ran to long ropes of pearls, pearl embroidery, pearl hair pins, and gems spread copiously across her bodice and skirt. Elizabeth had her gems set in delicate enamel mounts by English goldsmiths. Davis concurred with her costume designer in a desire to be true to the richly attired and well-coiffed queen, who was in her sixties at the time of her love affair with Essex. So that her wig could be positioned correctly, the thirty-year-old actress allowed her forehead to be shaved.

The romantic jewel turning the plot of the film is a ring given to Queen Elizabeth by her father, Henry VIII, as a pledge of his love. He instructed her to send it to him if he ever grew angry with her and forgot his pledge. After her father died, Elizabeth gave the ring to her favorite at court, the earl of Essex, with the same instructions. When he was accused of treason, she waited in vain for him to return the ring as a sign of their love. In a last passionate audience with her he explains why he did not do so—while he adores her, he yearns to share her throne. As a result, for England's sake, she sentences him to death.

Davis was a leading contender for the role of Scarlett O'Hara in *Gone with the Wind* (1939): She lost only because the previous year she had won an Academy Award for a similar character, the title role of *Jezebel* (1938). Many actresses in Hollywood auditioned for the part of Scarlett—including Tallulah Bankhead, Lana Turner, and Paulette Goddard—but it was an English beauty, Vivien Leigh, who landed the role. There was no debate over her leading man. Every woman in America who had read Margaret Mitchell's Civil War novel agreed that Clark Gable was Rhett Butler.

Rhett is the profiteer who falls in love with Scarlett at a prewar ball, where she wears a low-cut green and white dress and a carved coral necklace in a Neapolitan style. After the war begins, Rhett meets Scarlett again at a ball. This time she is dressed in black, mourning the death of a husband she married on the rebound from her true love, Ashley Wilkes (Leslie Howard). During the event, the women donate jewelry for the Confederate cause and Scarlett gives her wedding ring. Later, Rhett acquires Scarlett's ring and returns it to her, making it clear in a letter that he knew her marriage was a travesty. This paves the way for one of the greatest love stories in movie history.

Below: For *The Private Lives of Elizabeth and Essex* (1939), Joseff of Hollywood made the Renaissance-style jewelry worn by Queen Elizabeth (Bette Davis). Essex (Errol Flynn) wears a Tudor-style necklace with a pendant of St. George and the dragon, a famous English motif.

Right: Bette Davis wears a charm bracelet composed of watch fobs and seals from the eighteenth and nineteenth centuries. She made more romantic films and wore more antique jewelry than any other actress in Hollywood, contributing to the revival of historically influenced clothes and jewelry.

The Glamour Years

As the Depression began to lift in the mid-thirties, Hollywood emerged as the glamour capital of the world. Fashions that previously had been designed with daring and almost irresponsible extravagance for the cinema became a source of inspiration for day- and nighttime clothes. When asked by *Harper's Bazaar* in 1934 why American women for the first time chose American over Parisian fashion, leading Hollywood designer Adrian stated emphatically, the "change of viewpoint has been brought about very largely by the movies. The movies have popularized American design as nothing else could do."

It was not only the movies that influenced American women but also the movie stars, who modeled couture clothes and precious jewelry in the premier fashion magazines, *Vogue* and *Harper's Bazaar*. No ordinary models, they appeared in sophisticated pictures by the top photographers.

The stars were treated as uncrowned royalty wherever they went. Writing for *The New Yorker* in 1933, Janet Flanner reported from Paris that Marlene Dietrich "was the belle of the Baron de Rothschild's ball. . . ." Indeed, at the Comédie Française, Flanner wrote, "when the Comte de Segur made his debut as an actor, she [Dietrich] was more observed . . . in a box than he was on the stage." However, the stars did not have to leave Hollywood in order to buy precious jewelry. Fine New York jewelers Trabert & Hoeffer-Mauboussin and Paul Flato opened branches in Los Angeles, and the city generated its own jewelers, including Laykin et Cie. Many of the jewels that the stars bought made their way into the movies, and the jewelers publicized themselves by lending objects in exchange for a screen credit.

Trabert & Hoeffer-Mauboussin was a firm whose founder, R. J. Trabert, was a connoisseur of antique jewelry. Trabert purchased valuable European estates to sell on the American market, while his partner, William Howard Hoeffer, was the financial and marketing genius behind the firm's success. Individually, Hoeffer received one of the first jewelry credits in the movies — "Jewels created by William Howard Hoeffer" for Claudette Colbert's 1935 movie *The Gilded Lily*. Her principal piece in this film was an extraordinary ruby and diamond necklace called a jigsaw jewel, as it could be transformed into a necklace, bracelet, tiara, or brooch. Despite the Depression economy Hoeffer established branches in the resort areas of Atlantic City, Miami Beach, and Palm Beach — among the few places in the country where expensive jewelry was being purchased. Hoeffer could sell anything — the estate jewelry Trabert bought as well as the modern designs that made the firm famous.

Trabert & Hoeffer-Mauboussin fully embraced the Machine style so popular in the 1930s. Buildings, factories, cars, planes, ships, and appliances were all designed with sleek lines and smooth, rounded surfaces; ornamentation was

In a fashion portrait by Horst P. Horst for *Vogue* (1936), Miriam Hopkins reclines in a chiffon gown accented with a heavy gold and topaz cuff by Olga Tritt. One of America's few women jewelers, Russian-born Tritt had a retail salon in New York. Her firm created massive jewelry with a neo-Baroque look using semiprecious stones in large sizes and rainbow colors — an alternative to cabochons.

Opposite: Claudette Colbert wears a fancy-cut diamond necklace with flaring side panels, suspending enormous ruby cabochons. Colbert became known as one of Hollywood's greatest comediennes, winning an Oscar for her performance in Frank Capra's *It Hap-* *pened One Night* (1934). Though often costumed in large jewels, Colbert preferred smaller, more personalized pieces. A sea horse brooch that she wore in many movies was a gift from her husband. (Courtesy Paramount Pictures)

Martha Raye (*left*) wears a cabochon sapphire and diamond clip brooch; Clara Bow (*center*) has on a gardenia headband, a wide diamond and platinum bracelet set with a cabochon gem, and a pair of diamond and gem-set clip brooches. With them are June Lang and Michael Whalen.

Left: Mary Pickford wears her Star of India clip brooch. *Harper's Bazaar* reported that it weighed 200 carats and rarely left Pickford's vault.

Right: Advertised in *Harper's Bazaar* in 1935, Trabert & Hoeffer's star sapphire ring, Star of Bombay, was bought by Mary Pickford. The firm named large gems with their places of origin.

simplified or deleted altogether. This transformation, wrought by the rise of industrial design, could be seen in every aspect of the decorative arts, including jewelry. The intricate diamond geometric openwork associated with Art Deco gave way to pavé diamond surfaces set with huge cabochon gems and intersected by bombé and cylindrical knobs mechanical in look.

Through its purchase of Mauboussin, Trabert & Hoeffer-Mauboussin had gained access to Mauboussin's European offices, enabling it to dip into reserves of the large and unique precious stones necessary for this new style. A cache of Hungarian emerald cabochons, reputed to have been sold clandestinely by the House of Orange, the Netherland's royal family, as well as countless other stones from royal treasuries, were used to create big, bold, flashy American jewels.

The success of a new jewelry style depends on publicity—not just advertising, but endorsements by fashionable, glamorous, highly visible patrons. Trabert & Hoeffer-Mauboussin could afford not only to invest in and purchase large estates of jewelry and stones but also to create a style and lend important pieces indefinitely to the most dazzling Hollywood stars. The stars gloried in publicity and were constantly being photographed wearing this jewelry. To be close to its stellar clients, Trabert & Hoeffer-Mauboussin opened a Los Angeles branch in 1934, which soon became a favorite haunt of Hollywood actresses. Stars took to the new style: They happily traded the small, faceted, and fancy-cut stones of the previous style for cabochon emeralds, star sapphires, and star rubies whose domed surfaces and sugar-loaf forms loomed large in their rings, bracelets, clip brooches, and necklaces.

From Hollywood they launched the first American jewelry style. Like fashions of dress, this style would be picked up in Europe and New York. During the glamour years of Hollywood, cabochon stones became the mark of an extravagantly chic woman.

Marlene Dietrich was so attached to her suite of cabochon emerald and diamond jewels by Trabert & Hoeffer-Mauboussin that she used them in her movie *Desire* (1936), in which, as a perfectly attired jewel thief, she tricks an eminent jeweler and a psychiatrist and makes off with a 2.2 million-franc pearl necklace. Her getaway becomes a comedy of errors as she is forced to team up with an automobile engineer from Detroit, Tom Bradley (Gary Cooper).

Dietrich was the epitome of glamour in Hollywood, and her cabochon emerald and diamond suite, further enhanced by a second cabochon emerald and diamond bracelet by Paul Flato, signaled that she had arrived. Beginning as a plump dance-hall girl and minor film actress in Germany, Dietrich's first major film credit was as a sleazy, sexy performer in small-time dives in the German film *Der blaue Engel* (*The Blue Angel,* 1930), directed by Josef von Sternberg. Upon completion of this film, Dietrich went with Von Sternberg to Hollywood and Paramount Pictures, where he orchestrated her career by directing her every move and refining every detail of her appearance. Their relationship ended in 1935.

By contrast, Paulette Goddard was purely American, with an impish albeit sophisticated image seen often in magazines and tabloids modeling jewelry by Trabert & Hoeffer-Mauboussin. Goddard's love of jewelry is legendary; she was never without a diamond or two. On a flight from Paris to Geneva, an awestruck

Decked in feathers, Colbert flashes a ridged, barrel-shaped crystal ring.

This ridged, barrel-shaped crystal ring, similar to the one worn by Claudette Colbert, shows a horizontal row of French-cut onyx flanked by two rows of round diamonds in a platinum mount. Fashion editors dubbed 1927 "The Year of Crystal" as Parisian jewelers introduced this luminous material into Art Deco designs and created rectangular crystal links for bracelets, crystal circles for clip brooches, and crystal leaves for flower basket brooches. An easily carved, inexpensive material, crystal had a second vogue during the late thirties, when the Machine style inspired large, bulky, rounded shapes, and the platinum-crystal-diamond combination again became popular. The barrel-shaped crystal ring was heralded as the radically modern cocktail ring.

A "Reflection" jewel by Trabert & Hoeffer-Mauboussin has a polished 18K yellow gold bangle centering on a rectangular-cut citrine in a pavé-set diamond quatrefoil bordered by circular-cut amethyst and diamond domes. Trabert & Hoeffer-Mauboussin spread the firm's name by lending jewelry for movies and by introducing a new line of daytime jewelry. Since the Depression, the firm had been making a version of these jewels by mixing 18K gold and semiprecious stones and formalized the line as "Reflection" in 1938.

Trabert & Hoeffer-Mauboussin's "Reflection" line enabled clients to choose patterns, make a selection of stones and unassembled 18K gold elements, and go away with a unique, individually styled jewel, which previously only the most wealthy could afford. "Reflection" jewelry was displayed at the 1939 World's Fair in New York. Its design later became known as the Machine style.

Chanel model watched her take six wide diamond bracelets out of a cigar case, scrutinize each one thoughtfully, and start cleaning them with an airline towel. At a Hollywood dinner party, when Goddard dropped an earring, director Anatole Litvak disappeared under the table and crawled around her knees to retrieve it, an action he may have regretted when the story became a favorite bit of mischievous Hollywood gossip. Goddard never refuted the story, nor, for that matter, any other story—no matter how racy.

A Ziegfeld Follies girl at fourteen, Paulette Goddard retired while still a minor to marry timber magnate Edgar James, but the union did not last long. After a quick divorce in Reno, she drove straight on to Hollywood to begin a new career. One year later, in 1932, she was discovered by Charlie Chaplin, whom she was rumored to have married secretly at sea around 1933. She subsequently appeared in two of his films, *Modern Times* (1936) and *The Great Dictator* (1940). Her jewelry collection is studded with gifts from Chaplin, who shopped for her at Trabert & Hoeffer-Mauboussin.

With her ready wit, Goddard built up a reputation for teasing reporters with entertaining repartee about jewelry. One of her favorite subjects was her diamond-fringe necklace, which could be converted into two separate bracelets. Not only did she wear this jewel in numerous publicity stills, but she also combined it—paying no attention to historical detail—with Gainsborough-inspired gowns in the period movie *Kitty* (1945), set in eighteenth-century London. Legend has it that the central octagonal diamond of this necklace came out of her engagement ring from Charlie Chaplin, yet it appears that the story was her own fabrication. While still married to Chaplin, she was photographed wearing a section of the necklace as a bracelet, and also wearing her engagement ring. Once, when asked how she acquired this necklace of fifty diamonds, she replied, "I got it by getting engaged so often. I never give anything back."

There is an element of truth to her retort. Many engagement rings were sold during the Depression, and several may have ended up in this necklace, which looks as though it was made up entirely of such stones. With regard to valuables, the Depression in America had the effect of a revolution: jewelry changed hands over and over again. Stones were bought so cheaply that a jeweler could afford to put away enough of them to launch a new style when the time was ripe.

After losing the role of Scarlett O'Hara for *Gone with the Wind*, Goddard received consolation from Chaplin in the form of a massive gold bangle with cabochon emerald floral motifs transposed against diamond ones and earrings with a diamond flower and an emerald flower for each ear. The cuff is large, snug, and comfortable; Goddard wore it constantly. (A cuff in the same style was owned by Mary Pickford, who had matching ruby and diamond earrings.) Goddard's matching emerald and diamond earrings rarely went conventionally in her ears; instead, she pinned them to her blouses and dresses, where they gave the appearance of grandiose clip brooches. When Alexander Korda advised her to wear real jewelry in the period movie *An Ideal Husband* (1948), Goddard tucked her emerald and diamond earrings in the décolletage of her Victorian gown, adding to a rich array of jewelry, including a carved emerald bead necklace.

As Goddard gradually carved out a career of her own and became a guaranteed box-office hit for Paramount, the tabloids reported rumors that her marriage was on the rocks—and, in fact, it was. In 1942 Goddard divorced Chaplin. Two years later she married her third husband, actor Burgess Meredith. Meanwhile, she continued to shine as a successful comedienne in the movies. But by the mid-1950s, in the wake of the McCarthy trials, she retired for the second time, divorced for the third time, and moved to Europe. The House Un-American Activities Committee had come after her because of her marriage to Chaplin and her friendship with Mexican painter Diego Rivera. Undaunted, she declared to the press, "If anyone accuses me of being a Communist, I'll hit them with my diamond bracelets."

In 1958, finally left alone by the headlines and the scandal sheets, Goddard married renowned German writer Erich Maria Remarque, author of *All Quiet on the Western Front,* and lived quietly in Switzerland. Still a jewelry wearer, she assembled a collection of colorful ruby jewels by Van Cleef & Arpels, Bulgari, and other jewelers. Just before she died in 1990, she bequeathed more than $20 million and her fourth husband's papers to New York University, which came as a surprise to those who remembered her only as an enchanting prankster.

Trabert & Hoeffer-Mauboussin also lent its jewelry to moviemakers. The firm received screen credit for Columbia's comedy *It's All Yours* (1937), starring Madeleine Carroll, and *Stage Door* (1937), starring Katharine Hepburn and Ginger Rogers. Trabert & Hoeffer-Mauboussin also received screen credit for the musical *The Vogues of 1938,* which revolves around the love life of a couturier and drips with jewels. A gloved hand wearing a drop-dead star ruby and diamond bracelet pulls open curtains to reveal the credits. The bracelet is only the beginning of a movie that was the ultimate showcase of the cabochon style. The costumes were authentic haute couture: clothes by Omar Kiam, furs by Jaeckel, shoes by I. Miller & Sons, hats by John Fredricks and Sally Victor, and jewels by Trabert & Hoeffer-Mauboussin.

While fancy-cut diamond jewels make an appearance on subsidiary characters, the blues and reds of star sapphires and large cabochon rubies, dazzling and rich on the Technicolor screen, light up the major stars. The most impressive jewel in the movie is the eighty-three-carat star ruby called the Star of Burma. It came from Burmese mines that produced the finest rubies in the world and had a distinctive pigeon-blood color. The Star of Burma is set in a chunky diamond, Burmese ruby bead, and platinum necklace mount, with wide buckle-shaped panels and a substantial lozenge-shaped drop pendant, a masterpiece of haute Machine style.

For the movie *Vogue* models came from New York to appear in the filmed fashion shows, but a Hollywood star outshone them all—Joan Bennett, whose delicate, blond, patrician looks belied a decade of Hollywood moviemaking. She had begun her career at nineteen, starring opposite Ronald Colman in the smash hit *Bulldog Drummond* (1929), and Bennett consistently maintained her position as a fine leading lady. In 1938, after meeting and working with Walter Wanger, the producer of *The Vogues of 1938,* she started on the powerful second lap of her stardom. Wanger, whom she married two years later, directed her career and, among other things, suggested that she become a brunette. This switch was unexpectedly effective in creating a dramatic image. No longer locked into a fragile and aristocratic facade, Bennett accepted roles such as a Cockney

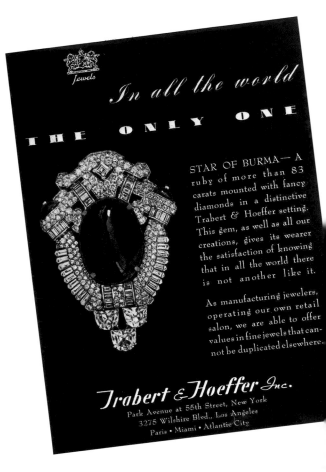

Trabert & Hoeffer-Mauboussin advertised the 83-carat Star of Burma ruby in 1935. The ruby was mounted in a necklace and worn by Joan Bennett in *The Vogues of 1938* (1937).

Marlene Dietrich's emerald and diamond jewelry suite from Trabert & Hoeffer-Mauboussin appeared in many of her films as well as in fashion portraits. The bracelet consists of pavé-set, baguette- and circular-cut diamonds centering on an oval cabochon emerald, accented with six emerald beads and mounted in platinum. The matching clip brooch features pavé-set, half-moon, circular-, and baguette-cut diamonds centering on an oval cabochon emerald mounted in platinum. The brooch could be separated into two pendants.

Marlene Dietrich wears two of her cabochon emerald and diamond bracelets in a publicity photograph by Clarence Sinclair Bull. The lower bracelet was by Trabert & Hoeffer-Mauboussin and the upper by Paul Flato. The Flato round cabochon, said to be the size of a bantam's egg, could be snapped into a ring. It was reported to weigh 128 carats, but the sizes of such gems were sometimes exaggerated in the press.

Seen at the theater with Douglas Fairbanks, Jr. Dietrich has on her emerald jewels by Trabert & Hoeffer-Mauboussin and Paul Flato.

Seldom without her emerald jewels, Dietrich appears at dinner with Cedric Gibbons and his wife, Dolores Del Rio, who wears a fan-shaped Art Deco brooch.

In a lobby card for the black and white film *Desire* (1936) Dietrich wears her cabochon emerald bracelet and a clip brooch by Trabert & Hoeffer-Mauboussin.

prostitute and a blackmailer, giving memorable performances in a series of movies directed by Fritz Lang, including *Man Hunt* (1941), *The Woman in the Window* (1944), *Scarlet Street* (1945), and *The Secret Beyond the Door* (1948).

Coming from a New York theatrical family, Bennett approached acting in a highly professional manner and would have continued season after season if her husband had not shot her agent, Jennings Lang, in a fit of jealousy in 1951. A woman of dry wit, she later noted that in the eighties this crime of passion would have enhanced her career instead of setting it back, as it did in the fifties.

When shopping for her cabochons in the 1930s, Joan Crawford went to an exclusive East Coast jeweler. Known for dramatic roles projecting inner strength, self-sacrifice, or sophisticated villainy, offscreen the actress projected a hard, knowing look. In a 1932 *Photoplay* article entitled "Spend!" she made it clear that she regarded spending as an almost sacred duty. In the depths of the Depression, she expressed a unique type of patriotism: "I, Joan Crawford, I believe in the Dollar. Everything I earn, I spend." In this pursuit she worked her way to the top, making her way by 1938 into the very select clientele of New York jeweler Raymond C. Yard, a firm that never advertised. From them, among other things, she picked out a wide fancy-cut diamond bracelet punctuated with star sapphires. The center stone weighed 73.15 carats and the two side stones 63.61 and 57.65 carats. The bracelet became the prime attraction of her suite of cabochon sapphires that the press dubbed Joan Blue in her honor.

In the boom years of the twenties and late thirties, and barely slowing down through the Depression, Raymond C. Yard enjoyed a continuing success. Beginning his career at fourteen at the venerable jeweler Marcus & Co., Yard founded the firm that bears his name in 1922 solely to provide jewelry services for the

Rockefellers, Harrimans, Vanderbilts, F. A. O. Schwarzes, and Flaglers, who followed him from Marcus. With this patronage, Yard's list of clients did not need to be long, but his stones, of course, had to be significant. The globe-trotting Americans who were Yard customers could easily compare them with those found on the rue de la Paix. Yard, perhaps the most respected figure in American jewelry history, was so preoccupied with important stones that he convinced the foremost Parisian stone dealer, Raphael Esmerian, to relocate in America and participate in the increasingly important American jewelry scene.

Yard took his sixteen-year-old golf caddy Robert Gibson into his business during the years that Joan Crawford was a client. Once, after young Gibson had finished nervously fastening a necklace around her neck, she turned and gave him a screen-style kiss, which he always said was his first. Gibson later became president of Raymond C. Yard.

Merle Oberon, a British actress, arrived in Hollywood in 1935 with a dazzling collection of jewels, notably several pieces by Cartier. Even among the well-bedecked Hollywood stars Oberon shone brightly, becoming almost as famous for her jewelry as for her films. Born Estelle Merle O'Brien Thompson, a Eurasian of Irish extraction, she grew up in Tasmania and India before emigrating to England. She was first a dance-hall hostess and then a bit-part movie actress before catching the eye of director Alexander Korda, who made her a star in his 1933 production of *The Private Life of Henry VIII*. In that movie she played

Merle Oberon wears a bracelet similar in style to a diamond and gem-set double flower cuff by Paul Flato. The bracelet, a diamond and gem-set shell necklace, and diamond cluster earrings are all mounted in platinum. Oberon included this bracelet in her jewelry selection for *'Til We Meet Again* (1940).

Anne Boleyn, a role that won her international recognition. Subsequently wooed by the Hollywood studios and advised by Korda, who sold part of her contract to Samuel Goldwyn, she began to make films in both London and Hollywood, including *Folies-Bergère* (1935) with Maurice Chevalier, *Wuthering Heights* (1939) with Laurence Olivier, and *A Song to Remember* (1945).

Korda and Oberon were married in 1939, and on their wedding day he gave her three Cartier diamond and gold roses. She wore them in *'Til We Meet Again* (1940), a tragedy in which she played Joan Ames, a mortally ill passenger on a San Francisco-bound ocean liner, who falls in love with murderer Dan Hardesty (George Brent) on his way to face the death penalty. Oberon opens the movie with the three rose brooches clipped to her suit; later, in the ship's bar, she puts them on a ribbon around her neck. In interviews for the film, Oberon revealed the sentimental value of the roses to reporters.

When Oberon became a transatlantic star, Cartier was pressed into service to make her a special pigskin jewelry case lined in caramel velvet. It had twenty-eight compartments for her travel collection, which included five necklaces, six bracelets, eleven rings, and assorted clips and brooches. Cartier also created Oberon's most famous jewel, her drop emerald and diamond necklace. When asked by a reporter if it was designed by couturiere Elsa Schiaparelli, she replied, "No, but she almost got it! I saw it in a Paris shop, and I went back a second time to look at it. The salesman said someone else was interested, but I only half believed him. The next time I went in, the necklace was not in the case. My mysterious rival had been looking at it in one of the little private rooms. Still I hesitated because the design was so exotic—so unlike the classic settings for precious stones. The next day I walked right by the shop, not intending to be tempted again, but Mme. Schiaparelli was just coming out. Instantly I knew why she had been there, and assumed she had the necklace right in her handbag. I must have looked my disappointment when I got back to the hotel, because Mr. Korda, in his direct way, put on his hat and went out. He walked across to the shop; the necklace was still there, and he bought it."

After Oberon settled permanently in Hollywood, she discovered American jeweler Paul Flato and transferred her affection from Cartier to him. He was the perfect Hollywood jeweler. The opening of his Los Angeles branch at 8637 Sunset Boulevard, opposite the Trocadero nightclub, in 1938 was attended by a bevy of local notables, and it received national attention. Flato kept the luminaries coming back by throwing annual fashion shows of his jewels, a tradition he started in New York by inviting the year's debutantes to model his jewels at the Ritz-Carlton Hotel.

The manager of the Los Angeles establishment was Constance Collier, one-time fiancée of Max Beerbohm and an English stage actress. Collier made her Hollywood debut in D. W. Griffith's *Intolerance* (1916). She played stately older ladies in several movies, including *Stage Door* (1937) and *An Ideal Husband* (1948). Then she had a third career, as a jeweler.

Flato and his flamboyant entourage won his jewelry firm a following of movie stars. Freed from the restraint of the jeweler's code of discretion, Flato came into the limelight in Los Angeles, partying with his clients and thoroughly enjoying the resulting publicity.

When big jewels were the order of the day, Cartier created some very distinctive ones, using large, unfaceted stones, mainly emeralds from India—which gave a name to the style. Since the first decade of the century, the Parisian firm had been collecting Oriental gems. Twenty-nine rock-size emeralds with small diamond rondelles make up Merle Oberon's Cartier necklace.

Above: An ink and gouache drawing of Joan Crawford's star sapphire bracelet shows an intricate design of star sapphires, rectangular, triangular, baguette, marquise, and half-moon-cut diamonds, mounted in platinum. Bracelets were a specialty of Raymond C. Yard. Their width gave ample opportunity for a harmonious repetition of color accents in fancy-cut diamond panels.

Crawford's favorite 70-carat star sapphire was the engagement ring from her second husband, leading man Franchot Tone. They married in 1935. Crawford also owned a 72-carat emerald-cut sapphire ring and frequently wore both on the same finger.

Below: The inventory of gems for Joan Crawford's star sapphire bracelet, dated February 11, 1938, is recorded in Raymond C. Yard's ledger.

Left: Joan Crawford, with a blue fox fur over her arm, wears a star sapphire and diamond ring, a star sapphire and fancy-cut diamond wide bracelet, and an 80-carat drop-shape star sapphire and diamond pendant, suspended from a baguette-cut diamond necklace, all mounted in platinum. Her star sapphire bracelet was purchased at Raymond C. Yard; the pendant came from Hollywood jeweler John Gershgorn.

Among Trabert & Hoeffer-Mauboussin jewels owned by Paulette Goddard were an 18K gold bangle with a cluster of pavé-set diamond and cabochon emerald flowers mounted in platinum, and large earrings with matching flowers—diamonds with emerald centers and emeralds with diamond centers.

He'd begun his career in New York. In the late twenties as a young student from Flatonia, Texas, he abandoned Columbia University's business school for an office in the jewelry district. His neighbor was Edmond E. Frisch, an established Swiss wholesaler. In no time at all the traffic was going in Flato's direction. His astonishing sales ability, Southern hospitality, and outrageous sense of humor brought vitality and spunk to the quiet, sometimes self-important, and serious corridors of the jewelry industry. One of his endearing characteristics was an ability to tell tall jewelry tales. A favorite involved the ex-chorus girl and bon vivant Florence Gould, daughter-in-law of railroad magnate Jay Gould. As Flato told it, Gould was seated at a dinner next to Louis Arpels, patriarch of Van Cleef & Arpels. When she remarked to him that Paul Flato was her jeweler, her necklace came unfastened and fell into her soup.

When asked about his fabulous designs, Flato said, "I don't know how to draw a line. I am a creator of jewels and guide my designers." Flato designers were an unusual group. Head designer Adolph Klety executed "French" designs—formal, feminine diamond and platinum jewelry characterized by curving lines and flower motifs. *Drippy* was the word Flato used for Klety's jewels. George Headley designed imaginative gold jewelry, but he was most identified with gold boxes and

For a *Harper's Bazaar* article in 1940, to publicize Goddard's new film *The Ghost Breakers*, Louise Dahl-Wolfe photographed the actress in her Trabert & Hoeffer-Mauboussin jewelry.

Goddard wore her Trabert & Hoeffer-Mauboussin bangle for a 1941 cover of *Screen Life*. Her earrings were clipped to a Mexican-style blouse.

JOHN'S OTHER WIFE THE ABSORBING SERIAL DRAMA OF RADIO AS AN EXCITING STORY IN THIS ISSUE

SCREEN LIFE

DECEMBER

SCREEN LIFE 10¢

PAULETTE GODDARD

bibelots. (Later he married socialite Barbara Whitney, who created a museum for his work.) Fashion leader, socialite, and heiress Millicent Rogers was known for her "fat-heart" designs, exaggerated and abstract heart shapes covered with a collage of stones. These were worn by Ginger Rogers and Alice Faye, among others. Socialite Josephine Forrestal, wife of James V. Forrestal, Secretary of the Navy under Franklin D. Roosevelt, conceived "wiggly" clips, with big, colorful stones. "Wiggly" was an Americanization of the French jewelry term *en tremblant* traditionally applied to jewelry elements that flutter delicately, such as the petals of a flower or the wings of an insect. Joan Bennett owned a signature Flato suite of Forrestal design: a pillbox, compact, and mirror shaped as little gold cushions with diamond buttons. The duke of Verdura arrived from the House of Chanel with a little jewelry expertise and a lot of social grace, clients, and friends. A titled Italian, he was responsible for designs of ornate, rococo character.

Flato produced some startlingly original themes for jewelry—sign-language gestures, ambulances, telephones, feet, envelopes, boxer shorts, corsets, and astrological symbols. Taken as a group, they constituted a Surrealist line—something new. Although Surrealism had been extremely popular as a movement in art, influencing fashion, film, dance, and social life, it had not before been explored by a precious jeweler. Flato's playful, whimsical, distinctive jewels popped up on the collars, necklines, and lapels of dresses of many Hollywood actresses. The only parallel to the Flato jewelry was the costume jewelry designed for Schiaparelli in Paris by her coterie of Surrealist artists.

One of Flato's most loyal customers was coloratura soprano Lily Pons, equally at home on the stage of the Metropolitan Opera and a movie set. Pons carried on the tradition of opera stars who made grand entrances wearing grand jewelry. With a reputation firmly established in the exclusive milieu of American and European opera, Pons was selected by RKO as its answer to Columbia's opera singer–movie star, Grace Moore, who had actually been nominated for an Academy Award. While Pons's first film, *I Dream Too Much* (1935), may have stirred controversy among opera buffs over the caliber of the recording of her voice, it was a box-office hit. Pons went on to make three more movies, *That Girl from Paris* (1937), *Hitting a New High* (1937), and *Carnegie Hall* (1947), all of which had very thin plots and swelling operatic arias. Pons continued performing in operas and recitals into the early 1970s. After she died, in 1976, a town in Maryland was named Lilypons in her honor.

Pons's fondness for stunning jewelry led her to many jewelers, but during the 1930s she stocked up mainly on Flato jewels ranging from modest daytime accouterments to spectacular formal jewelry in the naturalistic style. Pons owned a Flato necklace that spelled the last name of her husband, Andre Kostelanetz, and a charm bracelet with her initials.

Perhaps Flato's greatest contribution to contemporary jewelry was an infusion of naturalism. Not since 1889, when Tiffany exhibited a collection of enamel orchids at the World Exposition in Paris, had any such flowing, naturalistic designs been attempted by an American jeweler. Tiffany's orchids, universally praised for their original designs, had inspired Art Nouveau goldsmiths to create large-scale flower jewels in enamel and semiprecious stones. Paul Flato's large-scale floral and naturalistic designs were executed in platinum, white and yellow

Mae West's figure provided the inspiration for the Flato diamond and gold corset bracelet with diamond and ruby garters illustrated in *Harper's Bazaar,* November 1939. Part-time Flato designer Josephine Forrestal is credited with its ownership, if not its design.

gold, diamonds, and included both precious and semiprecious stones.

The Flato atelier and workshops reinterpreted the traditional French flower motifs—blossoms with buds and tendrils—as well as standard jewelry flowers such as roses and lilacs. The signature jewel of Flato's New York shop at One East Fifty-seventh Street, and the image for one of the firm's early advertisements, was a monochromatic diamond lilac brooch. Unlike Art Deco jewelers, who used stylized patterning and angle-cut gems to define their designs, Flato gave his flowers the appearance of animation with articulated detail and flexible mountings.

No sooner had Paul Flato opened in Los Angeles than his jewelry began to appear in the movies. It was ideal for the heroines of mid-thirties comedies. Married or single, these heroines were at variance with the mores of their class, but appeared perfectly dressed and bejeweled in their roles. The plots of these films revolve around the predicament of wealth and social stratification for those enmeshed in its unspoken rules and regulations. Although this may sound heavy-handed, the dilemmas presented in these movies and their inevitably cheerful resolutions created a genre—the screwball comedy.

Katharine Hepburn was the perfect heroine for the screwball comedies; her background paralleled that of the heroines she played. The daughter of a prominent doctor and a mother who was a suffragette, Hepburn was raised in Hartford, Connecticut, and educated at Bryn Mawr College. After a brief marriage that terminated when she told her husband, "My public needs me," she sailed to Broadway, where she was spotted by a talent scout and given a film contract at RKO. Her offscreen presence was as strong-willed and unconventional as the women she played. Shunning parties and interviews, wearing slacks, concentrating on active sports, she chose her own friends. She was linked romantically with Howard Hughes and Leland Heyward, but the romance of her life was her twenty-seven-year relationship with the married Spencer Tracy. In the face of the tough, regimented—and frequently brutal—studio system, Hepburn stood her ground with producers and would quit a production at a moment's notice if she did not get the terms she wanted.

Hepburn had been making films since 1932 with some success and starring roles, including those in *Little Women* (1933), *Mary of Scotland* (1936), and *Stage Door* (1937). Beginning in 1938 she was paired with Cary Grant in comedies that have become classics. Grant was also a Hollywood veteran, having appeared opposite Marlene Dietrich in *Blond Venus* (1932) and Mae West in *She Done Him Wrong* (1933), but he rocketed to stardom when he began making screwball comedies. From his early years with an English traveling acrobatic and comedic company, he had a flawless sense of timing and a physical grace manifested in suave, sophisticated good looks. This was topped by an accent combining an almost indiscernible Cockney twang with pure American diction and rhythm.

Hepburn and Grant started their duet in *Bringing Up Baby* (1938), a sophisticated mix that involved an heiress (Hepburn), a zoologist (Grant), a dinosaur skeleton, and a leopard. It was such a zany comedy of upper-class modes and mores that the audiences had no idea what to make of it, and initially it was a flop. Next came *Holiday* (1938), an equally fast-moving but slightly more

Goddard wears her wedding band and engagement ring from Charlie Chaplin and a section of her adaptable Trabert & Hoeffer-Mauboussin necklace as a bracelet. (Courtesy Paramount Pictures)

Goddard's diamond-fringe scroll necklace by Trabert & Hoeffer-Mauboussin was set with circular, rectangular, baguette, octagonal, and cushion-cut diamonds attached to a diamond-collet chain set with a single marquise-cut diamond mounted in platinum.

101

HOLLYWOOD GIVES A PARTY

All of Hollywood turned out as one man for the cocktail party Constance Collier gave at the Paul Flato shop in honor of Mr. and Mrs. Paul Flato. Above, you see Miss Collier (left) with John McCormack, Annabella (polka dots and a halo), and the guest of honor himself.

Among the guests were Douglas Fairbanks, Sr., with his wife, and the Duca di Verdura, who designs for Flato. Don't miss the chic of Mrs. Fairbanks's impeccably tailored tweed coat worn over a print, and her slender lotus hands tipped with mandarin nails.

NAT DALLINGER

On the staircase, Mrs. Lewis Milestone is holding a martini in one hand, and pointing with the other to the great aquamarine she had Flato flank with diamonds and reset as a clip. With her, Miriam Hopkins, Mrs. Richard Barthelmess and the Duca di Verdura.

Right: The Paul Flato salon at 8637 Sunset Boulevard in Los Angeles presented a California-style Neoclassical exterior.

Marking the opening of the Flato shop in Los Angeles *Harper's Bazaar* for March 1938 pictured a variety of Hollywood notables and the duke of Verdura, a Flato designer. Some guests loaned jewels to be displayed in the contemporary-classical salon, designed by Terance Robsjohn-Gibbings.

Right: At a 1939 party at the Flato salon, Fanny Brice, Virginia Zanuck, and Reginald Gardiner admire a jewel held by the manager, former actress Constance Collier.

Below: Cesar Romero and a friend leave the Flato shop with Kay Francis.

AT PAUL FLATO'S NEW SHOP

Here is the charming entrance of the new Paul Flato shop recently opened on Sunset Boulevard, just opposite the Trocadero, in Los Angeles. Witness the grace and proportion of the Ionic columns and the ordered feeling of the modern-Greek architecture.

erance Robsjohn-Gibbings did the interior of the shop with he magnificent success you see above. Essentially a twentieth-century room, it fuses into a new style Egyptian monumentality, Babylonian splendor and Greek subtlety of balance.

This close-up was taken during the opening exhibition of jewels designed by Flato. None was for sale. All were privately owned by his clients and appeared only as a record of his work. Note that the right wall has been scooped out for a showcase.

Above: A niece of screenwriter Anita Loos, Mary Anita Loos, shows her Flato jewels to Charlie Chaplin at the opening.

In the 1920s and 1930s, when giving and receiving charms was very popular, women mounted them in a variety of ways. Paulette Goddard had hers set in a gold compact: among the humorous and personal references were letters from her nickname, Peter, three pet Scotties, Charlie Chaplin as The Little Tramp, and two drummer boys that had been a gift from George Gershwin. In this close-up, Goddard wears a big diamond and aquamarine ring by Paul Flato. *Above, right:* Goddard later had her charms remounted in a gold and platinum bangle centering on a star sapphire.

thought-provoking comedy revolving around one of the sixty most prominent families of the United States. Two sisters, beautiful but prosaic Julie (Doris Nolan) and nonconformist black sheep Linda (Hepburn), fall in love, one after another, with a handsome bachelor named Johnny Case (Grant). Case wants to make his fortune quickly and take a holiday.

All the jewelry in *Holiday* was by Paul Flato. Hepburn's daytime jewel, a black enamel hand, is an example of unconventional, personalized Flato designs. The firm used the hand gestures of sign language to create initial clips of 18K gold and black enamel, with diamonds on the wrist. Hepburn wears one in the playroom, the only room in the family mansion that offers escape from the oppressive atmosphere. At the engagement party for her sister, Hepburn wears a diamond "toe" ring (named for an Egyptian ring worn on the foot), a sunburst brooch of canary diamonds, and a dazzling three-strand diamond collet necklace with a three-inch diamond loop that hangs gracefully down her back, a beautiful detail that complements the shoulder-length hairstyles of the period.

Hepburn told Paul Flato that of all the Flato jewelry she wore in *Holiday*, she was especially fond of the "toe" ring. The genesis of this design was Flato's purchase of a toe ring for two dollars while he was travelling in Egypt. On his return to New York, he gave the ring to one of his artisans to recreate in platinum and diamonds.

That Uncertain Feeling (1941), another screwball comedy with a Flato jewelry credit, starred Merle Oberon as Jill Baker, the wife of Larry Baker (Melvyn Douglas), a prosperous insurance man. While he gives his wife plenty of jewelry, Baker fails in the more mundane realm. He sleeps through his wife's insomnia, he does not bother to shave, and he behaves in other ways that Jill's psychiatrist tells her should be irritating. One day in the psychiatrist's waiting room, Jill meets eccentric pianist Alexander Sebastian (Burgess Meredith). Jill falls in love with the temperamental artist and goes through the motions of divorcing her husband, but Alexander proves too eccentric even for the romance-seeking Jill, and she returns with relief to her predictable husband.

Throughout the film, the heroine wears extraordinary Flato pieces—big rings, large pearl button earrings, diamond bracelets, and assorted eye-catching gem-packed brooches. One particularly striking brooch is a sculpted gold flower in Flato's naturalistic style.

The views of jewelry-splashed high life in New York, compliments of Paul Flato, could do little to save *Two-Faced Woman* (1941) from disaster. Although MGM had assembled the ingredients for an excellent production—players Greta Garbo and Melvyn Douglas, who had proved a bankable couple in Garbo's first comedy, *Ninotchka* (1939), director George Cukor, art director Cedric Gibbons, and costume designer Adrian—the movie failed miserably from start to finish.

In *Two-Faced Woman* Garbo plays a ski instructor, Karina, who marries publishing tycoon Larry Blake (Melvyn Douglas) after one ski lesson. Karina then pretends to be her own twin sister, the carefree gold digger Katherine, to test Blake's constancy in New York. Unlike the character part of Ninotchka, a serious and dedicated communist who discovers the joys of capitalism, the role of Karina was too simple-minded for Garbo, who was obviously miscast and could not apply any of her usual theatrics to the role. She was not enough of a physical comedian to do humorous stunts on a ski slope or drunken curves on the dance floor, nor could she translate her husky speech patterns into the glib delivery of wisecracks and asides. This was the last film Garbo would ever make; she retired from the screen at age thirty-six. Historians have speculated that her abrupt departure from Hollywood and the movies resulted from her experience with this movie, which bombed at the box office and was poorly received by critics.

Yet its failure was not entirely the result of Garbo's acting. Louis B. Mayer had wanted to change Garbo's ethereal image by casting her in different types of films and playing down her dramatic costumes. Designer Adrian became involved in the transformation until, infuriated by Mayer's interference, he tore up his sketches in the middle of a production meeting and resigned. (This may be an apocryphal story, as Adrian is credited with one more MGM movie, *Woman of the Year* (1942), starring Katharine Hepburn.)

Garbo's costumes for *Two-Faced Woman* only succeeded in making her look rather ordinary, wan, and unexciting. Her pajamas are matronly in intimate scenes, and her wide straw hat is out of place in the snow-covered mountains. In a

Above: When French couturiere Elsa Schiaparelli attended the Flato opening in Los Angeles she bought a number of his pieces with designs that reflected the special brand of fashion Surrealism she practiced in Paris—a gold addressed envelope with a pocket watch, a gold cactus, and gold nut-and bolt-cuff links. The 18K gold cuff links shown are similar to those purchased by Schiaparelli. The motif was made famous in America by bandleader Eddie Duchin.

In 1940 Flato and dancer Irene Castle examine an acorn necklace and bracelet made of light- to dark-color topaz.

nightclub sequence, she wears too much Flato jewelry: a diamond fringe necklace, a ring, two abstract butterfly brooches at her shoulder, and two swirl brooches in her hair—"diamond hair curls" that Flato made especially for her. Garbo played out her last film role wearing more precious jewelry than in any of her previous movies. Individually, the jewels are beautiful, but there were too many.

One of the delights of *Two-Faced Woman* is Constance Bennett, as the playwright who attempts to steal Karina's husband. She provides the few hilarious moments in the film. Bennett is resplendent in big, bold jewels set with huge semiprecious stones; the gold necklace she wears in the nightclub sequence covers her entire décolletage, calling to mind the breastplate of a female warrior. Joan Bennett's older sister Constance had been making films on and off since 1916. A popular actress of silent movies, she briefly retired from the screen in 1926 to marry a steamship and railroad heir and become a member of the international set of the Roaring Twenties. Three years later, divorced and ready to go back to work, she—like Katharine Hepburn—proved perfect for screwball comedies as an actress with firsthand knowledge of the world she depicted.

In one of her best comedies, *Topper* (1937), Bennett starred with Cary Grant as affluent socialites who die in a car crash. As ghosts, they must do one good deed before they can decently retire. They choose to enliven the life of banker Cosmo Topper (Roland Young). Bennett and Grant give an exquisite and uproarious portrayal of thirties chic and sophistication. Grant, in impeccably cut suits, carries on athletically, variously driving a car with his feet or walking across Topper's roof without a misstep.

Bennett's long, slim figure is swathed in evening gowns and furs that envelop her as she entices Topper to break his daily routine. In one scene she wears a large necklace that is a diamond ballroom dazzler—in contrast to the conservative jewels worn by Mrs. Topper (Billie Burke)—and its source is attributed to Laykin et Cie of Los Angeles, one of the jewelers that Bennett patronized.

Harper's Bazaar of December 1938 featured Flato three-part diamond and ruby rococo clips designed by Verdura. The magazine likened the clips to bits of plaster curling from crumbling Renaissance palaces.

• Left: Smartest of
all Chanel's midseason
evening dresses, this
one of dark blue lace made
in tiers and held up by a
ruched lace necklace. The gloves
are blue suede cuffed with lace.
Salon de Couture, Bonwit Teller.
eron.
k satin gown,
e with huge
e Carnegie.
n a brand-new
slipper satin, fitted
hips and then going
enri Bendel.
ps are made of
in a beautiful
bits of stucco
ococo palace.
e in i

Above: Syndicated gossip columnist Hedda Hopper (center) looks over jewels on a Flato model with Mr. and Mrs. Tom McAfee. *Right:* Anita Loos (center), author of the 1925 novel *Gentlemen Prefer Blondes,* views Flato jewels on a model.

Actor John Emery escorts Joan Crawford, who wears the Flato three-part rococo clips designed by Verdura.

Opposite, far right: Joan Bennett's Hand of God brooch by Paul Flato has an 18K gold hand and pavé-set diamond stars, and is based on a palm reader's diagram. The seven pavé-set diamond stars represent Venus, Jupiter, Saturn, Apollo, Mercury, Mars, and the Moon, symbolizing the seven virtues associated with the gods. Dimensions: $2 \times 1\frac{3}{4}$ in.

In 1934 Sol Laykin's jewelry business was located in the Alexandria Hotel in Los Angeles. On weekends, encouraged by Allen Breed Walker, a jewelry lover who managed La Quinta Hotel near Palm Springs, Laykin did trunk shows for the guests, who included a long list of actors and actresses headed by Marie Dresser. So successful were these shows that Walker gave Laykin a permanent place in La Quinta. When the jeweler arrived one Friday, Gloria Swanson's ex-husband (who later married Constance Bennett), the marquis de la Falaise, decided Laykin's boutique would be called Laykin et Cie. Everyone loved the European cachet and the name stuck.

In 1935 Laykin et Cie relocated to 8635 Sunset Boulevard in Los Angeles and became a familiar haunt of movie stars. (Paul Flato later became Laykin's next-door neighbor.) Being jewelers to the stars, Laykin et Cie acted as adviser and confidant in all varieties of jewelry purchases and sales. Once Sol Laykin took a thirty-carat yellow diamond over to Mae West's house; her pet monkey picked it up off the table when no one was looking and swallowed it.

Paul Flato went out of business in the early 1940s. The reason for the firm's demise has aroused curiosity in the jewelry industry for the past five decades. One story has it that when World War II broke out and jewelry sales plummeted, Flato had over-bought and could not meet its financial obligations. Faithful customer Doris Duke gave Flato $20,000, and his family from Texas also sent

Bennett wore her Flato Hand of God brooch on a chain for a 1946 RKO publicity photograph. Appreciative of Flato whimsy as well as the firm's craftsmanship, Bennett also commissioned an 18K gold and enamel replica of the cigar-band wedding ring she wore in *Trade Winds* (1939).

109

Sign-language initials were introduced by Flato in the late 1930s. As Linda in *Holiday* (1938), Katharine Hepburn wears a clip with the sign for W on her blouse. W was the initial of Linda's mother's maiden name.

The A and L sign gestures, illustrated in a *Harper's Bazaar* advertisement of 1938, were created for Anita Loos.

The original wooden maquettes for sign-language initial clip brooches are seen on a drawing for sign-language cuff links from the archives of Louis Tamis & Sons, who manufactured many Flato designs.

A critical moment in *Holiday* comes when Linda, seen with her brother Ned (Lew Ayres), realizes that the man she is in love with is already engaged to her sister. She wears a Flato suite: a yellow diamond sunburst brooch, a triple-strand diamond-collet necklace, and diamond "toe" ring.

Right: A Flato advertisement of 1938 in *Harper's Bazaar* depicts an Egyptian "toe" ring similar in style to the one worn by Katharine Hepburn in *Holiday*, with a matching bracelet.

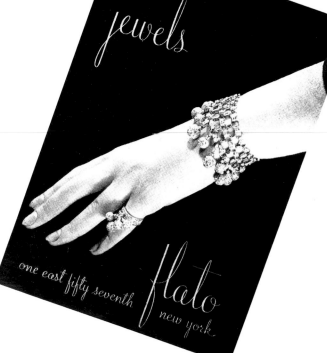

jewels

one east fifty seventh
flato
new york.

money, but it was not enough. Two Flato designers, however, remained prominent on the Hollywood scene: the duke of Verdura had opened his own business a short time before, and George Headley moved to Laykin et Cie.

In 1941 Gloria Swanson came out of a seven-year retirement to star in *Father Takes a Wife*. In this comedy, centering on the marriage and shipboard honeymoon of an actress and a shipping magnate (Adolphe Menjou), Swanson traded on her glamorous twenties image, wearing stunning outfits by RKO costume designer René Hubert. Movie posters blazed, "There's Glamour on the Screen Again, because Gloria's Back!" Laykin et Cie supplied her jewelry and received a credit in the film. Its contributions were eye-catching oversize brooches, one in the form of a pincushion created from stickpins, and the other a large gold Hellenistic head.

Just two years earlier, Laykin et Cie had accepted the invitation of Grover Magnin to move into I. Magnin, a leading department store in the West, in effect, inaugurating one-stop shopping for clothes and jewels. As Sol Laykin recalled, Grover Magnin, cosmetics queen Elizabeth Arden, and Darryl Zanuck's wife, Virginia, were all returning to the United States aboard the *Queen Mary*. At dinner, Magnin expressed his exasperation over the inability of "that firm with the three brothers" (Cartier) to decide whether they would open a salon in his

Below: An advertisement for a diamond and 18K gold lily brooch appeared in *Harper's Bazaar* in 1939.

Loretta Young wears a Flato 18K gold, diamond, and yellow topaz lily brooch and bracelet in a January 1938 *Harper's Bazaar* fashion portrait by George Hoyningen-Huene.

In *That Uncertain Feeling*, Melvyn Douglas surprises his wife, Merle Oberon, who mistakes him for her lover and faints when she discovers who it is. She wears a diamond and 18K gold lily with a bracelet and ring, all by Paul Flato.

store. Arden was proclaiming, "There is only one jeweler for you. That is Paul Flato," when Virginia Zanuck piped up, "You've been looking at my three little diamond and gold flower brooches all evening. Think I got them in Paris? No. I got them from Mr. Laykin of Laykin et Cie." Upon his arrival, Magnin contacted Laykin.

Laykin et Cie gradually achieved a national reputation. Like other large jewelers, Laykin started to advertise in *Vogue, Harper's Bazaar,* and *Town and Country.* Designer George Headley proved to be a great addition to the business. Headley contributed the light humor that had characterized the Flato establishment, attracting a broader range of customers. Many of these new customers,

Right: Opera singer and movie star Lily Pons had a Flato necklace with the last name of her husband, conductor Andre Kostelanetz, and a charm bracelet with her initials.

Above: Flato made catch-phrase bracelets in the gold block-letter, ribbon-chain style. The firm immortalized Jimmy Durante's expression "Hot-Cha," illustrated above in an ink and gouache drawing.

Right: An ink and gouache drawing for a Flato "Gold-Digger" charm bracelet shows charms representing objects of the miner's trade. The bracelet was inspired by a series of gold-digger movies directed and choreographed by Busby Berkeley.

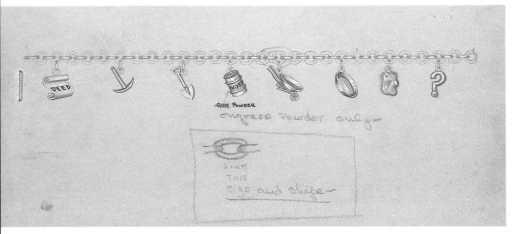

Pons poses after giving a concert at the Hollywood Bowl. She wears two pieces of Flato naturalistic jewelry, the double-apple cuff and the vine necklace.

Right: An ink and gouache drawing illustrates the 18K gold and diamond vine necklace in a Flato scrapbook. The leaves and flowers drape over the rigid band, which opens in front. In the nineteenth century this style was called the question mark by its originator, the French jeweler Boucheron.

Left: In a Flato scrapbook, the double-apple cuff is rendered in ink and gouache with textured relief on rich brown paper.

Lily Pons's double-apple cuff is extraordinarily bold in size and shape, every surface packed with circular- and baguette-cut diamonds set in platinum.

In *That Uncertain Feeling* (1941)
Merle Oberon and fellow patient-
in-therapy Burgess Meredith analyze an abstract painting. She
wears a Flato 18K gold, pearl, and
diamond abstract clip brooch. One
Flato collection was based on abstract design. The jewels were
splashed with color—diamonds,
emeralds, sapphires, rubies, aqua-
marines, and topaz—and varied in
texture, blending cabochons and
faceted cuts; black and white
pearls were sometimes added for
accents and dimension.

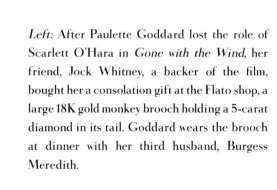

Left: After Paulette Goddard lost the role of
Scarlett O'Hara in *Gone with the Wind,* her
friend, Jock Whitney, a backer of the film,
bought her a consolation gift at the Flato shop, a
large 18K gold monkey brooch holding a 5-carat
diamond in its tail. Goddard wears the brooch
at dinner with her third husband, Burgess
Meredith.

unable to go to Paris because of the war, transferred their jewelry and couture
allegiance to Laykin et Cie and I. Magnin.

Henceforth, Laykin et Cie developed its own unique jewels, such as the brooch
composed of three ivory and gem-set monkeys representing the adage, "See no
evil; hear no evil; speak no evil," joined by a gold chain. Such jewels appeared
frequently in fashion reviews and gossip columns, where their owners were cited
by name. The Laykin et Cie triple monkey brooch, for example, was advertised
and illustrated in *Harper's Bazaar* in 1940 before it went into the collection of
Virginia Zanuck.

By the forties the success of Trabert & Hoeffer-Mauboussin's Reflection line,
Flato's surrealistic jewelry, and Laykin et Cie's playful baubles proved that less-

expensive, imaginative contemporary jewelry lured women into stores and promoted a jeweler's name in a way that expensive jewels did not. The duke of Verdura took the idea a step further. Harboring no desire to work with excessively valuable gemstones, which he dismissed as "rocks" and their connoisseurship as "mineralogy," he proceeded to make a name for himself with his own firm, Verdura. The detail and color of his work proved highly popular and increased the importance of such jewelry.

Born in Sicily, Fulco Santostefano della Cerda, duc di Verdura, was educated as a painter in Italy before becoming a designer in Paris at the House of Chanel, where Coco Chanel was experimenting on various lines of jewelry. His original costume jewelry line, launched for Chanel around 1926, was made in a rich Byzantine style, featuring bead necklaces, oversize cruciforms, and badges set with glass, semiprecious stones, and artificial pearls. When this line appeared,

Above: Verdura shows Coco Chanel the white enamel Maltese cross cuff that he designed for her.

Greta Garbo wears an array of Flato jewelry—a diamond-fringe necklace with scrolls, a ring, flower-clip brooches, and diamond hair curls—in *Two Faced Woman* (1941).

Top: Tyrone Power purchased a heart composed of cabochon rubies wrapped with a gold ribbon in 1941. This ink and gouache drawing of the jewel is from the Verdura archives.

Above: Mrs. Gary Cooper visited Verdura in 1947 and left with a gold mermaid sitting on a rock surrounded by sapphire waves and holding a diamond. The ink and gouache drawing is from the Verdura archives.

semiprecious stones were so plentiful that jewelers and the public alike considered them suitable for costume pieces and mixed them freely with colored glass and base metal backings. The 1926 Chanel line continues to be highly popular today and still influences costume and precious jewelry designers. The white enamel cuffs with Maltese cross motifs, which Chanel wore daily, are now replicated in many colors.

The Sicilian duke was not simply a costume jewelry designer but a connoisseur of the life-style in which jewelry played an important part. He was well educated, artistic, curious, entertaining, and impulsive — he spent his entire inheritance on one elaborate farewell ball in 1926 before leaving Sicily for Paris. In 1934, restless again, he and his good friend Baron Nicolas de Gunzburg traveled around America. In their Packard, they sought adventure in Palm Beach, Beverly Hills, and other watering spots, meeting people who could help them get ahead in the field of fashion. Everything about them reflected a certain style. Once, when they ran out of gas, Verdura was dispatched to find some; he returned with his silver hip flask full.

In New York, Verdura wandered into the orbit of Paul Flato, where he became a free-lance designer. There he was given the opportunity to improve on the beauty of his work through the use of precious stones. When Flato opened in Los Angeles in 1938, Verdura joined his design staff full-time. Fanfare and praise from the magazines may have come in part because Verdura's traveling buddy, De Gunzburg, had become a fashion reporter who went on to serve as fashion editor at *Harper's Bazaar* and *Vogue* and as editor-in-chief of *Town and Country.*

When Verdura worked for Flato in Hollywood, it was said that he ran Flato's establishment there. Flato later denied this. Verdura "was the sweetest man who ever lived," Flato said. "His breeding shone in every aspect of his designs, but he never ever ran anything—not even his own shop in New York."

With two partners, ex-Flato salesmen J. Byrd Mann and Joseph Alfano, Verdura opened his own salon at 712 Fifth Avenue in 1939. They were backed financially by socialite Vincent Astor and songwriter Cole Porter. Verdura had met Cole Porter and his wife, Linda, in Sicily in 1926, and they became and remained close friends. The Porters did everything to support Verdura's design career, and as soon as Verdura was established in the field of precious jewelry, he designed pieces for them and created wonderfully decorative cigarette boxes that Linda and Cole exchanged at the opening of each of Cole's shows. The most famous Verdura box from the Porter collection, named "Red, Hot and Blue," was commissioned by Cole for Linda in 1936 while Verdura was free-lancing for Paul Flato. With a cover of a diamond sunburst on a ruby and sapphire background, the box, always on display in the Porters' fashionable, much-visited New York apartment, was photographed by *Vogue* in 1937 and hailed as the "most talked-of bauble in town."

These Verdura boxes were special, not only for their materials and thematic designs, but also for the memories they conjured up of the devoted friends, composers, actors, and other artists who worked with Porter. A cigarette case Verdura made for the 1938 opening of *The Man Who Came to Dinner* has caricatures of authors George S. Kaufman and Moss Hart and leading actors John Hoyt and Monty Woolley. Cole Porter had written a song for the show. The

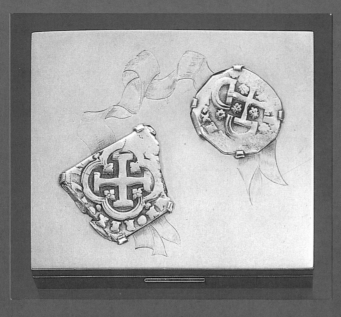

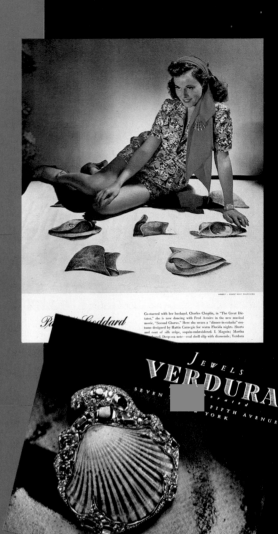

Above: A 14K gold cigarette case by Verdura, set with two gold pieces-of-eight joined by an engraved ribbon and inscribed "Mexican Hayride, Dec. 28, 1943," was given to Cole Porter by his wife, Linda. She gave the composer an inscribed case on each of his opening nights. When Porter's commemorative cases were auctioned at Parke-Bernet in 1967, among the top bidders were Frank Sinatra, Jean Howard, and Lauren Bacall, who owned this one. Dimensions: 3½ × 2⅞ × ¾ in.

Top: Paulette Goddard was photographed in a surrealistic beachscape by Horst for *Vogue* (January 1941) wearing a fiery orange Verdura shell clip accented with diamonds to hold down the scarf of her sporty Hattie Carnegie\cabaña suit.

Above: A Verdura advertisement in *Vogue* (February 1941) illustrates a seashell mounted in a diamond and gem-set clip brooch nestled in the sand.

In *Father Takes a Wife* (1941), Gloria Swanson dines with Adolphe Menjou. She wears a Laykin et Cie plaque resembling a pincushion studded with several stick pins.

Laykin et Cie was very proud of its movie-star clientele. An advertisement from *Vogue* (1941) features a gold and diamond bracelet and points out that it was "A new Laykin creation especially designed for Ann Sothern, MGM star."

gift to him is made in silver and lacquer, inlaid with yellow gold letters, and inscribed, "For Cole Porter, because we think you're wonderful. Moss and George."

Porter was a musical ace, and his songs for which he also wrote the lyrics were snappy, wicked, passionate, and sophisticated. They put glamour into music with sly innuendoes mixed with forthright American witticisms. Porter's music began to appear in film as soon as there was sound, and his long list of credits includes *Anything Goes* (1936) and *Kiss Me, Kate* (1953).

The Porters' life together seemed a thirties idyll, overflowing with talented friends and generated by solid accomplishment. Their dialogue and anecdotes were the stuff of screwball comedies, as when Linda Porter returned the Hope diamond to the jeweler, not because of the curse on it but because of its "dirty blue" color.

Cary Grant portrayed Cole Porter in a film biography, *Night and Day* (1946), which included a sequence of Linda giving Cole a cigarette case, an exchange that had become a ritual in their household. The tradition was carried on after Linda's death when Cole received a case made by Verdura and inscribed on the inside, "In Memory of Linda," with the names of Jean (Howard), Niki (De Gunzburg), (Howard) Sturges, Fulco (Verdura), and Natasha (Mrs. John C.) Wilson—all carrying on the Porter tradition. The 14K gold case that centered on a Russian gold coin surrounded by a sunburst motif honored Porter's last Broadway show, *Silk Stockings* (1955).

The onset of World War II turned Verdura's grand opening in New York into a bittersweet occasion. While Verdura himself was concerned about his beloved Paris and the financial forecast for precious jewelry, *Harper's Bazaar* voiced no reservations in its enthusiastic review of his jewelry exhibition in 1939, citing "a huge pear-shaped aquamarine, caught up at each side with a pair of diamond wings [and] a necklace of diamond eagle wings, stretching themselves out to encircle your throat."

Verdura's artistic finesse, whimsical flair, and knowledge of historical designs made for unforgettable jewels. His themes included beasts, birds, fish, chess figures, naiads, Neptunes, badges, different kinds of nautical knots, and Renaissance strapwork, for which he made not the usual jewelry renderings, but two-by-three-inch paintings capturing the colors of semiprecious stones. Verdura also made infinite variations on the scallop seashell brooch, taking jewelry naturalism literally by encrusting seashells bought at the American Museum of Natural History in New York with precious gems and setting them in gold. Many women bought them, and Verdura became identified with this motif; no two were exactly alike.

Even though Verdura emphasized semiprecious stones, he retained the respect of New York's precious jewelers. Clients with important jewels and gemstones would come to his small atelier and trade in their valuable pieces for his up-to-date bijoux. Their jewels and gemstones, out of place in Verdura's repertoire, were subsequently sold within the jewelry industry, thus making his two partners, Mann and Alfano, important dealers.

Even though Verdura never received an on-screen jewelry credit for a movie, he is rumored to have supplied the jewelry for *The Philadelphia Story* (1940). Katharine Hepburn had starred in the Broadway production of Philip Barry's play, and she had the foresight to secure the movie rights. Returning to Hollywood, she laid out her terms to MGM—leading man, Cary Grant, supporting actor, James Stewart, and director, George Cukor—before signing over the rights. The movie became Hepburn and Grant's supreme comedy, revolving around a Philadelphia heiress named Tracy Lord (Hepburn), who comes down to earth precipitously, learning about her own flaws and forgiving other people theirs.

In the movie, the camera pauses only for a second on Tracy's large diamond engagement ring and bracelet while the rest of the film jewelry receives no close-ups. However, costume designer Adrian tucked in a bit of insider Hollywood jewelry history and humor by including the imitation diamond girdle that had been used in the film *Marie Antoinette* (1938). It appears among the wedding presents at the Philadelphia mansion. Tracy's little sister (Virginia Weidler) picks up the enormous, elaborate jewel and says, "This stinks."

Vivien Leigh wears Verdura gold flame and knot jewelry in a fashion photograph by George Hoyningen-Huene for *Harper's Bazaar* (September 1940).

World War II Movies

World War II jolted the movie industry out of its complacent stories of wealthy life-styles and carefree ease. In the years since its inception, the movies had become America's eighth-largest industry, and its principals were a part of a success story that the rest of America had shared. And as had been the case during the Depression, all eyes were focused on Hollywood, which now exuded a spirit of patriotism and self-sacrifice.

The time had come for the film industry to contribute to its country. Leading men Clark Gable, James Stewart, Tyrone Power, and others joined the fighting forces, while Marlene Dietrich, Ray Bolger, and Jack Benny enlisted behind Bob Hope to entertain the troops on United Service Organization (USO) tours. Actors and actresses who stayed home sold war bonds to raise several million dollars every year.

Some of the biggest stars in Hollywood participated in a community project called the Hollywood Canteen, where they made and served soup and sandwiches for American servicemen and danced and talked with them, too. The project was so successful that it inspired a film, *Hollywood Canteen* (1944), starring Joan Crawford, Bette Davis, Barbara Stanwyck, Jane Wyman, and many other stars playing themselves.

Hollywood helped the government in its campaign to bring in materials necessary for the war and used its glamour to make the austerity of wartime shortages palatable. For the government, Twentieth Century–Fox made a newsreel featuring actress Alice Faye about its campaign to collect old silk and nylon stockings that would be used to make powder bags for heavy guns. Rita Hayworth posed on the hood of a car with a sticker that read, "Please drive carefully, my bumpers are on the scrap heap," encouraging co-workers and others to take unessential car parts to salvage centers.

The new Hollywood economy was summed up by Mae West, who made the supreme gesture of selling the diamond jewelry around which she had built her Gay Nineties look for the war cause. Her act set a good example and underlined the importance of platinum as a strategic metal. It was a catalyst for fuel and explosives, every scrap of which was useful to the military. The use of platinum for nonmilitary purposes was tightly regulated, making white and yellow gold the primary materials for the relatively meager number of precious jewels manufactured during the war. When men were fighting and dying for their country, jewelry was worn in moderation. The fashionable woman chose a new, patriotic brooch or one smart brooch from her collection to wear on the lapel of the suit that she donned for the office job she assumed from a man serving overseas.

Europeans fleeing the hostile regimes in Germany and Italy had begun arriving in America in the 1930s and continued to pour in during the war. Among them were members of the European jewelry industry. Once their escapes were

Mae West sold some of her diamond and platinum jewelry to aid a wartime cause. It was rumored that the beneficiary was the Royal Air Force, which had named its life vests after her. West's jewelry is a diverse collection that includes four wide bracelets and cabochon pieces, as well as the lacy Belle Epoque–period jewelry that she wore in her impersonation of Diamond Lil.

accomplished, they joined or opened firms in New York without skipping a beat. One Dutch diamond dealer remembered that his family drove from Amsterdam to Bordeaux, boarded a ship for America, anchored in Casablanca, and then sailed by way of the Dominican Republic to New York, where his father dropped the family in a hotel and was at work by ten o'clock the morning they arrived. A similar experience befell the two principals of Rubel Frères, manufacturers for leading Parisian jewelry firms. Jean and Robert Rubel arrived in New York from Europe by way of South America. They joined an American workshop that wholesaled jewelry to the Neiman Marcus department stores and the Van Cleef & Arpels branch in New York, established after the 1939 World's Fair. Then, in 1943, they opened their own retail firm, John Rubel Co.

Jean Rubel Americanized his name, although it was extraordinary that a French jeweler settling in the United States would let go of his French name, because American jewelers had always striven to create a European ambiance. The Rubel Co.'s appreciation of America was manifest in its designs, as the firm embraced American popular culture, taking jewelry motifs directly from the movie screen. The animated flowers that dance to Tchaikovsky's *Nutcracker Suite* in Walt Disney's experimental film *Fantasia* (1940) were the subject of the jewelry in the first John Rubel Co. advertisement and the inspiration for the Rubel "Dancing Flowers" line, which established Rubel as the jewelry darling of the wartime era. The little flowers fit in creatively with the spirit of patriotism.

Hollywood's share in the war effort was evident on the screen as well as off. A wide variety of wartime movies were produced, some portraying the sober aspects of the European theater and the heroism of military men, while others, wildly and exuberantly patriotic, lifted the spirits of the fighting men—and, incidentally, those left to cope on the home front—by introducing a bevy of young, shapely, well-endowed, long-legged starlets, who became the pinup girls of the armed forces. Many of these films were musical comedies, which the war-weary audiences favored. Other movies of the time had noble and uplifting happy endings and the movie industry experienced a boom as the war progressed. By 1944, 100 million Americans, two-thirds of the nation, were going to the movies weekly, up from 55 million in 1941. "All we had to do was open the doors and get out of the way" was a popular industry phrase.

One of the first films to deal with the onslaught of war in Europe was *Idiot's Delight* (1939). It opens with Clark Gable as World War I veteran Harry Van, making a rocky reentry into vaudeville. At a show in Omaha, Nebraska, he meets an acrobat, Irene (Norma Shearer), struggling to climb up from the world of vaudeville to make a career for herself. They have dinner together and fall in love, but the next day their work takes them in opposite directions. Years later, in 1939, when Harry is on tour in Europe with six women called Les Blondes, he meets Irene again. Impersonating a Russian countess, she is escorted by an arms dealer, Achille Weber (Edward Arnold).

Irene's relationship with the merchant of death keeps her in expensive clothes and magnificent jewelry. In her first scene alone in a hotel with Achille, Irene puts on two square gold bangles (which costume designer Adrian told the press had actually belonged to Russian nobility). After Achille says to Irene, "I hardly think you need to bother about jewelry in this place," she replies, "Only my bracelets, because you like them, Achille." The audience is aware that she is really thinking of Harry, whom she saw briefly when she entered the lobby.

In the concluding scenes, when Achille dramatically breaks his relationship with Irene and she reconciles with Harry, she wears a bracelet reminiscent of a sapphire and diamond jarretière (garter) bracelet by Van Cleef & Arpels. This style of bracelet had become world famous when the duke of Windsor gave Wallace Simpson one, engraved with the date of their marriage contract, as a wedding gift in 1937.

Another tale of political intrigue, *Casablanca* (1942) deals with political refugees escaping from Nazi Europe. Nearly everyone in Casablanca is raising cash for an escape. At the beginning of the film, a Moroccan merchant dismisses diamonds, saying they are a glut on the market. Exit visas are more precious than gems, and the difficulties in obtaining them in Casablanca becomes evident when a man is shot for two missing visas. The papers in his hand turn out to be documents of the French Resistance, identified by the Cross of Lorraine. That symbol reappears in the secret compartment of a ring shown to a member of the Czechoslovakian underground, Victor Laszlo (Paul Henreid), and his wife, Ilse Lund (Ingrid Bergman). A man called Berger turns up at Rick's Café Américain and pretends he is trying to sell them the ring. He is really identifying himself as a contact. Selling jewelry was so commonplace during the war, when people needed cash, that it makes a perfect cover for Berger.

The arrangements for Laszlo and Ilse's escape fail, but Rick (Humphrey Bogart), the proprietor of the cafe, intervenes. He saves not only Laszlo, but Ilse, with whom he had fallen in love when she was alone in Paris.

In a different category of war movies was the lighthearted *The Gang's All Here* (1943), which stands out for its exuberance. A patriotic musical comedy, it concerns a serviceman, Sergeant Andrew Mason, Jr. (Phil Baker), who falls in love with a show girl, Edie Allen (Alice Faye), although he is unofficially engaged

In *Casablanca* (1943) Paul Henreid and Ingrid Bergman, on the run from the Gestapo, identify a friendly contact through the Cross of Lorraine he reveals in the secret compartment of a ring he pretends to be selling.

125

For a Chesterfield ad, Claudette Colbert, Paulette Goddard, and Veronica Lake pose in their costumes from *So Proudly We Hail* (1943). Their patriotic jewelry incorporates stripes, shields, flags, wings, and anchors.

Below right: These ink and gouache drawings of World War II insignia clips are from the William Scheer archives. Patriotic jewels sold in large numbers in the 1940s and helped keep manufacturers in business.

AMERICA NEEDS NURSES ··· ENLIST NOW

CLAUDETTE COLBERT
PAULETTE GODDARD
VERONICA LAKE

PHOTOGRAPHED ON THE ACTUAL
SET OF PARAMOUNT'S NEW PICTURE

"SO PROUDLY WE HAIL"

AN EPIC OF THE NURSES
ON BATAAN

AT HOME and OVER THERE *It's* CHESTERFIELD

GOOD TOBACCO, Yes . . . the right combination of the WORLD'S BEST CIGARETTE TOBACCOS . . .

It isn't enough to buy the best cigarette tobacco, it's Chesterfield's right combination, or blend, of these tobaccos that makes them so much milder, cooler and better-tasting.

Good Tobacco, yes . . . but the Blend—the Right Combination—that's the thing.

Smoke Chesterfields and find out how really good a cigarette can be

Chesterfield CIGARETTES

LIGGETT & MYERS TOBACCO CO.

Norma Shearer, holding her spaniel Blackie, wears an American flag brooch. During World War II patriotic jewels were worn by many American women, and the stars and stripes often rippled with rubies, diamonds, and sapphires.

Below: An American flag brooch by Philadelphia jeweler J. E. Caldwell accompanies an ink and gouache drawing from the manufacturer Oscar Heyman & Bros., a prominent supplier of jewels to leading retailers.

At far left: Paulette Goddard wears a gold and enamel patriotic brooch on the lapel of her suit. She checks her makeup in a basket weave gold case called a minaudière, which has a diamond and cabochon gem-set clasp. A principal of Van Cleef & Arpels devised the oversized vanity after he saw the daughter-in-law of the railroad magnate Jay Gould toting daily necessities and makeup in a tin Lucky Strike cigarette box. The minaudière had compartments for cigarettes, a cigarette holder, a lighter, money, a watch, eye shadow, lipstick, powder, and rouge. Calibré-cut and cabochon gems usually enhanced the clasp.

In a *Harper's Bazaar* (1940) fashion portrait by Hoyningen-Huene, Joan Crawford wears a leopard outfit and a huge rectangular citrine ring, which was set in yellow gold, because of the shortage of platinum during the war.

to his childhood sweetheart. At a war bond garden party thrown in honor of his heroism in the Pacific, her entire theatrical company—including Carmen Miranda and Benny Goodman—arrives to provide entertainment at an estate on Long Island, where the romance between Andy and Edie winds to a happy end. The entertainment's choreography, by director Busby Berkeley and featuring the energetic Miranda, has become a classic.

The brooches worn by Faye and Miranda in the movie represent two types of wartime jewelry. Faye's sapphire, ruby, and diamond double-leaf brooch, which she wears in the Broadway USO canteen, is a refined jewel set with small precious stones, as is the diamond flame brooch that she later wears on the Staten Island Ferry. In contrast, Miranda's jewelry is in a whimsical vein, a style that continued through the war to lift spirits.

Carmen Miranda, one of Brazil's most popular exports to the United States, knew how to lift spirits. She had been brought to New York by the Shubert theater family in 1939 to star in *The Streets of Paris* and was snatched by Hollywood shortly thereafter. She played a wild, jewelry-wearing nightclub entertainer in all her movies, whose titles read like a travelogue of tropical hot spots: *That Night in Rio* (1941), *Week-End in Havana* (1941), and *Copacabana* (1947).

In most of her movies, the fiery South American played alongside an American leading lady whose looks were as natural as Miranda's were exotic. After America entered the war, the Hollywood studios featured several such actresses whose wholesome smiles, milk-fed good looks, and shapely figures won them millions of admirers in the fighting forces who posted pinups in their barracks and cockpits. This shift was reflected by the wartime publicity stills in which elaborate clothes accessorized by costly jewelry were replaced by tight, form-fitting outfits—often a bathing suit—accentuating the body. Betty Grable played the lead in *Pin-Up Girl* (1944) and posed for one of the most famous cheesecake photographs of the war, adding no diamonds to her curves.

The studios vied with one another to offer the most popular pinup girl. In one movie, MGM provided a steady stream of beauties. Signaling glamour through its

Joan Crawford loved rings — large rings — and when she purchased a new one from her favorite jeweler, Raymond C. Yard, in the early 1940s, she chose a step-cut amethyst of approximately 75 carats that is an exceptional deep violet hue. The stone is mounted in gold with delicate scroll supports.

The pearl necklace has remained a constant in jewelry fashion because of its beauty, femininity, and adaptability. The style of necklace worn here by Hedy Lamarr in the early forties is identical to that worn by Mary Pickford in the twenties and still seen today.

title, *Ziegfeld Girl* (1941) gave the studio the opportunity to update the Follies girl and stage a Busby Berkeley production using show girls wearing forties costumes, clothes, and jewelry. The lead singer was Judy Garland, who played Susan Gallagher. Drinking ice-cream sodas all the way, she reaches fame as a Ziegfeld headliner, and shows her kindness by taking her elderly father, a vaudeville actor, with her into the company. Garland's jewelry is demure and undistinguished except for the small cabochon sapphire clip brooch that she wears during an engagement in Palm Beach.

Hedy Lamarr glides through the movie as Sandra Kolter, a tall, stately beauty who is a professional show girl but who never ceases loving her jealous, estranged violinist husband. Of Austrian descent, Lamarr had become a celebrity because of her nude swimming scenes in Gustav Machaty's *Ecstasy* (1933). Later, her husband, Austrian arms dealer Fritz Mandl, tried to purchase all the prints. After divorcing Mandl in 1938, Lamarr went to Hollywood, where her classical beauty, rather than her talent, established her.

Lamarr's taste in jewelry was very specific. *Harper's Bazaar* reported that she cared only for pearls, and had assembled a collection that included pearl earrings, pearl rings, and a four-strand pearl necklace with one detachable strand. In *Algiers* (1938), a thriller set in the casbah of the North African city, Lamarr wears a pearl necklace when she meets the most-wanted French jewel thief, Pepe Le Moko (Charles Boyer). Le Moko's eyes shift back and forth from her beautiful jewels to her beautiful features. Later, in *Ziegfeld Girl,* Lamarr discreetly wears more modest pearl button earrings, pearl drop earrings, and a pearl necklace in the course of the story.

The third Ziegfeld girl is Sheila Hale, played by Lana Turner, a blond from Brooklyn, New York, who is discovered running an elevator in a Fifth Avenue department store by Flo Ziegfeld. At the premiere of the girls' first Follies, senior show girl Patsy Dixon, also known as Diamond Pat (Eve Arden), captures Hale's attention when she gives some free advice on how to navigate the staircase in the show's Mannequin Parade: "Take lots of time walking down and you'll gather plenty of moss." Diamond Pat waves an armful of wide bracelets. The next morning, Sheila walks down the staircase of her parents' house and asks her boyfriend, Gil (James Stewart), if she seems different now that she is a Follies girl. He replies in disgust, "A diamond don't have to be in no Tiffany settin' before I can see it," referring to the most famous design in American jewelry, the Tiffany engagement ring, whose six prongs lift a diamond above the band to expose the greater part of the stone to the light.

Sheila soon takes up with a wealthy man, Geoffrey Collis (Ian Hunter), who presents to her at their first dinner date a wide bracelet lit up by a huge,

In *Ziegfeld Girl* (1941) Lana Turner luxuriates in a bubble bath.

Carmen Miranda and Alice Faye appeared with Tony de Marco and Phil Baker in *The Gang's All Here* (1943). The large rooster and double-leaf brooches worn by the women were jewelry fashion's antidote to the sobriety of wartime. (The rooster brooch does not appear in the movie.)

Right: Carmen Miranda's famous number "The Lady in the Tutti-Frutti Hat," choreographed by Busby Berkeley in *The Gang's All Here* (1943), fixed her image in the minds of millions. Though she was associated with the tropical style of costume jewelry that was launched by this film and popular during World War II, Miranda herself wore precious jewelry.

Above: Carmen Miranda took time out from dining and dancing at Sherman Billingsley's Stork Club in New York to chat with Midshipman James A. Boswell. She wears a gem-splashed but-terfly brooch on her evening suit and a veiled hat with a star at her ear, a modi-fied version of her headdress in the opening scene of *The Gang's All Here.*

Below: A gold, gem-set rooster brooch, covered with rubies, dia-monds, sapphires, and emeralds, was made by American jeweler Seaman Schepps. The brooch ex-emplifies the representational style that evolved in the postwar era.

Left: The Brazilian star wears a Paul Flato sapphire, diamond, and platinum necklace to publicize her first Broadway musical, *Streets of Paris.* The portrait was made for *Vogue* in 1940 by Anton Breuhl in a set by Terance Robsjohn-Gibbings, who had designed the Flato Los Angeles shop.

multicolored center medallion that can be worn detached as a brooch. The jewel is shown in close-up resting on an appetizer plate.

The style of the bracelet, which drew on Art Deco and Machine styles in its design and construction, was labeled Retro by American jewelry historian Neil Letson in the 1980s. The term made its way into Christie's auction catalogues; François Curiel, head of the jewelry department, did not want to label this group Wartime. Retro style jewelry grew out of the wide gold bracelets, cuffs, and watch bracelets of the 1930s, which were originally created by French jewelers for daytime wear. In the forties the same styles, though a shade bolder and more elaborate, carried a woman through the day into the evening, creating a style called one-jewel dressing.

As *Ziegfeld Girl* unfolds, Sheila continues to love Gil but does not relinquish Geoffrey, who keeps her in a Fifth Avenue apartment with a maid and showers her with expensive furs and jewelry. When Gil visits her boudoir bearing a marriage license, Sheila complains about how tired she is of playing Cinderella, then trips on a diamond bracelet lying on the floor. Gil remarks, "People who wear glass slippers shouldn't walk on rocks." Geoffrey later breaks off his relationship with Sheila when he catches her professing her love for Gil, who has become a wealthy mobster and does not want her either.

Back in her New York apartment and facing a bleak future alone, made gloomier by her craving for alcohol, Sheila asks her maid, "How many of these service stripes have we collected?" The maid replies, "Addin' Mr. Geoff's signing-off present and deducting that one we pawned—I makes seven." Just before her last performance in the Follies, when she topples drunkenly down the staircase, Sheila is again counseled by Diamond Pat, who tells her, "I'd give my right arm, yeah, and everything on it [several wide bracelets] for a guy with an ice-cream wagon, if he really loved me."

Although *Ziegfeld Girl* ends on an upbeat note, with the reconciliation of Sheila and Gil, the film depicts jewelry as symbolic of indulgence that leads to misery—and worse. Unlike the previous era, when precious gem bracelets in movies signaled glamour and ease in the world, here it represents the spoils of immoral living.

Lana Turner entered show business in a way strikingly similar to her character in *Ziegfeld Girl*. She was discovered in Schwab's drugstore in Los Angeles while truant from school by an editor for *Hollywood Reporter*. At MGM she earned the title "Sweater Girl." Briefly married to bandleader Artie Shaw, she had roles in several wartime films, including an Americanization of *Grand Hotel* (1932), renamed *Weekend at the Waldorf* (1945), in which she portrayed the stenographer previously played by Joan Crawford. Finally, in *The Postman Always Rings Twice* (1946), she proved that her acting ability was equal to her sexy looks. In her maturity, Turner built up a substantial collection of diamond jewelry, primarily from Laykin et Cie.

Pinups of the Sweater Girl were highly popular, but America's most cherished pinup girl during the war was Rita Hayworth, whose *Life* magazine photo was reproduced a million times over—one was even affixed to the atomic bomb tested on the Bikini atoll. The daughter of a Ziegfeld Follies dancer, Hayworth was born

In *Gilda* (1946), Hayworth wears a platinum and square-cut diamond choker that she flings into the audience during a sultry rendition of "Put the Blame on Mame, Boys." The choker, called a rivière, is composed of a row of diamonds set in a flexible, articulated mount.

in Brooklyn, New York, and began her dancing career at twelve as one of the Dancing Cansinos. At the age of seventeen she was brought by Fox studio to Hollywood, where she made a series of "B" films until the studio entered financial hard times and merged with Twentieth Century and she lost her job. She then married a much older man, Edward Judson, who took charge of her career. He changed her name from Cansino to Hayworth and advised her to dye her raven-colored hair reddish brown and alter her hairline to give her face a more dramatic shape. Then he made sure she was photographed at all the Hollywood events.

His stewardship finally paid off when she received enthusiastic reviews for her role in the remake of the Valentino classic *Blood and Sand* (1941), directed by Rouben Mamoulian. Hayworth played Doña Sol, a Spanish heiress with a penchant for bullfighters, most especially Juan Gallardo (Tyrone Power), whom she leads to his doom. From the moment Juan spots Doña Sol in her blue suit, with a three-strand pearl necklace, cheering him from the box above the bullring, he is hopelessly under her spell. Later, Doña Sol invites Juan to a dinner party to retrieve the bullfighter's hat he gallantly threw her. For the occasion, she wears a white evening dress, a broad diamond necklace with side scrolls, a bracelet with a sapphire cylindrical motif, and a number of rings.

Hayworth's grand jewels, made by Paul Flato at the end of his career, are featured in the two dramatic scenes when she woos and wins the simple bullfighter, and when she leaves him. In the latter sequence, which takes place in a café, she dances with his successor, a bullfighter who replaces Gallardo both in the bullring and in Doña Sol's affections. Halfway through her dance she drops a ring, which the camera bears down on to show the diamond head of a cat with a caliber-cut sapphire smile and ruby eyes, symbol of a cunning enchantress.

After *Blood and Sand* Hayworth danced in several lighthearted wartime musical comedies, two with Fred Astaire, *You'll Never Get Rich* (1941) and *You Were Never Lovelier* (1942), and one with Gene Kelly, *Cover Girl* (1944). When

Rita Hayworth serenades matador Tyrone Power in an updated version of the Valentino vehicle *Blood and Sand* (1941). She wears a magnificent scrolled diamond necklace mounted in 18K white gold and a sapphire bracelet, earclips, and rings, all by Paul Flato.

Right: Rubel ink and gouache drawings were for dancing flower brooches, from 1943.

Below: John Rubel Co.'s first advertisement, from 1943, showed dancing flowers based on those in Walt Disney's feature-length animated film *Fantasia*.

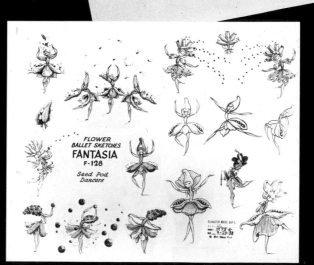

FLOWER
BALLET SKETCHES
FANTASIA
F-128
Seed Pod
Dancers

Left: Disney studio sketches depict the seed-pod dancers from the flower ballet in *Fantasia*.

© The Walt Disney Company

the war ended, Hayworth channeled her dramatic ability and statuesque beauty into her most electrifying performance in the title role of *Gilda* (1946). She plays a lovesick small-time American singer who is imported to Buenos Aires by her new husband, Mundsen (George Macready), an unscrupulous casino owner and postwar Nazi collaborator. Through a quirk of fate, Mundsen's manager turns out to be the man who left her—Johnny Farrell (Glenn Ford)—and drove her into making a loveless marriage.

After the mysterious death of Mundsen, Gilda marries Johnny, thinking that, once married, she will have the man she has always loved, but Johnny is infuriated by what he thinks he knows about her past behavior and treats her badly. The film reaches its crescendo when Gilda, now Johnny's prisoner and his wife only in name, goads him with a performance of "Put the Blame on Mame, Boys" in his casino. Turning the siren song into a striptease, she slowly peels down her elbow-length, black satin gloves, then takes off her baguette-cut diamond and platinum rivière, swings it like a lasso above her head, and flings it into the crowd before asking for help with the zipper of her tight black evening dress.

With the one exception of the diamond rivière, jewelry plays only a minor part in this simmering film. A large Retro bracelet is glimpsed around Hayworth's wrist, and other accessories blend with her tailored suits, dresses, and evening frocks. At one point, when Gilda produces a diamond clip brooch to taunt Johnny, Mundsen sneers at her offhand manner, "Fifty thousand pesos—and it's cute."

The Love Goddess of Hollywood, as Hayworth was known, never amassed a noteworthy jewelry collection, although she had more opportunity than any other star. After her divorce from actor/director Orson Welles, she married into a family whose vast wealth included some of the world's most extraordinary holdings of precious gems and jewelry. In 1949, over the objections of Harry Cohn—

Below left: Mickey Rooney beams as his bride of 1942, Ava Gardner, shows off her engagement ring. The ring, from Van Cleef & Arpels, centers on a 6.35-carat emerald-cut diamond surrounded by eight circular-cut diamonds. Because the ring was made during the war, it is mounted in gold instead of the traditional platinum.

Below: In a watercolor storyboard for Disney's *Snow White and the Seven Dwarfs* (1937), Doc is shown grading stones as Dopey looks on. The dwarfs were miners.

who suspended her from Columbia Pictures for it—Hayworth married Aly Khan, son of the Aga Khan, a Muslim spiritual leader whose people annually showed their devotion by giving him his weight in diamonds. Among many other spectacular jewels, the Aga Khan owned a legendary Cartier necklace composed of thirty-eight round diamonds and suspending diamond drops totalling 113 carats. Another daughter-in-law of his, a former Dior model, Nina Dyer, had a spectacular jewelry collection, including large diamond rings from Harry Winston, emerald and sapphire suites from Cartier, and bijouterie that ranged from a suite of Cartier panthers rendered in diamonds and sapphires (instead of black onyx) to a Siamese cat brooch with sapphire eyes designed for Dior.

MGM's contender for Hayworth's title of Love Goddess, Ava Gardner, was signed by the studio on the basis of a photograph taken by her brother-in-law. While the snapshot caught her gorgeous face and sensational figure, it gave no hint of her thick Southern drawl. Louis B. Mayer's legendary response to her screen test was, "She can't act. She can't talk. She's terrific!" Upon her acceptance by the studio, Gardner was enrolled in MGM diction courses and relegated to bit parts. She did, however, become familiar through her World War II pinups.

All of this changed when one of MGM's biggest stars, Mickey Rooney, fell madly in love with Gardner, bringing her into the limelight. Gardner agreed to marry Rooney only after her nineteenth birthday had passed. He threw an engagement party at Romanoff's on her birthday, Christmas Eve of 1941, and gave her a 6.35-carat diamond engagement ring from Van Cleef & Arpels in a graceful style enhanced by eight round diamonds that created a lace-doily effect.

At first, Louis B. Mayer refused to consent to the marriage, and both stars' contracts stipulated that Mayer's consent was required. A tearful confrontation between the lovestruck Rooney and the patriarch Mayer, who did not want to see his twenty-two-year-old boy-next-door star marry a pinup girl, did not dissuade Rooney. And so the happy couple wed in a small town near Santa Barbara, California, on January 10, 1942. Three members of Rooney's family, one friend of Gardner's, and Rooney's publicity man, who also accompanied them on their honeymoon, attended the ceremony. Gardner wore a tailored blue suit with a corsage of orchids, and Rooney presented her with a wedding band inscribed "Love Forever." The marriage lasted one year.

Before the war ended Gardner was married again, in a different blue tailored suit and orchid—this time to Artie Shaw, the bandleader and former husband of Lana Turner. Shaw encouraged Gardner to educate herself and go beyond the only book she had read, Gone with the Wind. Like many other starlets who had been seized by wartime Hollywood for their physical attributes, Gardner had no education and little experience of life.

Later, with a new approach to acting stemming from her maturity and the education Shaw had encouraged, she was ready to tackle dramatic roles. Costarring in the screen adaptation of Ernest Hemingway's The Killers (1946) with an unknown, Burt Lancaster, Gardner won over the critics and launched a career with some memorable performances. Praised by a reporter for her acting talent in 1985, she said, "Listen, honey, I was never really an actress. None of us kids who came from MGM were. We were just good to look at."

Alfred Hitchcock

An Englishman who had started out at twenty-one in the London branch of Famous Players–Lasky, Alfred Hitchcock became one of his country's most prominent directors, responsible for such classics as *The Man Who Knew Too Much* (1934) and *The Thirty-Nine Steps* (1935). His thrillers were said to be technically on a par with American films, an observation that Hitchcock took as a compliment. And in 1939, when David O. Selznick invited Hitchcock to Hollywood on a generous contract, he accepted eagerly, knowing that he would have access to the advanced technical equipment that he considered essential to the success of his work. The technical underpinnings of movies, camerawork and split-second timing, were so important to Hitchcock that he drew storyboards for each scene and, occasionally, for changes of emotion. These narrative maps helped Hitchcock weave inanimate objects—including precious jewelry and accessories—into his plots like no other director before or since.

In *Shadow of a Doubt* (1943) the emerald ring that establishes the guilt of a murderer is a gift from Charlie Oakley (Joseph Cotten) to his niece and namesake, Charlie Newton (Teresa Wright). Thrilled by his gift, Charlie holds it up and spots inside it a set of initials that later turn out to match those of a victim of the notorious "Merry Widow" murderer. After returning the ring to her uncle, she tells him to leave town, because the knowledge of his crime will destroy her mother. When he does not go, Charlie retrieves the ring and flaunts it at a party, forcing Uncle Charlie to announce his departure.

In the course of the film, the dialogue about jewelry shifts. At first, Uncle Charlie praises emeralds, "Good emeralds are the most beautiful things in the world." Then he dismisses his victims as "proud of their jewelry but of nothing else." In a grim confrontation between the two Charlies in a smoky bar, a waitress catches sight of the ring and says, "I'd just die for a ring like that," foreshadowing the successive attempts on young Charlie's life and the ultimate death of her uncle.

Hitchcock's *Lifeboat* (1944), an intense wartime film about human psychology and survival with a script by John Steinbeck, opens amid the floating debris of a World War II passenger ship that has just been torpedoed by a German U-boat. In the gloom Constance Porter, played by Tallulah Bankhead, appears in a lifeboat, wearing a Cartier diamond bracelet and flashing a gold cigarette case and lighter, with some of her other possessions—a camera, fur coat, typewriter, hand luggage, and pocketbook—surrounding her. The first survivor to join her is the crewman John Kovac (John Hodiak), who knows her by reputation as a famous reporter. When her camera accidentally falls overboard, he chides her to consider the human tragedy rather than bemoan lost photographs of the sinking ship and passengers. Bedraggled survivors who clamber aboard are a young army nurse (Mary Anderson), a self-made millionaire named Rittenhouse (Henry Hull), a

In *Lifeboat* (1944) Walter Slezak, the Nazi submarine captain, fixes the clasp of Tallulah Bankhead's Cartier wide bracelet and discusses the chemical composition of diamonds: "They're really nothing but a few pieces of carbon, crystallized under high pressure, great heat."

Bankhead sings "I'll Be Seeing You" for three hundred guests at a New York restaurant following her 1952 television debut and the publication of her autobiography *Tallulah*. She wears a Verdura shell clip brooch and an oversize oval-link gold bracelet.

black steward (Canada Lee), the ship's radio operator (Hume Cronyn), Gus, a seaman with an injured leg, (William Bendix), and a woman (Heather Angel) carrying her dead child. The last to arrive is a Nazi sailor (Walter Slezak).

Hitchcock's challenge in this movie was to keep the action flowing within the confines of only one set, the lifeboat. He employed unexpected devices to sustain the tension. Connie's luxury items become necessities for survival: her mink coat warms the shell-shocked woman who lost her child, her gold lighter sterilizes the knife used to amputate Gus's leg, and her pocket flask of whiskey provides a primitive anesthetic. The practical possessions of the German sailor, a small locket-type compass and a flask of drinking water, lead to his doom when the others discover he has been hoarding water in addition to directing them toward a German supply boat. Their compassion for him as a fellow human being turns to hatred, and in hysteria heightened by days at sea, lack of food, and no water, they kill him.

Near the end of the film, the only object left that can save the starving castaways is Connie's Cartier diamond bracelet, which was a gift from her first husband. It served as her passport out of the South Side of Chicago to the Gold Coast and functioned as her good-luck charm for fifteen years. She removes it from her wrist and offers it as bait for a desperate attempt at fishing.

Connie: Ye gods and little fishes. Fishes. Ye Gods. We haven't got energy pills, but the ocean is full of them, millions of fish swimming around. Well, why don't we catch some!

Rittenhouse: We tried that. We have no bait.

Connie: Sure we have bait—by Cartier.

Kovac: Are you kidding?

Connie: Kidding, my foot. I'm starving! Well, what are you waiting around for? Where's the fish line? Bait your line, chum.

After more dialogue, Connie wryly comments, "I can recommend the bait. I ought to know. I bit on it myself."

Bankhead won the New York Film Critics' Award for her performance in *Lifeboat,* and Hitchcock himself said that she towered over every other actor in the cast. The daughter of a Southern congressman, Bankhead won a beauty contest at age fifteen and made her stage debut in the same year, 1919, in *Squab Farm* at the Bijou Theatre in New York. A long career on the New York and London stage followed, during which she was an intimate of an elite circle of actors, playwrights, critics, and writers, including Lillian Hellman, whose play *The Little Foxes* (1939) provided Bankhead with one of her great roles. While Bankhead's film work never had the depth of her stage career, *Lifeboat* proved a superb vehicle for her talent and personality. Like the character Connie, Bankhead was known for outspoken wit and beautiful jewelry.

Her collection included pieces by Verdura and other New York jewelers, and among them was a striking three-strand pink cultured-pearl necklace, which she wears in a portrait by Augustus John. This style of necklace, made up of soft, sunset pink- or champagne gold-cultured pearls harvested in Burma and measuring ten to fifteen millimeters, was an alternative to the traditional pearl necklace (with white and smaller pearls) of earlier decades.

In *Spellbound* (1945), Hitchcock turned his fascination with the dark side of human nature into a thriller about psychiatrists and psychology. The movie opens in the antiseptic setting of the Green Manors sanitarium, where the young

While in Hollywood, in 1945, Salvador Dali painted a portrait of Mrs. Jack Warner. Seen in a surrealistic landscape with motifs alluding to the theater, she wears her half-moon diamond earclips, cabochon emerald ring, and her favorite Trabert & Hoeffer-Mauboussin cabochon emerald pendant.

Left: In 1941 Dali and Verdura collaborated on an exhibition of gold boxes and jewelry with surrealistic designs. Among the boxes, they presented this hammered gold cigarette case set with an ivory miniature depicting a spider with a Medusa head in a barren landscape. A beetle of sculpted gold, pearl, opal, and black enamel with garnet eyes lurks on the border. Dimensions: $3 \times 3\frac{1}{2} \times \frac{5}{8}$ in.

Dr. Petersen (Ingrid Bergman) falls in love with the new director, Dr. Edwardes (Gregory Peck). But it turns out that he is not Dr. Edwardes at all but an impersonator who is suffering from amnesia. Dr. Petersen's self-imposed mission to free the impersonator's memory and uncover his real identity becomes more urgent when he is accused of murdering the real Dr. Edwardes. The couple finally flees to the home of her former teacher (Michael Chekhov), where they analyze the amnesiac's dreams to find the solution to the crime.

Because Hitchcock wanted the sets in the dream sequence to be sharply focused, in contrast to traditional movie dream sequences with blurry outlines, he turned to Salvador Dali, a leading Spanish Surrealist artist who worked in many mediums. Dali created an eerie landscape whose strange features provided clues to the murder.

During the period that Dali collaborated with Hitchcock, he kept a part-time residence in Hollywood and experimented in designing precious jewelry. Although he did not use the finest stones and did not have the deftness and knowledge of a fine jeweler, his inventive motifs left an imprint on the history of jewelry. The titles of some of his jewelry, "Ruby Lips," "Leaf Veined Hands," "Pomegranate Heart" and "The Eye of Time," show a Surrealist preoccupation with transformation and hidden meaning, which endeared him to Hitchcock.

Hitchcock's *Notorious* (1946) opens in Miami, Florida, in 1946, with the sentencing of a Nazi collaborator to twenty years in the penitentiary. As the photographers converge, his beautiful daughter, Alicia Huberman (Ingrid Bergman), leaves the courtroom silently. The scene shifts to a late-night, somewhat debauched party in her Miami villa, where the camera lingers on a mysterious man, his features in the shadow—FBI agent Devlin (Cary Grant). Devlin later persuades Alicia to act on her patriotism and join him in cracking an undercover

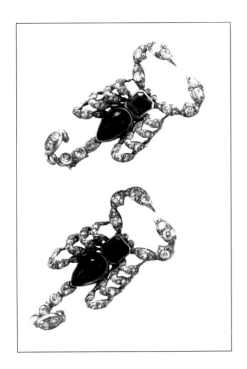

Top: In *Notorious* (1946), with FBI agent Cary Grant feigning disinterest, his superior, Louis Calhern, puts a diamond necklace by Harry Winston on Ingrid Bergman. Thus adorned, her mission is to win the heart of a Nazi ringleader. *Above:* Bergman's emerald and diamond scorpion brooches were a present from her husband, director Roberto Rossellini.

Nazi organization in Brazil. Her compliance culminates in her marriage to Nazi Alex Sebastian (Claude Rains) and her near poisoning when Sebastian and his mother figure out that Alicia has been spying on them for the American government.

Throughout the movie there is a strong attraction between Alicia and Devlin, but he refuses to allow himself to believe that she has changed for the better. His feelings grow turbulent when the operation calls for Alicia to seduce Sebastian. On the night Alicia is to have dinner with Sebastian, his mother, and Nazi associates, she shows off her evening dress to Devlin and his fellow agent Paul Prescott (Louis Calhern). Prescott fastens around her neck a large diamond necklace that he has rented for the occasion. Though there is no screen credit, the diamond necklace came from Harry Winston, whose trademark—leaf-shaped clusters of medium-size marquise, pear-shaped, and round diamonds—identifies it. Here, the diamonds are set in flexible platinum mounts inspired by a holly wreath. The Winston firm had been working steadily since the 1920s to amass a treasury of diamonds second to none. Later, in the postwar period, Harry Winston did for precious jewelry what Christian Dior did for couture, putting women in rich, romantic feminine styles.

Bergman's modest demeanor and seemingly tranquil marriage to Dr. Peter Lindstrom established her as a well-loved Hollywood actress. But Americans were stunned and repelled in 1950 by revelations of her sudden elopement and marriage to Italian director Roberto Rossellini. Damned as a free-love advocate and denounced even from the floor of the U.S. Senate, Bergman was banned from making films in America for seven years. She worshiped Rossellini and continued making artistic and avant-garde films in Europe with him and other European directors. In 1956, she returned to the American screen in *Anastasia*, winning the Best Actress Academy Award. In 1958, with her marriage annulled, she returned to the United States. A final honor was accorded her in 1974, when she was named Best Supporting Actress for *Murder on the Orient Express*.

Bergman's eclectic jewelry collection grew over the years. It shows how successfully twentieth-century jewelers had been in creating timeless, wearable styles that continue to have appeal: an emerald line bracelet, a diamond snowflake clip brooch and earrings, an Art Deco dinner ring, and a gold charm bracelet, with bells in honor of her role in *For Whom the Bell Tolls* (1943). Rossellini contributed an unusual and imaginative pair of emerald and diamond scorpion brooches made by an Italian jeweler in the 1950s. Individual pieces show that Bergman shopped at Tiffany, and Bulgari, Gucci, and other Italian jewelers. In Jean Renoir's film *Paris Does Strange Things* (1956), Bergman modeled jewelry in the same way she wore it in private, choosing small pieces, sometimes set with pale semiprecious or synthetic stones, as discreet beauty accents.

For *Stage Fright* (1950), Hitchcock chose Marlene Dietrich to play his heroine Charlotte Inwood, an aging actress who has driven her young lover, Jonathan Cooper (Richard Todd), to murder her husband in a fit of jealous agitation. Hitchcock decided that as an adored actress who was the recipient of many gifts, she would have a substantial jewelry collection. During the day Charlotte wears narrow diamond chokers, one combined with pearls. And for her performances on

Precious jewelry that appears in movies sometimes does not reappear in publicity stills because the jeweler will not risk bringing it back for photography. Alfred Hitchcock insisted that any jewelry he used in a film must also be used in its publicity. For *Stage Fright* (1950), Marlene Dietrich wears a variety of diamond jewelry borrowed from Cartier; her dress is by Christian Dior.

stage she wears two magnificent suites that enhance the extravagant costumes designed by Christian Dior, whose costumes for Dietrich, like the rest of his couture, were characterized by a wide décolletage, tapering bodices, cinched waists, and very full, long skirts.

Another director might have used important jewelry only as an accessory; Hitchcock made it a highly visible part of Charlotte's character. The clicking of a gem-studded compact in the first scene, the snapping of a pendant clip brooch and a large cuff in the confrontation scene, and the taking of a cigarette from a case in the last scene, where she acknowledges her role as a bystander and witness to a murder, are mannerisms that do not propel the plot but develop her persona.

In one scene in her dressing room, as Charlotte tells an enraged Jonathan to leave the country, she coolly attaches a ruby and diamond clip brooch to her diamond necklace. When he announces that he has not destroyed the blood-soaked dress that would implicate her in the crime, she snaps on a huge matching ruby and diamond bracelet and exits defiantly. This suite belonged to Dietrich, but the next set of jewels to appear in the film was borrowed from Cartier. It emerges in another dressing-room scene. When Charlotte tells her new maid, Eve Gill (Jane Wyman), that the police want to question her, the actress is repairing the clasp of a Cartier diamond bracelet. The only time jewelry actively enters the dialogue in *Stage Fright* is when Charlotte offers Eve £10,000 worth of jewelry as blackmail. At the end of the movie, when the police have her incriminating testimony on tape, she says ruefully to the inspector from Scotland Yard, "I'm what you call an accessory, I suppose," at which point she takes a cigarette from her gold cigarette case.

The Hitchcock masterpiece *Strangers on a Train* (1951) begins with a cigarette lighter picked up on a train. The lighter belongs to a world-class tennis player, Guy Haines (Farley Granger), and is inscribed "From A to G." The *A* is for Ann Morton (Ruth Roman), a senator's daughter and Guy's girl friend, whom he cannot marry because his wife will not grant him a divorce. The lighter is pocketed by psychopath Bruno Anthony (Robert Walker), who wears a tie clip with his name on it given to him by his mother. Bruno has suggested that he and Guy can help each other: Bruno will kill Guy's wife, and Guy in turn will kill Bruno's father. Having no motive, neither will be suspected of the crime. Guy is horrified. At the end of the story, Guy's lighter, which Bruno has taken, turns up again. Clenched in Bruno's hand, it proves that he, not Guy, is the murderer.

Hitchcock contrasts Bruno's chillingly eccentric family with the sane, warm Morton household. In keeping with her position and social agenda, which figures in the plot, Ann dresses with conservative precious jewelry. At a formal reception she wears a line bracelet and a wide bracelet. By the fifties, when the film was made, both styles were common and bracelets like these, often family heirlooms, were worn on formal occasions, when precious jewelry was de rigueur. A more contemporary touch is seen in Ann's large pearl button earrings. The shorter hair styles of the period, with the ear exposed, put a new emphasis on earrings.

The romantic leads of Hitchcock's *Rear Window* (1954) solve a murder together, basing their solution on a jewelry observation. Jeff (James Stewart), a photojournalist who broke his leg while photographing a car race lives in an apartment in Greenwich Village in New York City. Confined to a wheelchair, he

Posed with Michael Wilding in a publicity still for *Stage Fright*, Dietrich wears the bracelet above and a matching ring.

The huge cushion-cut ruby disk of Marlene Dietrich's bracelet, rimmed with baguette-cut diamonds, encircles a baguette, rectangular, and pavé-set diamond geometric motif. Attached to the diamond hexagon are twin tapering circular and baguette-cut diamond straps with a central graduated baguette-cut clasp. The extraordinary underside of the ruby disk is a flaring pavé-set diamond panel which rises to turret motifs, accented by baguette-cut diamonds, mounted in platinum. By family tradition, Louis Arpels, a principal of Van Cleef & Arpels and a close friend of Dietrich's, had the bracelet made from several jewels in her collection.

passes time watching his neighbors through a rear window that opens on a courtyard. His girl friend, Lisa (Grace Kelly), a fashion editor is eager to marry him. But Jeff has hesitated, thinking her perhaps too refined—as well she is, perfectly turned out in a series of daytime and evening New Look dresses by costume designer Edith Head. True to the fashions of the fifties, when white was the preferred color for jewelry, Lisa wears pearls exclusively—a pearl choker, a three-strand pearl necklace, and pearl earrings. This selection carries the chic and busy working woman through the day into the evening. The couple's difference in styles is summed up when Lisa tells Jeff that she is replacing the beat-up cigarette case he got in Shanghai with a plain, flat silver one with his initials engraved on it.

The two, however, begin to work in sync to solve a murder that Jeff believes has been committed in the apartment across the courtyard. Knives, rope, a trunk, a missing wife, and odd behavior by the resident, Mr. Thorwald (Raymond Burr), are the clues that lead Jeff to his suspicions, but the fact of murder is established when Jeff tells Lisa how Thorwald rummaged through his absent wife's handbag and pulled out her necklace and rings. Lisa says, "Women don't keep their jewelry in a purse, getting all twisted and scratched and tangled up," and "Why, a woman going anywhere but the hospital would always take makeup, perfume, and jewelry." Her supposition is correct. In a climactic scene, Lisa breaks into Thorwald's apartment to look for evidence and finds the wedding ring that confirms Thorwald's guilt.

In *Strangers on a Train* a cigarette lighter with the inscription "From A to G" tells Bruno (Robert Walker) that tennis pro Guy (Farley Granger) has a girl friend as well as a wife. The lighter becomes the evidence that proves a murderer's guilt.

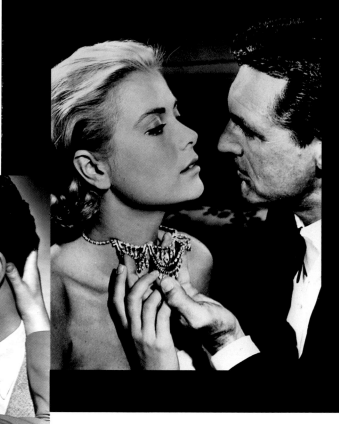

In *To Catch a Thief* (1955), Grace Kelly teases Cary Grant, whom she supposes to be a jewel thief, with an imitation diamond necklace. (Courtesy Paramount Pictures)

Left: This romantic pose, with a prominent jewelry accent—was seen repeatedly in publicity stills throughout the 1950s. For *Strangers on a Train,* Farley Granger embraced Ruth Roman, who wears a gold swirl earring.

To Catch a Thief (1955) is Hitchcock's jewel-thief thriller. It stars Grace Kelly as Frances Stevens, a beautiful American heiress visiting the French Riviera with her bejeweled mother, Mrs. Jesse Stevens (Jessie Royce Landis), the natural prey of jewelry thieves. The film incorporates one of Hitchcock's favorite scenarios, an innocent man who finds himself accused of a crime by the police. This time it is John Robie, "the Cat (Cary Grant)", a former jewel thief and expatriate American, who is suspected of a recent rash of thefts. To clear his name, he collaborates with a Lloyd's of London insurance agent, who produces a list of magnificent jewelry collections likely to attract the thief. The list begins with a group of two matching platinum and diamond bracelets, one platinum and diamond necklace, a platinum and diamond circle brooch, a blue sapphire ring—without doubt, the ultimate in costly trappings of the fifties. The entire collection appears on Mrs. Stevens when she and her daughter meet John Robie, who is keeping his eye on them. Even though he's using an alias, Frances guesses he is Robie the Cat and falls in love with the glamour of jewel thievery. She tempts him with dinner in her rooms and a splashy "diamond" necklace, which he studies with all the seriousness of a connoisseur before telling her, "You know as well as I do this necklace is an imitation." Later, when she realizes he has renounced his former occupation,

147

In *High Society* (1956) Grace Kelly wears the 12-carat, emerald-cut diamond engagement ring that she had received from Prince Rainier III of Monaco.

Frances apologizes for her behavior and aids John in solving the mystery of the thefts at a grand costume ball.

After filming *To Catch a Thief* on the Riviera, Grace Kelly was introduced to the ruler of the tiny principality of Monaco, Prince Rainier III. He was enchanted by the refined twenty-eight-year-old Hollywood star, daughter of a cover girl model and a famous American athlete, oarsman Jack Kelly of Philadelphia. Not only was Kelly exquisite, she was also an accomplished actress—she had won an Oscar nomination for Best Supporting Actress for *Mogambo* (1953) and took the Award for Best Actress for *The Country Girl* (1954). Soon after they met, Grace Kelly and Prince Rainier became engaged.

Van Cleef & Arpels was commissioned to create Kelly's wedding gift from the prince, a parure consisting of a necklace, bracelet, and earrings composed of pearls and diamonds. The jewels were not heavy royal concoctions but a very trim and luxurious suite of perfectly matched and graduated pearls—practical accessories for the princess's upcoming career of palace entertaining, family responsibilities, and charity appearances. After making these distinguished jewels, Van Cleef & Arpels became one of the official purveyors to Monaco, a royal appointment unrivaled at mid-century for its publicity value. Like other jewelers appointed to European courts, Van Cleef & Arpels also supplied jewelry for the stellar list of guests at the royal wedding and formal occasions thereafter. The appointment helped establish Van Cleef & Arpels as one of the most important jewelers of the 1950s both in Europe and in America.

The engagement ring Prince Rainier gave Grace was an extraordinary twelve-carat emerald-cut diamond that she wore in her next-to-last film appearance, *High Society* (1956), the musical rendition of *The Philadelphia Story*. Costar Celeste Holm described the stone: "Most diamonds I have seen look cold and icy, but the thing about this one was the colors in it."* The ring is given a Technicolor close-up when her ex-husband (Bing Crosby) remarks to her fiancé, "Some stone, George. Did you mine it yourself?" Kelly became Princess Grace when she married the prince in Monaco's Cathedral of St. Nicholas on April 19, 1956.

In *Vertigo* (1958) Hitchcock takes a woman's affection for jewelry and turns it into the human flaw that leads to the solution of a murder. James Stewart plays a San Francisco police detective, Scottie Ferguson, who has resigned from the force because his acrophobia and vertigo kept him from rescuing a fellow policeman, who subsequently fell to his death. Out of work, Scottie is persuaded by an old schoolmate, Gavin Elster (Tom Helmore), to follow his wife, Madeleine (Kim Novak). Madeleine has begun to show signs of mental instability, according to her husband: she seems to be possessed by her great-grandmother who committed suicide in 1855. Tailed by Scottie, Madeleine goes to Carlotta's grave, visits her house, which has become the McKittrick Hotel in a sleazy part of town, and sits in a museum studying her portrait, which depicts the woman in an open-neck dress with a Spanish-style ruby drop jewel pendant around her neck.

Scottie falls in love with Madeleine. But he helplessly witnesses her suicide when his acrophobia prevents him from stopping her fall from a bell tower. Soon after, the jewel from her great-grandmother's portrait reappears to him in a fevered dream, the first symptom of the madness that lands him in a sanitarium. Later, he meets a somewhat blowsy brunette, Judy Barton (also played by Kim Novak), who resembles the blond and elegant Madeleine so completely that he wonders if she is the same woman. He buys her clothes like Madeleine's, has her hair bleached and her nails and makeup done. He retains a lingering doubt, however, until she asks him to fasten a jewel—the jewel from the portrait—around her neck. Its lines resemble an eighteenth-century goldsmith's work at first glance, but a close-up shows the jewel is an imitation. This convinces Scottie that the suicide he witnessed was actually the murder of Gavin's real wife, whom he had hired Judy to impersonate. He forces her to return to the scene and reenact the walk up the bell tower's circular staircase, hoping to free them both from the past and, at the same time, to cure his acrophobia. As he breaks the news that he knows she was an accomplice to the crime, he says bitterly of the necklace, "You shouldn't keep souvenirs of killings."

* Gwen Robyns, *Princess Grace* (New York: David McKay, 1976), 138.

Kelly wears a suite of pearl and diamond jewelry commissioned as a wedding present by Prince Rainier from Van Cleef & Arpels.

French filmmaker François Truffaut paid homage to Hitchcock in his 1967 film *The Bride Wore Black*. In it, Jeanne Moreau wears an undulating hammered-brass bracelet by American sculptor Alexander Calder. It is similar to these bracelets by Calder.

Alfred Hitchcock was one of French director François Truffaut's favorite filmmakers. Truffaut paid homage to the master of suspense with his film *La Mariée Était en Noir* (*The Bride Wore Black*, 1967), in which, like Hitchcock, Truffaut used jewelry as clues and to heighten suspense. In an early sequence, shortly after Julie Kohler (Jeanne Moreau) packs a suitcase with black and white ensembles, she reappears in a wispy white ball gown and enters a modern apartment building, putting her hand on the registry book. A man's signet ring is on her forefinger.

In a series of flashbacks, it is revealed that her husband was shot on the steps of the church at their wedding by five carousing bachelors. She took the ring from his finger at that moment and put it on her forefinger as a sacred pledge of devotion—and revenge. At present she is systematically searching out and killing each murderer. The fourth murder finds her posing as the virgin goddess Diana in an artist's studio. One of her targeted five, the artist is shot with one of Diana's deadly arrows—but not before there has been a brief jewelry exchange. Julie, as Diana, stands in a white off-the-shoulder tunic. He says she looks like a tennis champion and gives her a bracelet by Alexander Calder, commenting, "It's not junk—it's by Calder," and takes off her ring.

Thus Truffaut and Moreau saluted Calder, who was a personal friend, by incorporating his jewel into the dialogue. Calder was a sculptor most famous for his large, abstract, biomorphic mobiles, but he also made jewels for his friends, who besides Moreau included Georgia O'Keeffe and Peggy Guggenheim. His bold designs were based on the spiral. They were executed in hammered brass, gold, and silver. The large, primitive, and abstract cuffs, brooches, necklaces, earrings, and rings were worn by women in ways that reflected their style and personality. In *The Bride Wore Black,* Moreau's cuff adds a pagan but contemporary touch.

In *The Bride Wore Black* Truffaut came the closest to imbuing jewelry with symbolic import in the style of the master. Many directors have imitated him, but only Hitchcock exploited the possibilities of jewelry in the movies, using it to reveal a person's love life or life-style, an unsavory past, or a passport to romantic success, not to mention a clue to a murder.

Dark Themes and Colorful Extravaganzas

As America emerged from wartime scarcity into one of the longest runs of prosperity in its history, Hollywood was going through radical changes, both financially, politically, and aesthetically. The steady flow of box-office returns ended when the government issued a regulation that effectively finished the studio system. The patriotism that had generated unprecedented profits during the war was discredited when Senator Joe McCarthy's witch-hunters began accusing members of the Hollywood community of communist sympathies. The pall that this cast on Hollywood was reflected in movies, including such introspective works as *Sunset Boulevard* (1950) and *The Bad and the Beautiful* (1952). At the same time, television, the new entertainment phenomenon, kept potential audiences at home, causing moviemakers to find new ways to pry viewers away from their sets. One solution was adult movies on themes that television could not touch—dark views of the underside of the Age of Affluence like *Sorry, Wrong Number* (1948) and *The Velvet Touch* (1948). At the other end of the spectrum, splashy, color extravaganzas, often presented on a wide screen, including *Gentlemen Prefer Blondes* (1953), *Funny Face* (1957), and *Pillow Talk* (1959), outperformed television in showmanship.

In the late 1940s the government declared the established practice of block

In *Sorry, Wrong Number* (1948), Barbara Stanwyck uses her telephone as a link to the outside world. Though dressed only in a negligee, Stanwyck displays a complete suite of diamond jewelry: an iris brooch, a wide diamond bracelet, ribbon earrings, and a rectangular-cut engagement ring. All the jewelry is by Ruser, who received a screen credit. (Courtesy Paramount Pictures)

booking an illicit activity and banished it by law. In the past the practice had guaranteed income for studios by forcing independent exhibitors to buy a package of films. Anyone who wanted the box-office draws was obliged to take others, usually of lesser quality, as well. After the new law went into effect, there were no reliable outlets for all the films distributed by the studios, and this created an atmosphere of financial uncertainty that undermined year-round, assembly-line filmmaking.

By 1948 the studios were retrenching, selling their real estate and allowing the long-term contracts of actors and actresses to lapse — a radical change of policy. Stars had been the most valuable assets of studios since Carl Laemmle made Mary Pickford a headliner. Now, without the very large, regular income that block booking had ensured, star contracts became too expensive. Nevertheless, actresses of the late forties and fifties were hardly left without jewels, on screen or off. Nor were there any fewer purveyors to cater to them. One Hollywood jeweler, John Gershgorn, who had prospered by selling jewels to actresses on studio sets out of a black bag, opened a retail establishment on Rodeo Drive in Beverly Hills. Henceforth, stars came to him like other clients.

In adult suspense thrillers, pearls and diamonds were the building blocks of jewelry styles for heroines played by such leading ladies as Rosalind Russell and Barbara Stanwyck. Their jewels range from a strand of pearls to a multi-tiered pearl necklace, or from a single diamond on a slender chain to elaborate diamond pendant-brooches, worn singly, in groups, or as pendants on a rivière. All jewelers kept a supply of the diamond rivières that were the staple of a precious jewelry collection. Diamond pendant and brooch designs matured beyond two-dimensional jewels to three-dimensional moving sculpture, making this monochromatic style a sight to behold.

In *Sorry, Wrong Number* (1948), Barbara Stanwyck showcased the sumptuous

Below: Barbara Stanwyck's Ruser gardenia brooch has three-dimensional, layered circular-cut diamond petals and pistils. At far right is a reverse view of the platinum mount of the gardenia brooch.

diamond jewelry of the postwar period. The movie tells the story of Leona Stevens (Stanwyck), a self-inflicted invalid, who spends her time in bed in a deserted luxury apartment on New York's fashionable Sutton Place. Though totally alone and dressed in a negligee, she wears a full suite of diamond jewelry—an iris brooch, a wide bracelet, ribbon earrings, and rings. The drama of the film centers on Leona overhearing a telephone conversation between two men plotting to kill a woman, first stealing her jewelry to make the death look like the result of a burglary. As Leona frantically makes and answers a series of telephone calls to prevent the crime she's heard planned, an oversize rectangular wedding ring flashes on her finger.

All the jewelry in the film was by William Ruser, whose firm received a screen credit. A second-generation Hollywood jeweler, Ruser was first employed at the age of seventeen by Howard Hoeffer in the Atlantic City, N.J., branch of Trabert & Hoeffer-Mauboussin. He rose to manager of the firm's Los Angeles branch, succeeding Dudley Ramsden, who had been wooed away by Stanley Marcus to head the precious jewelry division of his Dallas department store, Neiman Marcus. Ruser, on returning from service in World War II, opened a jewelry store at 300 Rodeo Drive in Beverly Hills with his wife, Pauline. The firm was known for its curvaceous, three-dimensional platinum and diamond jewelry, with subtle gradations of form and structure.

Top: A flashback in *Sorry, Wrong Number,* shows Stanwyck marrying Burt Lancaster. She wears her own Ruser suite, a gardenia-brooch suspended from a round diamond and platinum link chain with matching earrings. (Courtesy Paramount Pictures)

Above: Stanwyck wears all three of her Ruser gardenia brooches on a platinum and diamond chain, with matching earrings and a diamond and platinum picture frame ring centering on a rectangular-cut diamond weighing 9.37 carats.

On the set of *Remember the Night* (1940) director Mitchell Leisen (*right*) shows Stanwyck what has been selected for the production by Hollywood jeweler John Gershgorn (*center*). A discerning collector, Stanwyck approved the jewelry for her starring role.

In the film, a series of flashbacks helps build suspense for the final drama. In one scene, Leona appears as a manipulative, domineering wife, who drives her husband to crime while he is working in her own father's corporation. During a tantrum in their bedroom, the camera pans to an overflowing jewelry box. And in the last scene, Leona—bejeweled and terrified—is unable to summon the strength to leave her bed and escape death.

A polished dramatic actress, Barbara Stanwyck was known in Hollywood for her professionalism, for which Cecil B. De Mille singled her out in his autobiography: "I have never worked with an actress who was more cooperative, less temperamental, and a better workman." She began her career as a Ziegfeld Follies girl, then moved to Hollywood with her actor husband, Frank Fay, who was more established in the entertainment world than she was. Stanwyck soon overtook her husband in fame and popularity, playing tough, resilient leads.

Stanwyck married her second husband, Robert Taylor, one of Hollywood's most handsome and popular leading men, in 1939. Four years older than Taylor, Stanwyck quelled the gossip when she told the press, "The boy's got a lot to learn, and I've got a lot to teach." Five years later, she was the highest-paid woman in America. During the course of a long and successful movie career, she was nominated for four Academy Awards, for her performances in *Stella Dallas* (1937), *Ball of Fire* (1942), *Double Indemnity* (1944), and *Sorry, Wrong Number* (1948). While she never won, she was given an honorary Oscar in 1982 for the sum of her work.

In the 1960s, Stanwyck switched to television, starring in "The Barbara Stanwyck Show" and a popular series about the old West, "Big Valley," for which she won an Emmy from the Television Academy of Arts and Sciences. She garnered two more Emmys, working into her seventies on "The Colbys" and appearing in the mini-series "The Thorn Birds."

Rosalind Russell, the daughter of a lawyer and a fashion editor, was born in Connecticut and came to Hollywood via New York's American Academy of Dramatic Arts and the Broadway stage. She made her film debut in 1934 and established a reputation as a lively leading lady, adept at delivering witty lines — which she did to great acclaim in *His Girl Friday* (1940), a comedy costarring Cary Grant.

Cool chic distinguished Russell's performance in the melodrama *The Velvet Touch* (1948), produced by her husband, Frederick Brisson. In the film she plays Valerie Stanton, a stage actress who accidentally kills Gordon Dunning (Leon Ames), the producer of a play she is in. He had threatened to ruin her reputation and overturn her engagement to architect Michael Morrell (Leo Genn) if she left his play to appear in Ibsen's *Hedda Gabler.* Valerie's crime becomes attributed to Marian Webster (Claire Trevor), the producer's ex-girl friend, who kills herself in a mental hospital. Valerie appears safe from prosecution, but she cannot live with her conscience and, after a dramatic performance in *Hedda Gabler,* she confesses to police detective Captain Danbury (Sidney Greenstreet).

Russell does not wear a wide variety of gem-set jewelry in the movie, although she does appear in one scene in a pair of large diamond flower earrings and prominent bangle bracelet. She does, however, wear numerous large multi-strand pearl chokers and necklaces, some of them made of ten-to fifteen-millimeter cultured pearls from Burma — standard daytime wear.

All the jewelry in the movie was made by John Rubel of New York, who received a screen credit. Unfortunately, by the time of the movie's release, the firm had shut down, victim of a huge debt in unpaid federal taxes. During the war years, jewelers were assessed high luxury taxes, but they did not have to pay them at regular intervals. Allowing its tax debt to accumulate, Rubel was finally forced into insolvency. During its five-year lifespan, the firm had gained extensive coverage in fashion magazines. Along with whimsical brooches, Rubel's classic jewelry designs — flowers, swirls, and scrolls — proved extremely popular, and their dainty designs suited the postwar recovery period.

In the late 1950s, Rosalind Russell achieved perhaps her greatest popular fame playing the title role in the play and film *Auntie Mame.* To design the sets for the movie, Russell invited her friend Gene Moore, art director, jewelry designer and window display genius of Tiffany & Co. in New York. Moore was unable to accept the assignment, but his firm received a reference in the movie when Mame's best friend credits her ability to survive the 1929 market collapse to having bought jewelry at Tiffany when everyone else was buying stocks. For her role in *Auntie Mame* Russell was nominated for the Best Actress Academy Award, as she had been for *My Sister Eileen* (1942), *Sister Kenny* (1946), and *Mourning Becomes Electra* (1947). Like Stanwyck, she never won, but she did receive a special Oscar, the Jean Hersholt Humanitarian Award, for her charity work.

During the early 1950s the House Un-American Activities Committee (HUAC) in Washington, D.C., singled out Hollywood as the center of a communist conspiracy aimed at indoctrinating the American people through the persuasive medium of film. At the time filmmakers themselves were probing their industry in their films. The most famous saga about the dark side of Hollywood from this period was Billy Wilder's *Sunset Boulevard.*

Rosalind Russell rides to a party with Leon Ames in *The Velvet Touch* (1948). She wears large diamond and platinum flower earrings, a rigid bangle, and toys with a gold cigarette case; all by John Rubel Co.

Left: Joan Crawford's feather brooch by Ruser, of circular-cut diamonds on a tapered baguette-cut stem, evokes the look of a real feather ruffled in the wind. Crawford wore this brooch during her Academy Award–winning performance in *Mildred Pierce* (1945), but scenes showing the jewel ended on the cutting-room floor. Length: 6⁷⁄₁₆ in.

Below: Joan Crawford's marquise-cut diamond floret earrings with round diamond centers and her baguette-cut diamond rivière by Ruser, both mounted in platinum, are photographed with a Stork Club ashtray that she kept as a souvenir.

The movie starts with the dead body of a young man floating in the swimming pool of a twenties mansion. A voice-over, coming from the hereafter, begins the narrative, explaining that it is five o'clock in the morning, a murder has just been reported, and an old-time star is involved. The body and voice belong to Joe Gillis (William Holden), an out-of-work writer who had sought refuge from the men who wanted to repossess his car at the mansion of silent-screen star Norma Desmond. Gloria Swanson, who plays Norma Desmond, gives the movie a ghostly echo, as Desmond's life story in the movie in some respects parallels Swanson's own experience.

Appearing with Swanson in this half-fact, half-fiction film set in the fifties are famous members of the silent screen community—Cecil B. De Mille, Hedda Hopper, Buster Keaton, Anna Q. Nilsson, H. B. Warner, Ray Evans, and Jay Livingston, all playing themselves. Erich von Stroheim plays Norma's butler, ex-husband, and ex-director, Max von Mayerling. A highly controversial director in silent films, von Stroheim was known for his decadence and extravagant spending. As the director of *Queen Kelly* (1928), he went so far over budget that he nearly bankrupted Swanson's film company, forcing her to fire him midway through the production. In *Sunset Boulevard,* as the butler, he waits on Norma meticulously and preserves her exalted view of herself by sending her fan letters under assumed names.

For Joe, moving into Norma's mansion is an escape from his financial obligations. Norma sees in Joe not only an escort but, more important, the means of her comeback. She sets him to work editing the manuscript of *Salome* into a screenplay, which she hopes Paramount will make—with her in the starring role and with Cecil B. De Mille as director. Joe learns firsthand about the golden era of movies—the silent era—as Norma entertains him with her old silent movie *Queen Kelly,* performs Mack Sennett bathing-beauty routines, and organizes a card game with Anna Q. Nilsson and Buster Keaton.

Joe becomes reduced to a gigolo by Norma's expensive gifts—suits, shirts, shoes, platinum key chains, cigarette cases, and cuff links. On New Year's Eve she gives him a gold cigarette case inscribed, "Mad About the Boy—Norma." For the occasion of the gift she is ablaze in jewelry: two massive necklaces, one of which she pins to her hair, a couple of brooches worn on the hip, and several huge, wide bracelets. When Norma sets out with Max and Joe in an enormous twenties

At New York's Stork Club, actor Russell Nype lights a cigarette for Crawford, who wears diamond floret earrings and a baguette-cut diamond Ruser rivière, mounted in platinum.

limousine for Paramount Studios she wears her famous Cartier bangles.

The bangles, which entered Swanson's jewelry collection in 1930, were the inspiration of Jeanne Toussaint. A particularly close friend of Louis Cartier, Toussaint joined the firm around 1910 and became a creative and artistic director with an intuitive flair for fashion and precious jewelry. When Cartier had to make financial adjustments during the recession in the European jewelry business caused by the Depression in America, Toussaint's brilliant innovations in the realm of materials—rock crystal used in precious pieces for example—kept Cartier identified with luxury while offering a less-expensive product. Swanson's bangles are perhaps the finest example of a Toussaint jewel incorporating rock crystal.

Sunset Boulevard draws to a dramatic close when Joe tries to escape from the crazy household and Hollywood. Enraged by his desertion, Norma follows him out of the house and shoots him three times. He falls into the pool. As journalists, including gossip columnist Hedda Hopper, and television and movie crews converge on the mansion, Norma gets what she has craved: a chance to perform once more for cameras and an audience.

Another movie set in the stygian shadows of Hollywood, *The Bad and the Beautiful* features diamond jewelry by Laykin et Cie. It stars Lana Turner as Georgia Lorrussen, an actress made famous by the brilliant, obsessed producer Jonathan Shields (Kirk Douglas). He has also made the careers of director Fred Amiel (Barry Sullivan) and scriptwriter James Lee (Dick Powell). The question facing all three as they gather late one night for an overseas call from Douglas is whether they will ever again make a movie with him. While they wait for the call, each of them tells a story.

Georgia remembers that she was nothing but a depressed alcoholic trying to follow in the steps of her famous-actor father. She walked onto the set of one of Jonathan's productions as a bit player, wearing a large Laykin et Cie diamond butterfly brooch, a diamond barrette, and wide bracelets. Before her first starring role, she goes on a binge. After throwing her into his pool to sober her, Jonathan gives her a single-strand pearl necklace to boost her confidence.

With alcoholism behind her, Georgia delivers a magnificent performance. She looks stunning at the party after the premiere in spectacular Laykin et Cie diamond earrings and a wide bracelet. But the thrill and trappings of stardom cannot shield her from that shattering moment when she rushes to Jonathan's house to share the success and finds him with another woman, an extra in the film, who tells her, "You're business. I'm company."

The "Sweater Girl" during World War II, Lana Turner became a seasoned dramatic actress in the postwar period, winning an Academy Award nomination for Best Actress in *Peyton Place* (1957). An American beauty with blond hair and blue eyes, she appeared in film after film perfectly attired, and with an impressive number of jewelry changes. One of her favorite jewelers, Laykin et Cie, is credited with the jewelry in *The Bad and the Beautiful* and *Imitation of Life* (1959), but no one jeweler supplied the prodigious number of suites Turner wore in each of her films. Undoubtedly she drew from her own substantial collection, which she built in the course of eight marriages.

These marriages, each lasting about three years or less, provided the gossip columnists with as much dirt as other stars' love affairs. Several of her husbands were celebrities: bandleader Artie Shaw, actor Stephen Crane, socialite Bob Topping, and star of Tarzan movies, Lex Barker.

In 1958, in a real-life drama equal to a film noir scenario, her fifteen-year-old daughter, Cheryl Crane, stabbed to death with a kitchen knife underworld thug Johnny Stompanato, Turner's lover and longtime companion. The teenager was acquitted of the murder because the jury believed that she thought her mother's life was in danger at the moment of the stabbing. Turner behaved with aplomb during the highly publicized trial and was able to give a cool performance in *Imitation of Life* (1959). After the film was released, however, when Laykin et Cie sought to sell the jewelry from the movie, it found only one buyer because of the scandal surrounding Turner. The actress herself bought the pearl necklace she wears in the final scene.

To Hollywood, the downfall of the studio system and the devastation caused by the HUAC's investigation was compounded by the runaway success of television. Adding insult to injury, TV recycled Hollywood actors, actresses, and even directors in its programming. Loretta Young in "The Loretta Young Show," Lucille Ball in her weekly sitcom "I Love Lucy," and Alfred Hitchcock in "Alfred Hitchcock Presents" were just a few. To meet the challenge, Hollywood adopted expensive wide-screen processes first developed in the twenties, among them CinemaScope, VistaVision, and Technorama; the cost was offset by the number of customers they drew. Also, because television had yet to master color transmission, Hollywood made color standard in film. Color movies, often musicals, featured such rising stars as Marilyn Monroe, Audrey Hepburn, and Doris Day.

By the end of the fifties, when film was awash in color, the prosperity of the country was manifest on the screen in rich jewelry styles that displayed a wide variety of colored stones. But when the decade began, Marilyn Monroe sang for many women when she celebrated the coveted white stone in "Diamonds Are a Girl's Best Friend," a song from *Gentlemen Prefer Blondes* (1953):

Marilyn Monroe as Lorelei Lee sings "Diamonds Are a Girl's Best Friend" in *Gentlemen Prefer Blondes* (1953). Lorelei's passion for diamonds made memorable jewelry comedy, though Monroe did not wear real diamond jewelry in the film.

A kiss on the hand may be quite Continental
But Diamonds Are A Girl's Best Friend,
A kiss may be grand,
But it won't pay the rental on your humble flat
Or help you at the Automat.
Men grow cold as girls grow old
And we all lose our charms in the end.
But square-cut or pear-shape,
These rocks don't lose their shape,
Diamonds Are A Girl's Best Friend.
There may come a time when a lass needs a lawyer,
But Diamonds Are A Girl's Best Friend,
There may come a time
When a hard-boiled employer thinks you're awfully nice,
But get that "ice," or else no dice.

He's your guy when stocks are high,
But beware when they start to descend.
It's then that those louses
Go back to their spouses,
Diamonds Are A Girl's Best Friend.

In the film, Marilyn Monroe plays the show girl Lorelei Lee, who is dedicated to a quest for men who will give her diamonds. Her best friend, show girl Dorothy Shaw (Jane Russell), comments on Lorelei's radarlike eye for diamonds:

Lorelei: Didn't you notice his pocket was bulging?

Dorothy: Ahh. That could be a bag of gumdrops.

Lorelei: No. It was a square bulge, like a box for a ring. I think he's got a present for me.

Dorothy: You know I think you're the only girl in the world that can stand on a stage with a spotlight in her eye and still see a diamond inside a man's pocket.

When Lorelei and Dorothy set sail for Europe, Lorelei snares a married man who she thinks is a diamond magnate. Envisioning his plump face as a large faceted stone, she dreams of his potential as a supplier of jewelry and presses him to give her his wife's diamond tiara. The gift backfires when his irate wife and the father of Lorelei's fiancé from New York almost succeed in jailing her as a jewel thief. But in the end, both Lorelei and Dorothy find true love, and Lorelei finds wealth and diamonds as well.

Perhaps the living embodiment of Lorelei Lee, Hungarian-born Zsa Zsa Gabor, became better known through the tabloids for her diamonds and her husbands than for her movies. Without the notoriety that she happily provoked, most of her pictures would have been overlooked, with the exception, perhaps, of the cult classic *Queen of Outer Space* (1958).

One of her vehicles, a B film originally shown in Technorama, *For the First Time* (1959), presents Gabor as Contessa Gloria, jet-set friend and longtime companion of Tony Costa (Mario Lanza), a famous opera singer who has fallen in love with a deaf girl. As a mature woman, Gloria adds a worldly footnote to this idyllic love story set mostly in Capri. For a port-side tea dance, she appears in a bright red ensemble with a high collar that enhances a broad diamond collar with a central diamond dome motif (probably detachable), a large diamond ring, diamond earrings, and a diamond wave barrette in her teased blond hair.

When Tony leaves Capri, he tells the countess that he wants to marry the deaf girl. He reveals that he is organizing his singing tour in order to consult all the great ear specialists of Europe. Gloria retorts that in Capri everyone falls in love. She looks particularly glamorous when she says this, in a five-strand necklace combination of a large three-strand cultured-pearl necklace, a string of jade beads, and an additional oversize single-strand cultured-pearl necklace. But Tony marries the deaf girl.

Rejected, the countess nevertheless follows Tony to Vienna, and after his

Opposite, top: In *Sunset Boulevard* (1950), the butler, Erich von Stroheim, presents Gloria Swanson with a silver tray of fan mail he has written to prop up the faded star's ego. Her young escort, William Holden, looks on. Swanson wears a necklace in the late thirties style, brooches on her hip, and two Cartier-Paris bangles designed by Jeanne Toussaint. (Courtesy Paramount Pictures)

Opposite, center: Swanson's bangles, made of rock crystal disks with circular and baguette-cut diamonds and crystal beads, threaded on elastic, are an example of dextrous mating of materials by Jeanne Toussaint, Cartier's artistic director for almost half a century. The bangles are oversized, but the tapered diamonds spread over the surface like shimmering rays give the impression of lightness. They were revolutionary at the time because of their massive size and the imaginative blend of semiprecious and precious materials—rock crystal, diamonds, and platinum.

Opposite, at lower right: There was a special poignancy in *Sunset Boulevard* as Swanson made the film when the glamour machine of Hollywood was a thing of the past. (Courtesy Paramount Pictures)

Opposite, at lower left: At a New York party on March 29, 1951, Gloria Swanson, Judy Holliday, and Jose Ferrer heard the announcement of the 1950 Academy Awards on the radio. Wearing her Cartier-Paris bangles, Swanson covers her eyes after learning that she has not won the Oscar for Best Actress in *Sunset Boulevard*. Ferrer, however, won an Oscar for *Cyrano de Bergerac* and Holliday won for *Born Yesterday*. *Sunset Boulevard* had received nominations for best director, picture, and actress, but it won only the award for best script. Coincidentally, and sadly for her, it was Swanson's birthday.

performance, she prepares for an evening on the town wearing a soft pink floral evening dress and a pink satin stole with a ruby and diamond triangular collar. But Tony does not have time for her, as his wife's ear operation has just been successfully performed.

What should be a triumphant return to Capri becomes a nightmare for Tony when his wife suffers a relapse. After a drunken brawl in a bar precipitated by his agonized concern, he lands in jail, where Countess Gloria makes a final appearance. She wears a black dress, a double-strand cultured-pearl necklace, a triple-strand cultured-pearl bracelet, and a leopard-patterned chiffon scarf. She provides an eloquent character reference at the crucial juncture to get her friend out of jail, saving his career.

A plausible reason for the absence of a jewelry credit in this film is that the jewels belonged to Zsa Zsa herself and not a jeweler. Beginning at age fifteen with Burhan Belge, the Turkish ambassador to Hungary, Gabor tied the knot with eight rich men, including hotelier Conrad Hilton, actor George Sanders, and Prince Frederick von Anhalt. One of the great shoppers at Van Cleef & Arpels, dictator Rafael Trujillo showered her with so many expensive jewels that an American congressman called her the best-kept woman in the Northern Hemisphere and compared her to Madame de Pompadour. Not content with just these gifts, Gabor astonished a Beverly Hills jewelry salesman by attempting to buy jewelry from clients shopping in his salon.

Though Zsa Zsa Gabor had an enviable one hundred-carat diamond necklace from Winston, her jewelry collection surpassed Lorelei Lee's fixation on only one stone. By the late fifties, monochromatic white jewelry—diamonds and pearls in platinum mounts—intermingled with diamond styles featuring emeralds, sapphires, and rubies set in gold and platinum. After India received its independence in 1947, the maharajas opened their vast treasure stores of rubies, sapphires, and emeralds to merchants in an effort to raise cash. Not since the teens and twenties had so many precious stones become available to jewelers, but the dimensions of the stones were smaller than those of the twenties, and carved gems were scarce. Jewelers responded by mixing red, blue, and green gems of different sizes and cuts in broad necklaces. As a result, the Indian-style jewelry of the fifties makes up in color what it lacks in size. A contemporary version of the twenties and thirties Indian-style necklace proved as popular as its predecessors.

Reflecting the era's penchant for blended color, the semiprecious stone turquoise enjoyed a vogue in formal diamond jewelry. During the late fifties and sixties jewelers used large quantities of turquoise, which they freely incorporated into formal jewelry. Its opaqueness, in contrast to the sparkle of diamond and ruby accents, brought a fresh look to precious jewelry design, and suites of turquoise jewelry became an integral part of a precious jewelry collection. For her twenty-first birthday, for example, Princess Margaret of England received a parure of turquoise and diamonds from her mother, the queen.

In a period of nontraditional colors, turquoise assumed an ascendancy and supplanted precious stones, if only momentarily. Although the merchants who regulated the turquoise mines in Iran were reliable, the demand for it was so great that in approximately ten years the supply was depleted. The truth is, however, that the heyday of turquoise would have been brief no matter what, because the

In *For the First Time* (1959) Zsa Zsa Gabor starred with Mario Lanza and in one scene appeared wearing a contemporary Indian-style emerald and diamond choker and matching earrings.

Below: In a publicity still for *The Bad and the Beautiful* (1952), producer Jonathan Shields (Kirk Douglas) embraces his protégée, Georgia Lorrussen (Lana Turner). She wears pear-shaped, pavé-set diamond drop earrings and a diamond circular brooch in a garland motif, both mounted in platinum and by Laykin et Cie.

For a brief moment in the late fifties and early sixties, turquoise was the most popular stone in precious jewelry. Turquoise necklaces are seen on Lana Turner in *Imitation of Life* and on Doris Day in *Pillow Talk*. The tiered turquoise, diamond, and ruby necklace shown is composed of star-shaped motifs intersected by floral motifs. Mounted in gold and platinum, it has matching earrings.

stone presents jewelers with special problems: it is very brittle, it breaks easily, and it sometimes changes color on contact with the skin oils. While the finest-quality turquoise proves almost impervious to discoloration, in stones of just slightly lower quality changes do occur. One of the services Van Cleef & Arpels offered during the turquoise fashion was to replace any stones that broke or discolored.

The jewelry of the fifties often updated styles of the past, such as the Garland and Indian styles, but some jewelers, such as Julius Cohen, David Webb, and Jean Schlumberger, began to break away from the traditional with designs that would distinguish the next decade. A perfect example of ingenuity in design is Cohen's diamond necklace Flame of Gold, purchased by Hollywood celebrity Greer Garson. The necklace was inspired by traditional diamond ribbons, but here they surprisingly terminate in a fiery burst of metal and gems centering on a 28.68-carat canary diamond.

For informal day wear, many Hollywood stars sported a variety of charm bracelets and whimsical brooches. One of their favorite sources for these items was Ruser, which specialized in customized, sculptured gold jewelry. Joan Bennett's daughter, Shelley Wanger, had a Ruser brooch of a small cherub called Sunday's Child from a jewelry series that appealed to every age. Loretta Young had a swan with a baroque pearl body, and Joan Crawford had several variations on her favorite poodle design.

A very different sort of actress from Joan Crawford, Doris Day, born Doris von Kappelhoff in 1924, started her ascent to stardom when she took Betty Hutton's place in the 1948 musical *Romance on the High Seas*. Previously she had been a successful singer, working with Bob Crosby and Les Brown, and, as a recording

A unique jewel, the Flash and Roll necklace-bracelet by Julius Cohen is composed of five segments of cylindrical gold rope-twist motifs set with multicolored diamonds. It won an award at the 1958 Diamonds International Exhibition in New York, and was bought by Charles Revson for his wife, Lyn. Julius Cohen won numerous jewelry awards for his creative designs with unusual gem combinations after he opened his salon in 1955 at 17 East Fifty-third Street, next to the Stork Club.

star, had changed her name to Day, inspired by her favorite song "Day by Day." She starred in the bubbly bedroom farces of the late fifties and sixties, and her popularity nationwide translated into a successful television career, with "The Doris Day Show." Day appealed to young girls who dreamed of being as vivacious and pretty as she was and women who appreciated her pert repartee with men and her wardrobe and jewelry.

The colorful jewelry style of the period was very much in evidence in the Doris Day–Rock Hudson comedy *Pillow Talk* (1959), which gave a jewelry credit to Laykin et Cie. Made in CinemaScope, *Pillow Talk* starred Day as an interior

MGM film star Greer Garson sent Julius Cohen a photograph of herself wearing his Flame of Gold necklace as she won the Golden Globe Award in 1962. The necklace is composed of a ribbon chain with pear- and oval-shape diamond flames, suspending a 28.86-carat pear-shape canary diamond in an asymmetrical flame, and mounted in 18K gold and platinum. The necklace won an award in the 1957 De Beers Diamonds International Competition.

decorator, Jan Morrow, who cannot use her own phone because the party line is monopolized by bachelor-composer Brad Allen (Rock Hudson), who spends his day serenading and sweet-talking all his adoring girl friends. Dubbing him a sex maniac, Jan complains to her client Jonathan Forbes (Tony Randall), a wealthy divorcé three times over who has fallen in love with her.

As a businesswoman, Jan wears jewelry that is neither large nor overpowering. In Jonathan's office she wears pearl button earrings and a sunburst brooch with radiating lines of diamonds set in gold. Later in the same place she wears a high-waisted two-tone green sheath and matching fringe hat brightened with gold earrings, and a necklace of pearls intersected with orange glass beads.

Jan's colorful, coordinated attire reflects the shift in business dressing from sober suits to more feminine ensembles—sheaths with short jackets and three-quarter-length coats, matching hats, handbags, sleek pumps, and long gloves. The clothes followed the creations of three famous Parisian designers, Dior, Balenciaga, and Mainbocher. Their broad areas of color, clean lines, and lack of fuss inspired jewelry that was made with more diamonds and colored gems than had been seen in daytime jewelry since the 1920s. In general, gold was not part of the overall design but simply a mounting for the gems. The thirties custom of wearing gold for daytime, platinum for evening—a rule of jewelry dressing advocated by the duchess of Windsor—was already obsolete; since World War II, when to wear gold and platinum had been a matter of personal choice.

A key moment in *Pillow Talk* comes when the lovestruck Jonathan is singing Jan's praises. He makes the mistake of confiding in his best friend, Brad, and complaining about his inability to get a call through to her because she shares the line with a sex maniac—at which remark Brad registers a flicker of recognition. Later that evening, completely by chance, Brad sits in a booth next to hers at the Copa Del Rio where she is coping with a client's drunken son. He watches her dance in a tight white sheath accessorized with a pendant diamond brooch and diamond drop earrings with sapphires, and when her drunken escort passes out on the dance floor, Brad rushes up to rescue her, assuming an alias: Rex Stetson.

Rex begins to pay court to Jan. On their first date she wears a fringe diamond and turquoise pendant necklace, turquoise cluster earrings, and a turquoise cuff. On a date in a piano bar called the Hidden Door, Jan wears a wine-red, crushed-velvet cocktail dress and a matching coat with a slender choker of ruby beads and diamond rondelles (small diamond spool-shaped motifs). When Jan consents to go with Rex to Connecticut for the weekend, her country clothes are elegant: a white fur-collared, beige-checked, loose, cream-colored coat that matches her cream-colored sheath, and her sunburst brooch and pearl button earrings. The jewels and clothes draw attention to her in a diner where Jonathan takes her after she discovers that Rex is really Brad. She cannot stop sobbing, and when Jonathan slaps her to stop her hysteria, two men at the counter rise to her defense and knock him out. Jonathan's ensuing pain and dental work knock out his passion for Jan, and he dourly observes the hilarious reconciliation of Brad and Jan.

Doris Day herself always wore precious jewelry, which may explain how New York jeweler David Webb creations snuck into a movie which had a Laykin et Cie credit. Suspicion of this was raised several years after the completion of *Pillow Talk,* when an article attributed some of Day's jewels in the movie to David Webb. It did not mention which ones, but the attribution may be correct because Doris Day is known to have shopped at David Webb and may have worn a suite from her own collection. Webb definitely supplied jewelry for her next movie, *Midnight Lace* (1960), and for other actresses and movies, including Lana Turner in *Portrait in Black* (1960) and Susan Hayward in *Back Street* (1961). In the late fifties, Webb was wholesaling to Bergdorf Goodman and Bonwit Teller, leading New York department stores, and designing for private clients as well. The flamboyance and vivacity that set his work apart is evident in bold, oversize jewels, of which the multi-strand pearl necklace with a large pale aquamarine clasp worn by Aunt Bea (Myrna Loy) in *Midnight Lace* is a good example. In 1963, David Webb moved from a walk-up on West Fifty-Seventh Street to a street-level salon

In *Pillow Talk* (1959) Doris Day has a beautiful collection of Laykin et Cie jewelry. As Jan Morrow, dining with Brad Allen alias Rex Stetson (Rock Hudson), she is wearing a diamond fringe necklace with a line of pear-shaped turquoise pendants and diamond and turquoise cluster earrings.

167

Joan Crawford's fourth and last husband, Alfred Steele, was chairman of the board of Pepsi-Cola. At a birthday celebration for him, she wore her Ruser poodle brooches.

Opposite: Ruser charms accent three bracelets that belonged to Joan Crawford. At center, her 14K gold bracelet of sculpted links suspends a gold poodle with sapphire eyes in a sapphire and pearl oval frame by Ruser; a gold heart; a Greek lamp; a horseshoe; and a gold sun hat with a diamond accent on the top, which opens to reveal a tiny gold sun hat. At top, her 14K gold woven double-link bracelet suspends a pearl and gold heart outlined in rope twist, a sign of Capricorn, a gold heart inscribed, "For You My Heart," with a gold and ruby bow, a gold poodle with sapphire eyes standing under a heart initialed JC, a monogrammed medallion inscribed, "JCT," on the front and "To Joan, All my love Franchot, Oct. 11, 1937" on the reverse. Below, Crawford's "I Love You" charm bracelet suspends a three-dimensional heart inscribed, "Aimons aussi longtemps que nous vivons et vivons aussi longtemps que nous aimons," an Academy Award medallion, a St. George medallion, an Academy Award in a circular frame, a tragedy and spinning comedy mask in a circular frame inscribed, "To Joan," on the front and, "Happy Face Vincent," on the reverse.

at Seven East Fifty-Seventh Street. There, in collaboration with his designer, Donald Claflin, Webb completely broke with tradition by introducing a menagerie of jeweled animals and a line of formal jewelry inspired by costume. This gave the firm's work a young, funky look that it has never outgrown.

One of the most strikingly colorful movies of the fifties is *Funny Face* (1957), which features VistaVision, high style, and the striking Audrey Hepburn. She plays Jo, a drab intellectual working in a run-down Greenwich Village bookshop, who is transformed into a beautiful international model by fashion editor Maggie Prescott (Kay Thompson) and photographer Richard Avery (Fred Astaire). In Paris, where her transformation begins in earnest, Jo is fitted by a leading French couturier and groomed to model his clothes for the international press. She and Dick Avery do fashion shoots all over Paris, culminating in a session on a staircase in the Louvre under the wings of the *Nike of Samothrace.* Jo sweeps out of a portal wearing a strapless red evening dress, with matching shoes, a chiffon scarf, and long white gloves. At her neck gleams an emerald fringe necklace in a fifties version of the Indian style. This jewel was a diamond choker with small irregular-shaped emerald drops.

Hepburn's film wardrobe was supplied by leading Paris couturier Hubert Givenchy, and his clothes were not the only authentic touch in this classic fashion

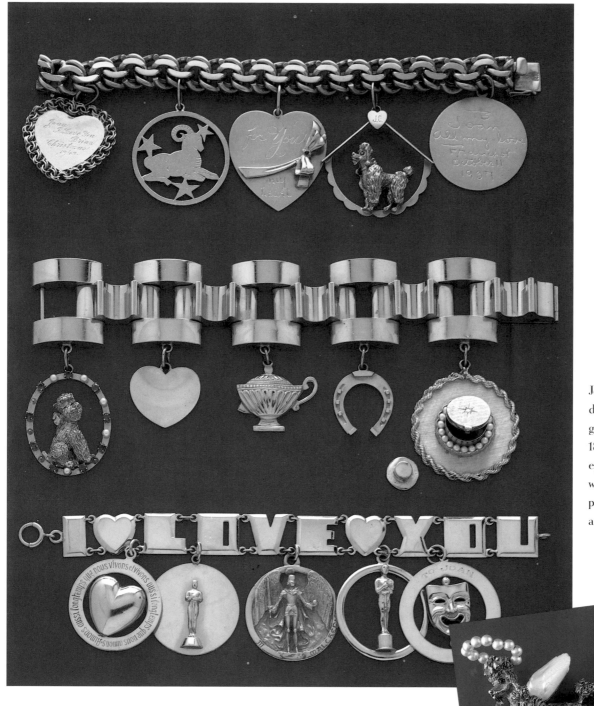

Joan Crawford's Ruser poodle brooches in 18K white gold with sapphire eyes and 18K yellow gold with ruby eyes have pearl halos, freshwater pearl wings, and a pearl base. Both brooches are under two inches long.

movie. The entire plot was a thinly veiled reference to the dynamic editor-in-chief of *Harper's Bazaar*, Carmel Snow, and photographer Richard Avedon. Photographs by Avedon previously published in *Harper's Bazaar* set the tone in the film's opening credits, and Snow is generously thanked for her contributions.

By the 1950s fashion magazines, especially *Harper's Bazaar*, went from using Hollywood stars as their most spectacular mannequins to finding extraordinary-looking women who soon became famous in their own right as professional models. One of the best known, named Dovima, was discovered by a fashion editor, waiting for a lunch date on Lexington Avenue. Instantly recognizable to movie audiences, Dovima made a cameo appearance in *Funny Face*, posing and reading a comic book during a fashion shoot.

Fashion had become an all-consuming pursuit. An exceptional group of editors, art directors, photographers, couturiers, and models promoted it systematically, and fashion magazines wielded incredible power. Their influence is parodied in *Funny Face* when Maggie Prescott and Dick Avery make a radical decision to replace grace, elegance, and pizzazz, represented by Marion (Dovima), with character, spirit, and intelligence, represented by Jo. After protesting against chichi fashion magazines and spouting her philosophy, however, Jo falls for Dick, and the world of high fashion wins.

By the time Audrey Hepburn starred in *Funny Face,* she was a leading ingenue who added a Continental flair (she had an English father and Dutch mother) to American movies. For her first American film, *Roman Holiday* (1953), she received an Academy Award, and she received four more Oscar nominations, for *Sabrina* (1954), *The Nun's Story* (1959), *Breakfast at Tiffany's* (1961), and *Wait Until Dark* (1967).

Hepburn had begun her career as a dancer in England, and while working in cabarets and nightclubs she inched her way into the movies. An insignificant role in the French film *Monte Carlo Baby* (1951) brought her to the attention of Colette, who insisted she play the title role in the Broadway production of her play *Gigi.* In one year she was signed by Gilbert Miller for the play and then brought to Hollywood by William Wyler for the role of the princess in *Roman Holiday.*

Hepburn allied herself with a prominent East Coast family after she married actor-producer Mel Ferrer, who was the son of a New York socialite and a Cuban doctor. He directed her in *Green Mansions* (1959) and *Wait Until Dark* (1967). Although they were never year-round residents of Hollywood, the Ferrers socialized with other young members of the film community, such as Elizabeth Taylor and Eddie Fisher. After *Wait Until Dark* Hepburn divorced Ferrer, married an Italian psychiatrist, Luca Dotta, and retired for almost a decade to raise two sons in Switzerland. Presently, she has come back into the spotlight as an ambassador for UNICEF.

No matter what role she played, Audrey Hepburn always came across as a woman of refinement and sensibility. When she was cast as Holly Golightly in *Breakfast at Tiffany's* (1961), the author of the short story the movie was based on, Truman Capote, was appalled. He had envisioned the dizzy and provocative Marilyn Monroe in the role. But Hepburn's distinctive personal style was to make Holly Golightly the ideal of every young woman in America; she transformed the movie into an immortal New York tale of youth and dreams. As in *Funny Face,* and despite the title, the fashion emphasis in *Breakfast at Tiffany's* is on couture, not jewelry, and because of Givenchy's smashing clothes for Hepburn in both films, she became an international fashion icon.

In Holly's ceaseless efforts to find stability in her madcap life—and simply to cheer herself up—she often goes to Tiffany's, which is represented in the movie as an institution with a heart that can purvey more than diamonds by making dreams come true. Largely because of the movie, Tiffany has become the one jewelry store in New York that is a tourist attraction.

In a 1953 studio portrait, Audrey Hepburn wears distinctive diamond and pearl button earrings, a typical fifties style. (Courtesy Paramount Pictures)

Elizabeth Taylor

Through great talent, luminous beauty, numerous well-publicized marriages, an extraordinary life-style, and the most exceptional jewelry collection ever assembled by a Hollywood star, Elizabeth Taylor almost single-handedly links the pre- and post-studio system eras in Hollywood and provides a continuity with the great stars of the past. Taylor has long lived a high-profile life punctuated by the display and acquisition of jewels celebrating her romances, movies, and commitment to humane causes.

Taylor came into her own in the fifties. At the same time, a group of young actors including Paul Newman, James Dean, and Montgomery Clift from the New York Actors Studio was practicing Stanislavsky's method acting—as taught by Lee Strasberg—probing the subconscious for memories and feelings to bring authenticity to their roles. Their approach was appropriate for movie scripts based on best-selling plays and novels by Theodore Dreiser, Tennessee Williams, John O'Hara, and Edna Ferber, among others. The performances of the method actors drew critical praise that Hollywood's producers, directors, and backers could not easily dismiss. As this new genre of film acting took off, it created a growing need for actresses whose dramatic abilities could bring intensity to female roles. The paradox was that Elizabeth Taylor, a product of the studio system, found her way to greatness among this revolutionary group of actors.

Taylor was a veteran performer before she ever set foot on a studio lot. The offspring of American parents living in London, she attended Madame Vacani's ballet classes with the future queen of England and danced for the British royal family at the age of three. When her parents relocated to Los Angeles at the beginning of the Second World War, Taylor was spotted by a talent scout. It was 1940; Taylor was eight years old. In 1943 she was put on long-term contract to MGM, which lasted until 1960. A beautiful child whose dark curly hair framed an ivory complexion and set off unique violet eyes, Taylor won great fame and enthusiastic praise with her fifth film, *National Velvet* (1946), and the public settled in for an enduring relationship with her in the old Hollywood tradition.

Audiences watched her mature on screen, her preteen charm developing into feminine radiance. At sixteen she made the transition to leading lady roles, first as Peter Lawford's fiancée in *Julia Misbehaves* (1948). In two adorable comedies, the type that Hollywood once churned out in abundance to showcase the next generation of young stars, she appeared as the daughter of Joan Bennett and Spencer Tracy, first as the fiancée in *Father of the Bride* (1950), then as the expectant mother in its 1951 sequel, *Father's Little Dividend*. While filming *Father of the Bride,* Taylor married playboy and hotelier Nick Hilton, and her new husband, along with MGM, presented her to the world as a full-fledged Hollywood star, with a Cadillac, a wardrobe, jewelry, and every other accouterment of a successful actress.

On February 18, 1952, nineteen-year-old Elizabeth Taylor showed her engagement ring—a sapphire in a double diamond surround—to a newspaperman. She was about to board a plane in New York for London to marry forty-one-year-old English actor Michael Wilding.

Taylor's image and trappings caught the eye of director George Stevens when he was casting the film adaptation of Theodore Dreiser's *An American Tragedy*, renamed *A Place in the Sun* (1951). Stevens was not interested in Taylor's acting ability—he had never even seen her on film. He thought she embodied what he was looking for: "Not so much a real girl as the girl on the candy-box cover, the beautiful girl in the yellow Cadillac convertible that every American boy sometime or other thinks he can marry."* As Angela Vickers, the irresistible American heiress who enchants George Eastman (Montgomery Clift), Taylor is a vision of loveliness in dresses with heart-shaped necklines and minimal jewelry—simple pearl necklaces and diamond pendant earrings.

She impressed the public and critics alike with her performance in *A Place in the Sun,* the film that established her as the ideal young heroine for the soul-searching, wrenching American dramas of the fifties. A photograph of Taylor from the 1950s appears on the cover of *Premiere* magazine's 1991 *Special Issue of 100 Years of Moviemaking,* and inside, film critic Bruce Bibby writes, "The Method may have conquered Hollywood in the 1950s, but even the Actors Studio's most staunch supporters were in awe of Elizabeth Taylor's luscious movie-star grandeur."

From the start, her private life held the public enthralled. It paralleled her screen roles with no dip in excitement, providing running copy and headlines not only for the fan magazines but for the leading newspapers and all the other media as well. Though all but the most recent of Taylor's husbands were known to the public before she married them, two were of legendary stature at the time of their unions. When Taylor married Mike Todd, an international businessman and showman of the fifties, he propelled his wife from star status to superstardom with publicity appearances and lavish gifts. Then, when she married Richard Burton, celebrated stage actor of the 1950s, their relationship, professional and private, eclipsed every other piece of theatrical news. Burton's numerous gifts of historic and important jewelry were covered in detail worldwide. Whereas Todd had given Taylor a collection of fine jewelry, it was Burton's gifts, with their wit, romance, and history, that associated Taylor with magnificent jewelry forever.

From her first marriage, a crescendo of publicity began to build around Elizabeth Taylor. For *Father of the Bride* she received dual coverage for her film and her marriage to Hilton, which heightened the public's sense of identification with her, even though the marriage was short-lived. In 1952 she married British actor Michael Wilding, a veteran of London and Hollywood films, and in 1953 bore the first of their two children.

Through the hectic years of young motherhood and living on two continents, Taylor stuck to a rigorous schedule of moviemaking. Even as she and Wilding were separating, she turned in a stellar performance with Rock Hudson and James Dean in *Giant* (1956). During the film's climax, at a banquet, all the Texan women wear flashy jewelry, but Taylor outshines them all in a gray evening dress with an understated but stunning Garland-style diamond suite.

The scene is absolutely true to life. Capitalizing on the oil boom, precious jewelers traveled to their clients all over the Lone Star State: Harry Winston took his "Court of Jewels" exhibit to Dallas and San Antonio; Winston's salesman Julius Cohen honed his skills with royal jewelry at the Texas State Fair; and

* Dick Sheppard, *Elizabeth* (New York: Doubleday, 1974), 90.

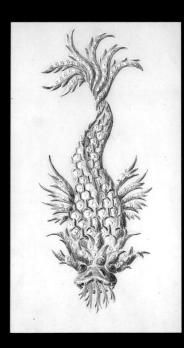

Dudley Ramsden, traveling by small plane, sold jewelry for Neiman Marcus.

Another Southern drama, this one set in the nineteenth century, *Raintree County* (1957), won Taylor an Oscar nomination for Best Actress. While making this film, Taylor initiated divorce proceedings, had a serious operation on her spine, and witnessed her close friend and costar Montgomery Clift's near-fatal accident in her driveway. She finished the movie with Clift after his surgery. No matter how full her private life became, Taylor established a pattern early on of completing the project at hand.

When he met Elizabeth Taylor, Mike Todd appeared to be at the height of his financial and theatrical success. An original partner in Cinerama, he sold the company at the zenith of the demand for wide-screen processes, going on to form a corporation to develop an even wider process, a sixty-five-millimeter cinematic device called Todd-AO. This technology was used for many movies, among them the smash hit *Oklahoma!* (1955), which Todd financed.

The whirlwind courtship of Taylor and Todd sparkled with splendid jewelry. Todd began with a pearl ring delivered to Taylor on the set of *Raintree County* by her costar, Montgomery Clift, with the message that the engagement ring would be along later. The next ring was an antique gold band set with garnets, which

Todd bought Taylor in Atlantic City, N.J. A month later, Todd gave her a huge emerald-cut diamond ring, which, teasing, he loved to tell Elizabeth and the press was not quite thirty but only twenty-nine-and-a-half carats. Taylor maintained that it was a friendship ring, but Todd called it the official engagement ring when it was first spotted by the press. On February 2, 1957, Taylor and Todd were married in Acapulco, and for this occasion the groom gave the bride a magnificent diamond suite consisting of earrings, a bracelet, and a ring.

During their marriage, Taylor lived the life that every fan imagined was the destiny of a great star. When Todd bought two theaters, he named them Liz and His. When Liz went to the hairdresser, he had champagne brought to her under the dryer. He reportedly gave her a gift every day and a special one on Saturdays, the day of their first meeting.

Todd's jewelry gifts ushered Taylor into the ranks of world-class jewelry wearers. At the London premiere of *Around the World in Eighty Days* (1956), one of Todd's productions, Taylor wore a red chiffon dress by Dior and a ruby and diamond necklace and earrings. Todd gave the duchess of Kent a roundabout compliment on her splendid jewelry by referring to his wife's suite and saying, "I'm in trouble — she'll be throwing these away tomorrow."* His straightforward wit and ironic humor made him a favorite of reporters, who regularly spiced their columns with his repartee. Hedda Hopper could not resist printing his retort after she nettled him about Liz's tiara for the Oscar ceremonies of 1957. He looked her in the eye and said simply, "Doesn't every girl have one?"**

The tiara wearing of the 1950s was stimulated by the marriage of Princess Elizabeth of England in 1947 and her subsequent coronation in 1953. Both ceremonies attracted many American guests, who turned to contemporary and estate jewelers to procure diamond headgear like the family heirlooms of British and European nobility. The tiara remained popular after the royal events and became an item in the formal parures seen at galas. Gloria Swanson wore a tiara to the New York Knickerbocker Ball of 1950, and Paulette Goddard borrowed a tiara from Van Cleef & Arpels for the 1951 New York Art Students League Diamond Jubilee. The style was parodied in *Gentlemen Prefer Blondes* (1953) when Lorelei tries to fit a tiara around her neck; on being corrected, she gushes that she loves finding new places to wear diamonds.

The tiara Todd bought Taylor was not seen at the Oscar ceremony the following year, as Taylor did not make an appearance. Four days before, on March 22, 1958, Mike Todd's private plane — "The Lucky Liz" — crashed, killing him, as he was flying to New York to receive the Friar's Club award for showman of the year. When she received the news, Taylor was two weeks into the shooting of Tennessee Williams's *Cat on a Hot Tin Roof* (1958). Although she was paralyzed with grief, she managed to turn in an Academy Award–nominated performance.

Taylor's marriage to Todd, although brief, was lasting in its effect on her approach to life and Hollywood. While he encouraged her to live up to her star status, and even to be extravagant, he also taught her how to negotiate contracts — as he had done for her on *Cat on a Hot Tin Roof* — and how humorously to deflect the sometimes cruel questions and comments of the press.

In the transitional period following Todd's death, Taylor turned for solace to his

* Alexander Walker, *Elizabeth, The Life of Elizabeth Taylor* (New York: Grove Weidenfeld, 1990), 183. **Mason Wiley and Damien Bona, *Inside Oscar* (New York: Ballantine, 1986), 278.

best friend and protégé, the singer, Eddie Fisher. Their subsequent marriage grew out of their mutual affection for Todd. Once more Taylor showed her mettle, picking up the pieces of her career despite the venom heaped on her by the press, led by Hedda Hopper, who championed Fisher's ex-wife Debbie Reynolds.

Distancing herself from the scandal at home, Taylor moved to London to make *Suddenly Last Summer* (1959), in which she plays Catherine Holly, who is committed as a mental patient by her Aunt Violet Venable (Katharine Hepburn). As a wealthy widow, Mrs. Venable wears delicate diamond jewelry throughout. Catherine puts on a large, eye-catching brooch when Dr. Cukrowicz (Montgomery Clift) permits her to wear her own clothes at the institution. Both Katharine Hepburn and Elizabeth Taylor were nominated for Best Actress for this film, but neither won the Academy Award.

To free herself from the studio and gain independent status, Taylor agreed to make the screen adaptation of John O'Hara's *Butterfield 8* (1960), the last film under her MGM contract. She felt no empathy for the character Gloria Wandrous, who seduces the husband of an East Coast heiress (Dina Merrill). Making the best of what she felt was a bad situation, Taylor insisted on certain changes in the script and demanded a role for Eddie Fisher. After a nearly fatal bout of pneumonia, Taylor finished *Butterfield 8*. To her astonishment, she won the Academy Award for Best Actress that year, prompting her to comment, "I won the Oscar because I almost died—pure and simple."

All the while, she was negotiating a mega-contract with Twentieth Century–Fox—over a million dollars, plus perks—for appearing in Walter Wanger's spectacular *Cleopatra*. By 1962, the year Taylor arrived in Rome to film *Cleopatra*, she was a living idol. Along with Marilyn Monroe and Marlon Brando, she was immortalized by Andy Warhol in his silk-screen paintings celebrating American popular culture. Her costar, Richard Burton, on the other hand, was among a handful of famous British stage actors including Laurence Olivier, John Gielgud, and Ralph Richardson. *Cleopatra* was intended to be a splendid union of the glory of Hollywood—its most beautiful female star, its art directors, costumers, and special-effects teams—with the prestige of the British stage, personified by Richard Burton, Rex Harrison, and Roddy McDowall. Grand epics were money-makers in the 1950s, and because of their large returns, no expense was spared—but *Cleopatra*'s budget topped every other one to date.

Dismissive of Taylor's acting ability and Hollywood background, Burton began by flirting with her mercilessly on the set. However, by the time a saffron-robed Cleopatra (Taylor) welcomes Marc Antony (Burton) to her villa, halfway through the production, Taylor and Burton had fallen in love, and everybody knew it. As the Rome reporters covering the birth pangs of the cumbersome epic—which was not turning out as planned—caught wind of the breaking romance, they sent the news out on the wires. *Cleopatra* had inadvertently become the site of a romance that was more exciting than the script. The story of the mismanaged production, in conjunction with the comings and goings of the stars' spouses, medical attendants on the set, and the scrutiny of the press—all contributed to a flurry of interest. As it turned out, however, the four-hour epic proved too boring for the public. Taylor summed it up succinctly: "Surely the most

In *Cat on a Hot Tin Roof* (1958), as Maggie the Cat, Taylor wears a single diamond collet necklace, diamond and pearl earrings, and two gold bangle bracelets in a confrontation with her husband, Brick (Paul Newman).

bizarre piece of entertainment ever to be perpetuated."

Rising above the disaster, Taylor and Burton went on to mesh their lives and careers as the most sought-after couple in the movie industry. Their next film together was *The V.I.P.s* (1963), the drama of a husband and wife who triumph over financial catastrophe through their love for each other. Although the film attracted a celebrity-filled cast—including Orson Welles and Maggie Smith—it was primarily a vehicle for its two leading stars. As both were in the process of conducting divorce proceedings, this film marked the moment the public had been anticipating. Burton asked Taylor to marry him. His engagement present to her was an important brooch centering on an emerald in a marquise-cut diamond surround. She was so thrilled that she begged the producers to let her wear it, but the film was too far into the production to alter the star's jewelry wardrobe.

For the premiere of his film *The Night of the Iguana* (1964), a screen adaptation of Tennessee Williams's play, Burton presented Taylor with a very different type of jewel—an enormous four-and-one-half-inch dolphin brooch. It was made by Schlumberger, a jewelry enterprise at the peak of its popularity. Beginning in the 1930s as a designer of abstract printed textiles in Paris, Jean Schlumberger was snagged by Elsa Schiaparelli, Chanel's archrival, to design jewelry, while Verdura was creating jewelry at Chanel. Some twenty years later, in 1956, Schlumberger moved triumphantly into a second-floor boutique with its own private elevator at Tiffany & Co. This move served to link the traditional New York jewelry giant with artistic jewelry, which was on the rise in popularity.

At his Tiffany address, Schlumberger designed jewelry within a stone's throw of the duke of Verdura. And, because some of their smaller pieces had some features in common, they were rumored to be rivals. In fact, however, they were friends who admired each other's work and shared similar themes—images from nature, art history, and mythology. The dainty and feminine brooches of Verdura could never be mistaken for the enormous fantasy jewels that Schlumberger created. In typical Schlumberger designs, gems wind around the edge of the jewel and protrude from the surface, lending a rich feeling to the whole. Verdura, by contrast, minimized the importance of stones and often used enamel for color.

Overseeing the production of these creations, Schlumberger's partner, Nicolas Bongard, bought and matched stones, ever on the lookout for unique shape and unexpected color, and presided over the various stages as Schlumberger's two-dimensional drawings took sculptural form.

The Schlumberger salon had a history of coming up with wildly original ideas for its jewelry. To celebrate the opening of Garson Kanin and Ruth Gordon's play *The Rat Race,* Schlumberger devised a rat brooch of gray cabochon sapphires. When artist Salvador Dali complained to Jean Schlumberger about his cumbersome handlebar moustache, the jeweler created little gold crutches to hold it up. While not a great collector of precious jewelry, *Vogue* editor-in-chief Diana Vreeland had a legendary piece by Schlumberger, which she kept on her night table when she was not wearing it. This objet d'art/jewel was a trophy of love with fringed armor, shield, and spears, conjuring up a medieval code of dress and honor. The brooch that Burton bought for Taylor was meant to bring back memories of Puerto Vallarta, then a romantic Mexican fishing village on the sea,

Taylor's 33.19-carat Krupp diamond, flanked by triangular-cut diamonds, was mounted in a platinum ring by Cartier.

176

where they lived during the filming of *The Night of the Iguana.* After Burton told Schlumberger and Bongard the background and occasion for the gift, the dolphin, with its wiggling body, waving fins, shining diamond scales, darting tongue, emerald lips, and sapphire eyes, became the Night of the Iguana brooch.

On March 15, 1964, Taylor and Burton were married. For the occasion Taylor commissioned Irene Sharaff, her wardrobe designer for *Cleopatra,* to make her a yellow gown similar to the one she wore during the production when she and Burton first fell in love. *Cleopatra* was more of a fashion statement of the sixties than one might suspect. The charged colors of the robes, large jewels, and extravagant hairdos (enhanced with switches) were the epitome of contemporary style. At the end of the filming, Taylor kept sixty of the Sharaff gowns, seeing in their flowing lines and plunging necklines potential evening dresses and in their solid colors the perfect background for jewelry.

Burton's wedding gift to Taylor, an addition to her emerald and diamond engagement brooch, was a lavish necklace with a progression of square-cut emeralds set in pear-shaped diamond clusters, joined by stylized diamond flower motifs. For her thirty-second birthday he had given her a pair of diamond and emerald earrings in the extra-long, drop-shaped outline that originated in the sixties. Her array of emerald and diamond jewels made a set, which was further augmented by a large emerald and diamond cocktail ring and emerald and diamond bracelet. These amazing emeralds were called the Grand Duchess Vladimir suite by the press, as some of the emeralds came from a legendary collection in Russia.

Once married, Taylor and Burton intensified their pace, making movies and partying all over the world with a circle of financiers, politicians, and aristocrats. Taylor stood out as unique. Although Sophia Loren, Maria Callas, Claudia Cardinale, and Gina Lollobrigida were receiving publicity, there were few news-worthy Hollywood stars for the press to follow. In the twenties, Taylor and Burton would have been filming in Hollywood and socializing in Beverly Hills, but, as it was the sixties, they were making movies on location and relaxing on the slopes of Gstaad, swimming in Sardinia, enjoying life in Sussex and Dublin, and spending

the fall in New York, Paris, London, or Rome. In 1964 they were mobbed in Boston when Burton performed in *Hamlet*. In 1965 they went to Dublin for Burton's film *The Spy Who Came in from the Cold* and worked together in Paris and Los Angeles on a romantic film, *The Sandpiper*, directed by Vincente Minnelli.

In retrospect, their work together was a preamble to their most celebrated collaboration, on the screen adaptation of the brutal Edward Albee play *Who's Afraid of Virginia Woolf?*, directed by Mike Nichols and produced in Hollywood. Although the film was not a box-office success, film critics respected Taylor for taking on the role, which was well out of the usual range of Hollywood parts. She had to put on weight and deepen her voice for the part. Her performance generated critical acclaim, and the movie was nominated for several Academy Awards. It won three, including one for Taylor. Although the press hypothesized that the couple's antagonistic roles in that film reflected their own married life, Taylor has since said it was one of their most tranquil periods together.

After this collaboration they accepted two classics that were filmed in Rome, *The Taming of the Shrew* (1967) and *Dr. Faustus* (1968). Both pieces presented Elizabeth Taylor in rich Renaissance costumes first, as Katharina and then as Helen of Troy. Irene Sharaff provided Taylor's costumes in Franco Zeffirelli's production of *The Taming of the Shrew*, and Alexandre, the leading hairdresser of the jet set, who was based in Paris, conceived Taylor's hairstyles for both films. Buoyant waves of hair invited resplendent jewelry and headpieces, and in *The Taming of the Shrew*, a Renaissance necklace with curling gold scrolls set with cultured pearls and semiprecious stones and with matching earrings was commissioned by Zeffirelli for Taylor. In the final scene Taylor wears a gold mesh, cushion-shaped hair ornament set with a jeweled motif, a long gold medallion necklace, and gold grillwork earrings with suspended pearls.

In addition to film projects, Taylor and Burton invested in a few commercial ventures, among them the Harlech television station in Bristol, England. For its 1968 grand opening, Burton presented Taylor with the Krupp diamond. Only two days before, on May 16, he had been engaged in a bidding war for the stone with none other than Harry Winston at Parke-Bernet Galleries in New York. The diamond was named for its previous owner, Vera Krupp, the widow of the German steel magnate Alfried Krupp von Bohlen und Halbach. Considered one of the most perfect diamonds in the world, the 33.19-carat emerald-cut diamond is superb. It has a heavy table (a large, wide surface), with perfectly cut and proportioned facets that beam brilliance and display a rich inner life.

To this day, the Krupp diamond appears on Taylor's hand daily. Set in a Cartier platinum mount, it is flanked by two triangular-cut diamonds. The ring's size and beauty precipitated a now-famous interchange at a wedding when Princess Margaret asked if she could try it on. Once it was on her finger, the princess said, "How very vulgar!"

Taylor countered, "Yeah, ain't it great!"

Taylor's light-hearted attitude toward her jewelry has given rise to many stories. It is said, for example, that every maid at the Dorchester Hotel in London has had the Krupp diamond on her finger—briefly—at one time or another. Like stars of the past, Taylor has created entertaining fictions for the press about her jewelry. Once she said that the Krupp was her prize for beating Burton at Ping-Pong.

The parties celebrating the premieres of Taylor and Burton's films in Europe were productions in themselves. The party for *The Taming of the Shrew* took place in Paris with members of the French government in attendance, and during the festivities a message was read from President Charles de Gaulle. Van Cleef & Arpels created Taylor's tiara for the occasion. The Rothschilds and the Windsors threw parties in their honor. Inspired by jewelry worn at these parties that came from European collections with royal lineage, Burton proceeded to bid on a historic pearl for Taylor when it came up for auction at Parke-Bernet.

La Peregrina is a pear-shaped drop pearl weighing 203.84 grains, suspended from an antique diamond and silver leaf mount which has oxidized. Translated as "The Wanderer," La Peregrina was one of the most-loved jewels of the Spanish royal family. Philip II of Spain gave it to his first wife, Mary Tudor of England, and, after her death, it was returned to the Spanish treasury. Margarita of Austria, wife of Philip III, wore it in a portrait by Velázquez. From the Spanish royal family, the pearl passed into the Bonaparte family, going from Joseph Bonaparte, king of Spain, to Louis Napoleon, who sold it in 1848 to the English marquess of Abercorn. The heirs put it up for auction in January 1969.

Burton bid anonymously through his lawyer, Aaron R. Frosch, and wrested the jewel from Prince Alfonso de Bourbon Asturias. After the auction, the prince let it be known that he wanted the jewel for the former queen of Spain and told the press he would buy it from Taylor if she tired of it. A friend of Taylor's told the *New York Post* (January 25, 1969), "Elizabeth will make no secret of owning it once she gets her hands on it. She buys jewelry to wear, not as an investment."

Soon after La Peregrina was delivered to Burton and Taylor at the Dorchester in London for her thirty-seventh birthday gift, it promptly vanished. After a frantic search, Taylor saw something white in the mouth of her Pekingese that looked too small for a bone. None the worse for wear, La Peregrina was mounted magnificently by Cartier three years later in a double-strand Oriental pearl choker intersected with diamond and ruby quatrefoils, with an additional diamond and ruby flame pendant to complement the original setting.

Taylor wore La Peregrina suspended from the Cartier necklace in the period movie *A Little Night Music* (1977). She enters wearing the necklace during a scene when her ex-lover discovers that her daughter has the feminine equivalent of his first name. They proceed to a dinner party where the assembled house-guests begin to discover whom they truly love. This film, a screen adaptation of Stephen Sondheim's Broadway hit, was sumptuously costumed and filmed on location in Vienna.

After buying La Peregrina, with its pedigree, Taylor and Burton made their own official entry into jewelry history the same year with the acquisition of a 69.42-carat pear-shaped diamond that immediately became known as the Taylor-Burton diamond. The original diamond, 240 carats in the rough, was purchased in 1966 from the Central Selling Organization, De Beers (which specializes in diamonds), by Harry Winston, whose workshop took more than eight months to cut it. Shortly after, Winston sold the pear-shaped diamond to Mrs. Paul A. Ames, sister of Walter Annenberg, then the American ambassador to the Court of St. James. After a robbery scare, Mrs. Ames decided to put it up for auction.

Interest in the diamond was especially intense, for the buyer would have the

The Taylor-Burton diamond accents a necklace of cascading pear-shaped diamonds, mounted in platinum.

opportunity to name it. Aristotle Onassis had dropped by the Parke-Bernet Galleries in New York to inspect the stone, leading the press to speculate that he intended to buy it for his wife, Jacqueline Kennedy Onassis. He had promised to buy her a diamond of at least forty carats for her fortieth birthday, to go with her collection of rubies. Richard Burton was also known to be in the running, since he had asked Parke-Bernet to send it to Gstaad for his inspection.

Bidding from England, Burton gave his lawyer a ceiling price of a million dollars. For the first time Burton was the underbidder; Cartier carried off the prize for $1,050,000, the highest price paid to date for a diamond. But Burton could not stand defeat, and he got on the phone to buy the stone. Cartier agreed. On October 24, 1969, the *New York Daily News* trumpeted, "A Diamond Goes for a Million and Change." After it was transferred to the Burtons on October 25, the headlines read, "Liz Gets That Peachy Pear." *The New York Times* quoted Richard Burton, "It's just a present for Liz."

The diamond, named the Taylor-Burton diamond, went on exhibit at Cartier's New York and Chicago stores, where, the papers reported, more than six thousand people a day came to see it. When Taylor finally received her gift, she wore it briefly as a ring, flanked by two diamonds. Then she asked Cartier to design a necklace for it. The firm sent a salesman to measure her neck and present her with a sketch of a cascade of a single row of pear-shaped diamonds set on the bias. When the necklace was completed, as a security measure three men with identical suitcases were dispatched to deliver the jewel to the Burton yacht *Kalizma,* which was anchored in Monaco. Presently, wearing the most expensive and best-publicized jewel in the world, Taylor attended the fortieth birthday party of Princess Grace at the Hotel Hermitage in Monte Carlo, escorted not only by Burton but also by detectives carrying machine guns—as stipulated in her

insurance policy from Lloyds of London.

On February 27, 1972, Taylor celebrated her own fortieth birthday in Buda-pest, attended by celebrities including Princess Grace and Ringo Starr, members of her family, and a handful of poets, artists, and intellectuals. *Women's Wear Daily* reported, "One image can portray the whole Saturday night party— Princess Grace swinging through the vaults of the old cellar near the Duna Hotel on a rapid congo line to the gypsy orchestra's version of 'Hava Nagila.'" While the party was publicized for its extravagance, Burton matched the party's cost with a donation to UNICEF.

Taylor's birthday gift from Burton was a heart-shaped yellow diamond, which he bought from Cartier. The diamond, mounted as a pendant in a gold-braided tassel necklace, was originally a gift from Shah Jahan in 1621 to his favorite wife, Mumtaz Mahal, the queen who inspired the Taj Mahal. Naturally, the press covered the jewel, one daily observing, "When you're married to Cleopatra and her crucial fortieth birthday is coming up, you need a grand gesture." Cartier whispered subtly in an advertisement run in *The New York Times*, "Cartier is for Lovers," with an illustration of the jewel and a small paragraph beneath that said, "This heart-shaped diamond was an expression of love when first presented centuries ago to Queen Mumtaz Mahal, and again, when recently given to another famous lady on a very special birthday."

Often considered the last star of the studio system, Elizabeth Taylor has continued to be of interest to a fascinated public. After her divorce, remarriage and second divorce from Burton in 1976, she married U.S. Senator John Warner in an outdoor ceremony in Virginia and changed her profile from a movie star to a politician's wife, campaigning and traveling by bus throughout the state. After her divorce from Warner, she was seen with such escorts as the late Malcolm Forbes. Now married again, to Larry Fortensky, Taylor remains in the public eye.

In 1987 Taylor launched her successful perfume Elizabeth Taylor's Passion for Parfums International, a division of Elizabeth Arden. The Passion campaign advertising was photographed by Norman Parkinson, with a jewelry credit for Harry Winston. In one photograph Taylor wears a diamond necklace and dangling diamond earrings, the various cuts shining like pinpoints of light, while the Krupp diamond gleams on her finger. For her next line of products, Elizabeth Taylor's Passion Body Riches, Gary Bernstein photographed her wearing an emerald and diamond cluster necklace with matching earrings, rising from a marble bath in a setting reminiscent of *Cleopatra,* with a leopard in attendance. The jewelry was again credited to Harry Winston.

The success of these ads and personal appearances prompted the House of Taylor, as Parfums International dubbed her division, to add Passion for Men and another perfume, White Diamonds. For the advertising campaign of her new scent for women, New York jeweler Louis Glick supplied Taylor with a necklace composed entirely of "D flawless white diamonds," a term that defines gems of supreme quality and fine color. The perfectly matched 142.95-carat necklace took three years to assemble. Taylor wore it for one ad photograph dressed in a white Elizabeth Emanuel evening gown and seen waving to fans from a limousine. Another photograph by Bruce Weber finds Taylor in an Isaac Mizrahi coat, wearing delicate diamond floral drop earrings, also supplied by Louis Glick, as well as the Krupp diamond.

At the debut of the perfume in stores across the country, a video was shown with clips from her films *Cat on a Hot Tin Roof, Butterfield 8,* and *Rhapsody* (1954). After the announcement of White Diamonds, *Vogue* magazine, leading the rest of the media, published a substantial article on Taylor. It was illustrated with photographs by Herb Ritts, in which the Krupp was the only jewel.

Since 1984 Taylor has been identified with one major cause, the American Foundation for AIDS Research (AmFAR), of which she is the founding national chairman. Literally traveling the globe, Taylor confers with doctors and visits hospitals and patients and engages in energetic fund-raising. In 1990, Dr. Mathilde Krim, the cochairman of AmFAR, told *People Weekly,* "Elizabeth is a smart, sincere, compassionate woman who commands enormous respect and prestige with the public. No one can match her."

In 1987, after the duchess of Windsor died, her jewelry collection was put up for auction at Sotheby's in Geneva to benefit the Pasteur Institute, a pioneer in AIDS research. Notables from all over the world converged on the auction tent and bought at prices that were double the original projections. Taylor herself bid over the telephone from her house in Bel Air, California, for one jewel, a circular and baguette-cut diamond clip called the Wales Plumes. She and Burton had admired it in Paris when they were dining with the Windsors, who were their good friends. As the price for the Wales Plumes rose higher and higher, Taylor held on. When it was finally hers, she told the press that she was happy the price had soared because, while it was the first jewel she had ever bought for herself, the money went to a fine cause.

Afterword

Although Hollywood began simply as a good location for making movies, it has come to connote much more than a place in southern California. In every decade, the meaning of Hollywood changes with new generations of actors and actresses, advances in technology, different approaches to movie-making, and shifts in the economy and politics, to say nothing of social mores and fashions. The image it projects to the rest of America and the world varies. Likewise, the relationship between the movies, the stars, and their jewelry has taken different forms over the years. In the late thirties, when Hollywood spelled glamour, jewelry's importance was clearly at its peak. Movie stars launched the cabochon style worldwide. The 1950s ushered in another high, when jewelry was celebrated on screen in Technicolor. Marilyn Monroe sang "Diamonds Are a Girl's Best Friend," and summed up a national preference. Then Audrey Hepburn made a film paean to a jewelry store, *Breakfast at Tiffany's*.

Nostalgia notwithstanding, trends and cycles continue to work their alchemy; jewelry credits abound in films again. Stars model jewelry in magazine photographs, and jewelers provide diamond suites for actresses at the Academy Awards, demonstrating that the bond between Hollywood and jewelers remains strong. The remaining pages are a few jewelry highlights from the last thirty years to round out this survey and guide the viewer to some recurring themes: the importance of movie cycles to style, the relationship between young stars and jewelers, and, ultimately, the influence of Hollywood on the jewelry industry.

Just as the romantic revival of the 1930s helped to bring antique jewelry into vogue, so the Roaring Twenties revival in the late 1960s and 1970s brought back the Art Deco jewelry of that period. Movies were very much a part of this revival, with an influx of films drawing inspiration from the twenties and thirties. One of these, a spoof on flappers called *Thoroughly Modern Millie* (1967), starred Julie Andrews as Millie. A running joke throughout the film is that Millie's long bead necklaces will not lie flat on her unfashionably ample chest. Julie Andrews followed this movie with *Star!* (1968), a film recreation of the life of Broadway and London actress Gertrude Lawrence. Throughout the film Andrews wears several wide diamond bracelets, brooches, and earrings and is shown shopping at Cartier, which is credited with the jewelry for the film. A 1968 Cartier catalogue illustrates a pair of marquise- and circular-cut diamond cascade earrings with a note that they were worn by Julie Andrews in the film. However, while lavish, the jewelry for *Star!* is not true to its time.

On the other hand, the jewelry Barbra Streisand wore for her role as the Ziegfeld Follies comedienne Fanny Brice in *Funny Girl* (1968) and its sequel, *Funny Lady* (1975), was truly authentic. As one of the first actresses to espouse the style offscreen, Streisand amassed her own Art Deco jewelry collection, and, as the jewelry-loving Brice, she paraded it on screen with a special flair and eye for

In recreating the glamorous and free-spirited 1920s, the makers of *The Great Gatsby* (1974) chose Cartier jewelry. On his Long Island estate, Jay Gatsby (Robert Redford) entertains Daisy Buchanan (Mia Farrow), who wears a pearl necklace and a marquise-cut diamond engagement ring. (Courtesy Paramount Pictures)

Left: In the opening scene of *The Great Gatsby* (1974), Lois Chiles as Jordan Baker wears a cabochon emerald and diamond clip brooch with a seed pearl sautoir intersected by emerald beads, suspending pearl and emerald tassels, all by Cartier. The sautoir is shown here on a still from the film. (Courtesy Paramount Pictures)

detail. Streisand shopped at Fred Leighton, an estate jeweler in a boutique on upper Madison Avenue in New York. Infusing the historical pieces with the magic and romance of their glorious past, Fred Leighton became a major player in the creation of the estate jewelry market.

To complement Irene Sharaff's gowns and costumes for her role in *Funny Girl*, Streisand wore a collection of dainty diamond jewelry: a lapel brooch pendant, a geometric diamond openwork brooch that she wore vertically instead of horizontally, a slender platinum chain, pearl necklace, and diamond rings. *Funny Lady* picks up Brice's life after her divorce from gambler Nicky Arnstein (Omar Sharif) and her marriage to showman Billy Rose (James Caan). This time, in costumes codesigned by Bob Mackie and Ray Aghayan, Streisand wears large Art Deco jewelry, pearls that wrap around her body and drape down her back, a large dome ring, diamond clip brooches, and a diamond wedding ring. She carries a delicate cigarette case of red and black enamel, which pops open at a touch.

For the filmed version of the Jazz Age novel *The Great Gatsby* in 1974, the ranking jeweler of the 1920s, Cartier, was asked to provide the jewelry. Of all the twenties revivals, this one received the most publicity, both for its stars, Robert Redford, Mia Farrow, Sam Waterston, Lois Chiles, and Bruce Dern, and for the intensive research that went into the costumes, props, and jewelry. The jewelry of Daisy Buchanan (Mia Farrow) consisted of multiple pearl necklaces, pearl-drop earrings, a diamond circle pin, a diamond rivière, a diamond service stripe, a diamond and black onyx cigarette holder, and a marquise-cut diamond engagement ring similar to Norma Shearer's. Daisy's friend Jordan Baker (Lois Chiles) wears a long pearl and emerald sautoir, a carved emerald and pearl necklace, a cabochon emerald brooch, a sapphire ring, and a diamond necklace. The Cartier inventory for the production reveals that the firm went beyond accessorizing the stars to supplying equally precious jewels for the numerous "jazz babies" milling about in the background as well.

As the Art Deco revival won adherents, Cartier reestablished its supremacy in this area of jewelry. Acquiring important estate pieces, Cartier reclaimed its heritage, put its archives in order, and started a museum collection. The firm held its first Art Deco retrospective in its New York store in 1976, followed by one at the Los Angeles County Museum in 1982, and then at the Musée du Petit Palais in Paris in 1989. In addition to the exhibitions, *The Great Gatsby*, though not successful, played a role in helping to acquaint the public with magnificent Art Deco jewelry. In fact, the marquise-cut diamond engagement ring worn by Daisy Buchanan in the film was bought out of the Cartier window by a woman who walked in the store one day and said simply, "I want Daisy's ring."

If movie stars were dancing the Charleston on screen in the 1970s, they were dancing with equal abandon at the New York club Studio 54. One of the busiest participants in New York night life was Liza Minnelli, daughter of film director Vincente Minnelli and Judy Garland. She was just coming into her own in the seventies, starring in Bob Fosse's *Cabaret* (1972) and Martin Scorsese's *New York, New York* (1977). She won an Academy Award as Best Actress for *Cabaret*.

At discos, Minnelli was the embodiment of seventies chic—best friends with clothes designer Halston and part of the circle that included Andy Warhol,

Elizabeth Taylor, Bianca Jagger, and Halston model and jewelry designer Elsa Peretti. After Halston died in 1990, Minnelli told *Vogue* (July 1990), "I've been wearing Halston's clothes since I was twenty years old. . . . And I didn't have one piece of gold or one piece of jewelry, it was all just that silver he had Elsa Peretti make for me." What Marlene Dietrich did for Trabert & Hoeffer-Mauboussin, Liza Minnelli did for Elsa Peretti.

In 1974, when Halston felt that Peretti was ready to be on her own, he went to Walter Hoving, chairman of Tiffany, and suggested that he give Peretti an exclusive design contract. Not only did Hoving give her a contract, he also gave her a designer's monopoly on silver jewelry as well, which the firm had not promoted in years. A beacon to lure the new generation of jewelry wearers to Tiffany, Peretti was to the seventies what Schlumberger had been to the sixties. Her sterling silver teardrop charms, equestrian buckles, asymmetrical hearts, and massive biomorphic cuffs became best-sellers. By 1979, Peretti had moved from the middle of the Tiffany catalogue, the "Blue Book", to the front as the most sought-after designer of the firm.

Funky, flashing metal—gold, silver, and steel—surged into fashion at the same time as it appeared on movie stars. Cartier introduced Les Must de Cartier, a line of mass-produced jewelry and accessories. One of the firm's jewelry designers, Aldo Cipullo, caused a sensation with a romantic trick jewel called the love bracelet, a solid gold band that could only be put on and taken off with its accompanying vermeil screwdriver. Paramount film producer Bob Evans gave one to his then wife, Ali MacGraw. Not long after, she fell in love with Steve McQueen on the set of *Getaway* (1972). During the filming and the ensuing scandal, as well as the couple's separation, the screwdriver remained in Evans's possession. Ali MacGraw's love bracelet could not be removed; it flashed on her wrist from the first to the last scene.

While all jewelers participated in the increasingly casual jewelry styles of the seventies, Bulgari, the Italian jeweler, which opened its New York branch at the Pierre Hotel in 1970, elevated its popular metal designs by adding gems. The gold and steel jewels issuing from the firm were studded with precious and semi-precious stones in violets, pinks, and yellows. The firm accommodated Art Deco fashions with a radical paring down of jewelry elements, bold geometrical shapes, and rectangular gem cuts. Bulgari's success led to many film credits.

While Bulgari had catered to movie stars from Kay Francis to Shelley Winters, Jessica Lange was the actress most identified with the firm in the 1970s. The association stemmed from her contract with producer Dino de Laurentiis. It was a generous seven-year exclusive contract in the old Hollywood tradition and provided the customary trappings for a star. Although Lange spent most of her first movie, *King Kong* (1976), clutched in the fist of an oversize ape, Bulgari still receives credit for her jewelry.

One final testament to the impact of Hollywood on the jewelry industry is the translation of screen icons and images into precious materials. Following in the footsteps of John Rubel, who thirty years earlier had transformed the dancing flowers from Walt Disney's *Fantasia* into a series of gem-studded brooches, Julius Cohen went to another segment of the movie, the "Prima Ballerina Hippo Ballet," for the chorus lead, Hippo Hyacinth, and recreated her in gems. Julius Cohen's

Top: Liza Minnelli wears silver cuffs by Elsa Peretti. *Above:* On the cover of *Interview* magazine for April, 1979 to publicize her role in Bob Fosse's movie *All That Jazz* Jessica Lange wears paneled 18K gold Bulgari earrings set with a square-cut yellow diamond and rectangular-cut emerald.

A Dancing Hippopotamus brooch by Julius Cohen, set with diamonds, emeralds, rubies, and a yellow beryl, paid tribute in 1974 to Walt Disney's classic 1940 film *Fantasia*.

In 1989, to celebrate the fiftieth anniversary of *The Wizard of Oz*, Ron Winston, president of Harry Winston, designed a pair of ruby slippers.

As a jeweled homage to Hollywood history, Rachelle Epstein of Shelle Design, Ltd. created two 18K yellow gold movie star cuffs, set with amethyst, and white and canary diamonds. The names of actors and actresses are engraved on the surfaces.

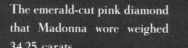

The emerald-cut pink diamond that Madonna wore weighed 34.25 carats.

18K gold hippo ballerina brooch has a yellow beryl tummy, emerald eyes, a ruby tutu, and ruby toenails. When Cohen ran an ad for the coy hippo, a flood of letters poured in. One from California expressed astonishment in a poem, which ended, "It's one thing they [burglars] would never steal!/Who would believe the thing was real?" One of the distinguishing features of Cohen's jewelry is his daring wit with exotic gems and precious materials.

An armful of rubies made their way into Harry Winston's ruby slippers to mark the fiftieth anniversary of *The Wizard of Oz* in 1989. Ronald Winston, chief executive officer and president of Harry Winston, conjured up this extravagant piece of nostalgia in honor of the film—and as a tribute to the collaboration between Winston and Hollywood that began in 1935 when Shirley Temple posed for publicity with the Jonker diamond. This diamond was an emblem of Harry Winston, who became the top retailer of diamonds in the world. Ron Winston, Harry's son, designed the recreation of Dorothy's ruby slippers with 7,600 rubies weighing 1,350 carats and a diamond trim of fifty carats. They were displayed in the Harry Winston windows in New York and shown on television in a special, "The Making of *The Wizard of Oz*." The ruby slippers also traveled to a charity event for which Ron Winston dressed up as the Cowardly Lion.

Yearly, at the end of the Academy Awards television presentation, one or all of the Fifth Avenue jewelers—Harry Winston, Cartier, Van Cleef & Arpels, Bulgari, and Tiffany—receives a credit for providing an actress with jewelry. With less fanfare, the ceremonies also showcase the work of young designers—most notably in 1991, Rachelle Epstein's movie star cuffs, which capture the essence of Hollywood—its stars, its bold color, its larger-than-life glamour—in its dramatic design. With a master's degree in painting from Yale, Epstein has adroitly played on contemporary themes throughout her jewelry-designing career, from her first bobby-pin necklace for jewelry retailer Willie Woo, to her Return to Glamour collection for Tiffany, to her own line, Shelle Design, launched in 1990.

The movie star cuffs, on exhibit at Bergdorf Goodman in New York, were snapped up for the Academy Awards by the wife of a production chief whose film had received a nomination. The cuffs are based on the knot-of-Heracles design, and their 18K gold coils center on matching Siberian amethysts of clear, brilliant purple, one encircled by white diamonds and one by canary diamonds. The engravings on each are different: One cuff is for actresses, the other for actors, and their names cover every millimeter of gold.

One of the biggest names in the entertainment industry, Madonna arrived at the same ceremony to sing the Academy Award–nominated song from *Dick Tracy* (1990), "Sooner or Later (I Always Get My Man)," wearing four wide diamond bracelets and a one hundred-carat diamond necklace, all by Winston. In addition, on her finger she wore a ring centering on an emerald-cut pink diamond.

In retrospect, it is much easier to look back at movie stars' choice of jewelry than it is to predict what their tastes will be. The range of possible combinations—stones, materials, designs, and jewelers—is limitless. However, many experts are in accord that colored stones, led by fancy-colored diamonds, are the way of the future. The presence of the pink diamond in the Winston ring and the combination of the Siberian amethyst and canary diamonds of the movie star cuff are proof that Hollywood has already caught on.

After her performance at the Academy Awards ceremony in 1991, Madonna appeared for the reception wearing a diamond necklace, several wide diamond bracelets, and a pink diamond ring, all by Harry Winston.

Acknowledgments

To assemble *Hollywood Jewels,* we received generous assistance from a cast of characters that included jewelers, the Hollywood community, private collectors, curators, librarians, photographers, and special individuals, as well as our photographer, editor, picture editor, designer, and project director.

First and foremost, we would like to express our gratitude to Ralph Esmerian for his unabated enthusiasm for jewelry history. We are grateful to the jewelry industry for making their jewelry and archives available: Steven Schonebarger of Black, Starr & Frost; Alain Boucheron and I. Marmin of Boucheron; Nicola Bulgari, Veronica Bulgari, and Denise Deluca of Bulgari; Ralph Destino and Bonnie Selfe of Cartier, Inc., New York; Eric Nussbaum of Cartier, Inc., Geneva; Andre Chervin of Carvin French, Inc.; Julius Cohen of Julius Cohen Jeweler; Gregory Coster; I. B. Dobry; Paul Flato; John Gershgorn; Paul Henry of Greenleaf & Crosby; Adam C. Heyman of Oscar Heyman & Bros., Inc.; Josie at Place, Inc.; Michael J. Kazanjian of Kazanjian Bros., Inc.; Sol Laykin of Laykin et Cie; Eric Laykin; Fred and Gloria Leighton of Fred Leighton, Ltd.; Michel de Robert of Mauboussin; Alfred Montezinos; Lynn Ramsey of the Diamond Information Center at N. W. Ayer, Inc.; Robert Saling; Nicolas Bongard of Jean Schlumberger; Walter Scheer and Mrs. William Scheer; Patricia Vail of Seaman Schepps; Rachelle Epstein of Shelle Design, Ltd.; Nicholas Silver; Bill Tamis of Louis Tamis & Sons; Peter Schneirla of Tiffany & Co.; John J. Martin of Trabert & Hoeffer, Inc.; John Ullmann; Veronique Ma'Arop of Van Cleef & Arpels, Inc.; E. J. Landrigan of Verdura, Inc.; Robert M. Gibson of Raymond C. Yard, Inc.; Young and Stephens, Ltd.; Douglas Weintraub; Ron Winston and Bridgette Divine of Harry Winston, Inc.; François Curiel, Patrizia Ferenczi, Eric C. Valdieu, Jane Wong, and Diana Kunkel of Christie's and John Block, Jacqueline Fay, and Valerie Vlasaty of Sotheby's were generous with information and jewels from Hollywood estates.

We wish to extend our warmest appreciation to the Hollywood community who shared their jewels and memories: Elizabeth Taylor and her assistant Roger Wall; Joan Bennett and her daughter, Shelley Wanger; Claudette Colbert; Marlene Dietrich, her daughter Maria Riva, her grandson and his wife, Peter and Sandy Riva; Greer Garson Fogelson; Gloria Swanson's granddaughter, Brooke Young; Jane Bovingdon Semel; King Vidor's daughter, Sue Parry.

The contributions of Lily Cates, Miani Johnson, Lilly Millard, Lyn Revson, Holly Solomon, and Jay Spectre have been invaluable to the production of the book.

For assistance with our research, we would like to thank Mary Corliss and Terry Geesken of the Museum of Modern Art Film Stills Archive, Dr. Roderick Bladel at the Billy Rose Theater Collection of the Performing Arts Research Center, and Dr. Robert Kaufmann of the Costume Institute of the Metropolitan Museum of Art.

Special assistance came from individuals who deserve acknowledgment: Lorenz Baumer, Edouard Dermit, Jeffie Pike Durham, George Fasel, Mrs. Coleman Jacobson, Dorinda Healy, Hilda Janssens, Chikara Motomura, Helen O'Hagen, Bahman Maghsoudlou, Elena Shematoff, Trudy Tripolone, Michael Yip, Jim Walrod, and our agent, Nancy Trichter.

Our profound thanks go to photographer David Behl, who gave his time generously. His artistic and technically superb photographs add immeasurably to the visual drama of the book.

We wish to single out Lory Frankel for her clear view of our complex material. Through her editing questions and directives, our narrative of movie and jewelry history came to fruition.

At Abrams, picture editor Susan Sherman was paramount to making our vision of an illustrated book incorporating various types of images a reality. We are grateful to Carol Robson for her sensitivity to the material and striking book design. For keeping us on track when the obstacles seemed insurmountable, we are deeply indebted to Bob Morton, Director of Special Projects.

PENNY PRODDOW
DEBRA HEALY
MARION FASEL

Select Bibliography

The Art of Cartier. Exhibition Catalogue. Musée du Petit Palais, October 20, 1989–January 28, 1990.

Bailey, Margaret J. *Those Glorious Glamour Years.* Secaucus, N.J.: The Citadel Press, 1982.

Ball, Joanne Dubbs. *Jewelry of the Stars, Creations from Joseff of Hollywood.* West Chester, Pa.: Schiffer Publishing, 1991.

Becker, Vivienne. *Art Nouveau Jewelry.* New York: E. P. Dutton, 1985.

Cantor, Eddie. *As I Remember Them.* New York: Duell, Sloan and Pearce, New York, 1963.

————. and David Freedman. *Ziegfeld, The Great Glorifier.* New York: Alfred H. King, 1934.

Charles-Roux, Edmonde. *Chanel and Her World.* New York: The Vendôme Press, 1979.

Cocteau, Jean. *Souvenir Portraits, Paris in the Belle Epoque.* New York: Paragon House, 1990.

Culhane, John. *Walt Disney's Fantasia.* New York: Harry N. Abrams, 1983.

Dali, A Study of His Art-in-Jewels, The Collection of Owen Cheatham Foundation. Livingston, Lida, ed. Greenwich, Ct.: New York Graphic Society, 1959.

De Gary, Marie Noel. *Les Fouquets, Bijoutiers et Joailliers a Paris, 1860–1960.* Paris: Musée des Arts Decoratifs, 1983.

Erté. *Things I Remember.* New York: Quadrangle/New York Times Books, 1975.

Flanner, Janet. *Paris Was Yesterday, 1925–1939.* New York: Harcourt Brace Jovanovich, 1988.

Franklin, Joe. *Classics of the Silent Screen.* Secaucus, N. J.: The Citadel Press, 1959.

Gabler, Neal. *An Empire of Their Own: How the Jews Invented Hollywood.* New York: Crown, 1988.

Gardner, Ava. *Ava, My Story.* New York: Bantam, 1990.

Grundberg, Andy. *Brodovitch.* New York: Harry N. Abrams, 1989.

Hall, Carolyn. *The Forties in Vogue.* New York: Harmony, 1985.

Halliwell, Leslie. *Halliwell's Film Guide.* 5th ed. New York: Charles Scribner's Sons, 1987.

Hopkins-Joyce, Peggy. *Men, Marriage and Me.* New York: Macauley, 1930.

Hurlbut, Cornelius S., and George S. Switzer. *Gemology.* New York: John Wiley & Sons, 1979.

Katz, Ephraim. *The Film Encyclopedia.* New York: Harper & Row, 1979.

Kobal, John. *The Art of the Great Hollywood Portrait Photographers, 1925–1940.* New York: Harrison House, 1987.

La Vine, W. Robert. *In a Glamorous Fashion, The Fabulous Years of Hollywood Costume Design.* New York: Charles Scribner's Sons, 1980.

Le Grand Negoce. Organe du Commerce de Luxe Français. *L'Exposition des Arts Décoratifs 1925.* Catalogue. Paris: 1926.

Marchesseau, Daniel. *The Intimate World of Alexander Calder.* Paris: Solange Thierry, Éditeur, 1989.

Mast, Gerald. *A Short History of the Movies.* 4th ed. New York: Macmillan, 1986.

The Master Jewelers. Snowman, A. Kenneth, ed. New York: Harry N. Abrams, 1990.

Morell, Parker. *Lillian Russell, The Era of Plush.* New York: Random House, 1940.

Muller, Priscilla E. *Jewels in Spain, 1500–1800.* New York: Hispanic Society of America, 1972.

Nadelhoffer, Hans. *Cartier, Jewelers Extraordinary.* New York: Harry N. Abrams, 1984.

Neret, Gilles. *Boucheron, Four Generations of a World-Renowned Jeweler.* New York: Rizzoli, 1988.

Proddow, Penny, and Debra Healy. *American Jewelry, Glamour and Tradition.* New York: Rizzoli, 1987.

Professional Secrets, An Autobiography of Jean Cocteau. Phelps, Robert, ed. New York: Farrar, Straus & Giroux, 1970.

Purtell, Joseph. *The Tiffany Touch.* New York: Random House, 1971.

Raulet, Sylvie. *Art Deco Jewelry.* New York: Rizzoli, 1985.

————. *Van Cleef & Arpels.* New York: Rizzoli, 1987.

Rhode, Eric. *A History of the Cinema from its Origins to 1970.* New York: Da Capo Press, 1985.

Robyns, Gwen. *Princess Grace.* New York: David McKay, 1976.

Sheppard, Dick. *Elizabeth.* New York: Doubleday, 1974.

Skinner, Cornelia Otis. *Madame Sarah.* Boston: Houghton Mifflin, 1967.

Spencer, Charles. *Erté.* London: Studio Vista, 1970.

Thomas, Bob. *Clown Prince of Hollywood: The Antic Life and Times of Jack L. Warner.* New York: McGraw-Hill, 1990.

Truffaut, François. *Hitchcock.* New York: Simon & Schuster, 1985.

Vermilye, Jerry. *The Films of the Twenties.* Secaucus, N.J.: The Citadel Press, 1955.

Vever, Henri. *Histoire de la Bijouterie Française au XIX Siècle.* Paris: Imprimerie Georges Petit, 1908.

Walker, Alexander. *Elizabeth, The Life of Elizabeth Taylor.* New York: Grove Weidenfeld, 1990.

West, Mae. *Goodness Had Nothing to Do with It.* Englewood Cliffs, N.J.: Prentice-Hall, 1959.

White, Palmer. *Elsa Schiaparelli.* New York: Rizzoli, 1986.

Wiley, Mason, and Damien Bona. *Inside Oscar.* New York: Ballantine, 1986.

Index

Page numbers in *italics* indicate illustrations and text in captions

A

abstract design 150; *116*
Academy Awards, for jewelers and designers 190
acting, method 171
Adrian (designer) 7, 27, 51, 72, 75, 81, 105, 121, 124
Affairs of Anatol, The (1921) 20, 23
Affairs of Cellini, The (1934) 73
Aga Khan 138
Aherne, Brian 75; *77*
aigrette *22, 25*
Albee, Edward 178
Alexandre (hairdresser) 178
Alfano, Joseph 118, 121
Algiers (1938) 131
All That Jazz (1979) *187*
Aly Khan 138
American Foundation for AIDS Research (AmFAR) 183
American jewelers 50–57, 81, 83; *49*
American popular culture 124
Ames, Leon 155; *155*
Anastasia (1956) 143
Anderson, Mary 139
Andrews, Julie 185
Angel, Heather 140
Anhalt, Prince Frederick von 162
Anything Goes (1936) 120
Arden, Elizabeth 112–13
Arden, Eve 131
Arnold, Edward 72, 124; *71*
Around the World in Eighty Days (1956) 174
Arpels, Louis 96; *145*
Art Deco 33, 49, 185, 186, 187; *30, 41, 45, 47, 55, 58;* jewelry 33–39, 45–46; *44*
Art Nouveau 9–11, 98; *6, 11, 18*
ashtray, Stork Club *156*
Astaire, Fred 135, 168
Astor, Vincent 118
Aucoc (jeweler) 10
Auntie Mame (1958) 155
Avedon, Richard 169
Ayres, Lew *111*

B

Bacall, Lauren *119*
Back Street (1961) 167
Bad and the Beautiful, The (1952) 151, 158; *163*
Baker, Phil 125–26; *132*
Balenciaga 167
Ball, Lucille 159
Ball of Fire (1942) 154
bangle 96; crystal 158; *160*
Bankhead, Tallulah 78, 139–41; *140;* jewelry 141
Banky, Vilma 26, 27
Bara, Theda 16; *18;* jewelry 16
Barker, Lex 159
Barnes, Binnie *71*
Barrymore, John 31, 45, 54
Barrymore, Lionel 63, 71, 73
bead: bracelet *40;* necklace *51*
Beardsley, Aubrey *25*
Bendix, William 140
Bennett, Constance 73, 106–108
Bennett, Joan 87–90, 171; jewelry 98; *93, 109*
Benny, Jack 63, 123
Bergdorf Goodman 190
Bergman, Ingrid 125, 142–43; *142;* jewelry 143; *142*
Berkeley, Busby 63, 129, 130; *114, 132*
Berlin, Irving 66
Bernhardt, Sarah 7–11; *7, 8;* jewels 9–11; *6, 10*

Bibby, Bruce 172
Biograph 11–12
Black, Maurice 61
Black, Starr & Frost 39, 43, 69; *33;* jewelry by 75; *46, 47, 48, 75*
Blackmer, Sidney 61
block booking 151–52
Blond Venus (1932) 99
Blood and Sand (1922) 25; *27*
Blood and Sand (1941) 135; *135*
Blue Angel, The (1930) 83
Bogart, Humphrey 125
Bolger, Ray 123
Bombshell (1933) 60
Bongard, Nicolas 176–77
Born Yesterday (1950) *160*
Boswell, James A. *133*
Boucheron, jewelry by *115*
Bow, Clara 39, 82
bow, diamond *17*
box: gold *141;* Verdura 118–20
Boyer, Charles 75, 131; *76*
bracelet 88; bead *40;* charm 165; *114, 169;* geometrical *41;* line 144; *49;* love 187; Retro *122;* ruby *145;* slave 25; wide 33–35, 49, 134, 144; *38, 51, 94*
Brady, Diamond Jim 62, 68–71; jewelry 68–69; *70*
Breakfast at Tiffany's (1961) 170, 185
Brent, George 92
Brice, Fanny 185; *61, 103*
Bride Wore Black, The (La Mariée Était en Noir) (1967) 150; *150*
Bringing Up Baby (1938) 99
Brisson, Frederick 155
Brock, jewelry by *65*
brooch 152; *30, 88;* circular *163;* clip *42, 184;* dancing flower *136;* Dancing Hippopotamus 187–90; *188;* dolphin 176–77; emerald and diamond 177; *177;* feather *156;* flag *127;* flower-basket 35–39, 49; *38, 43, 44, 45;* gardenia *152;* lily *112;* patriotic *126, 127;* poodle *169;* rooster *133;* shell clip *140;* triple-monkey *116;* whimsical 165
Brown, Clarence 26
Brown, Les 165
Bulgari 49, 87, 187, 190
Bulldog Drummond (1929) 87
Burke, Billie 106
Burr, Raymond 146
Burton, Richard 172, 175–82; *173, 177*
Bushell, Anthony 46
Butterfield 8 (1960) 175, 183

C

Caan, James 186
Cabaret (1972) 186
cabochon gems 39, 83, 87, 185; *42*
Cagney, James 60
Calder, Alexander 150; *150*
Caldwell, J. E., jewelry by *127*
Calhern, Louis 143; *142*
Callas, Maria 177
Call Her Savage (1932) 39
Camille (1921) 25
Camille (1936) 72–75; *73*
Cantor, Eddie 20, 62, 63
Capote, Truman 170
Capra, Frank 83
Cardinale, Claudia 177
Carnegie Hall (1947) 98
Carroll, Madeleine 87
Cartier, Jacques 14; *13*
Cartier Company 13–15, 33, 47, 49, 91–92, 112, 158, 180, 190; *33;* jewelry by 138, 139–41, 144, 179, 180, 182, 185, 186, 187; *58, 66, 93, 140, 144, 180, 184, 185;* watches *28, 29*
Cartier-Paris, jewelry by *54, 58, 122, 160*

Casablanca (1942) 125; *125*
Case, Anna 13
Castellani (jeweler) 78
Castle, Irene 106
Cat on a Hot Tin Roof (1958) 174, 183; *175*
Cavalieri, Lina 7; *17;* jewelry 13, 15
censorship 20
chain, emerald-and-diamond *50*
Chanel, Coco 117–18; *117*
Chaplin, Charlie 12, 86–87; *101, 103*
charm bracelet 165; *169;* gold-digger *114*
charms *104*
Chekhov, Michael 142
Chevalier, Maurice 92
Chiles, Lois 186; *184*
choker *36, 47, 67, 135;* Indian-style *163;* pearl 155
Christie's 134
cigarette case *119, 141*
cigarette lighters and holders *58*
Cinerama 173
Cipullo, Aldo 187
Claflin, Donald 168
Clarke, Mae 60
Cleopatra (1917) *18*
Cleopatra (1963) 175–77
Clift, Montgomery 171, 172, 173, 175
clip: diamond *183;* shell *119*
clothes, women's, for business 166–67
Coconuts, The (1929) 31
Cohen, Julius 165, 172, 187–90; jewelry by 165, *188*
Cohn, Harry 137–38
Colbert, Claudette 81; *83, 84, 126*
Colette 170
Collier, Constance 92; *103*
Colman, Ronald 87
color in jewelry 162–65, 190
color movies 63, 151, 159, 185
Columbia Pictures 138
comb, jewelled 63
comedies: jewelry 159–62; screwball 99–121
compacts *54*
Conquest (1937) 75; *75, 76*
Cooper, Gary 83; *39*
Cooper, Mrs. Gary *118*
Copacabana (1947) 129
Cosmopolitan Films 63
Costello, Dolores 45–46; *30*
costume designers 7
costume jewelry 117–18
Cotten, Joseph 139
Country Girl, The (1954) 149
Cover Girl (1944) 135
Crane, Cheryl 159
Crane, Stephen 159
Crawford, Joan 32, 49–51, 54, 63, 90, 123, 165; *53, 108, 128, 129, 168;* jewelry 49, 94, 95, 156, 169
Crews, Laura Hope 73
Cronyn, Hume 140
Crosby, Bing 149
Crosby, Bob 165
crystal 84; bangle 158; *160;* ring 84
cuff links *105*
cuffs: double-apple *115;* forearm 11; *6;* gold movie star 190; *189;* silver *187*
Cukor, George 105, 121
Cullinan diamond *64*
Curiel, François 134
Cyrano de Bergerac (1950) *160*

D

Dali, Salvador 142, 176; *141*
Damita, Lily 38
Dancing Cansinos 135
dancing flower, brooch *136*

Dancing Hippopotamus, brooch 187–90; *188*
Daniels, Bebe 26, 62; *27*
Davies, Marion 62, 63
Davis, Bette 65, 75–78, 123; *77, 79*
Day, Doris 159, 165–67; *164, 167;* jewelry 167
Dean, James 171, 172
"Dearest" dance 62
de Gunzburg, Niki 118, 120
de la Falaise, Marquis 108
de Laurentiis, Dino 187
Del Rio, Dolores *90*
de Marco, Tony *132*
De Mille, Cecil B. 19–23, 154, 157; jewelry *29*
Dern, Bruce 186
Desire (1936) 83; *90*
diadem, diamond *22*
Diamond Jim (1935) *71*
Diamond Lil (play) 72
diamonds 152, 159–62, 185; baguette-cut *67;* colored 190; jewelry 153; mines *17;* yellow 182
Diamonds and Pearls (1918) 16
Dick Tracy (1990) 190
Dietrich, Marlene 81, 83, 99, 123, 143–44; *144, 145;* jewelry 144; *88, 89, 90, 145*
Dinner at Eight (1934) 60
Dior, Christian 144, 167; *144*
discos 186
Disney, Walt 124, 187; *136, 137, 188*
Divorcee, The (1930) 31
Dr. Faustus (1968) 178
Don Juan (1926) 31
Don't Change Your Husband (1919) 20
Dotta, Luca 170
Double Indemnity (1944) 154
Double Whoopee (1928) 60
Douglas, Kirk 158; *163*
Douglas, Melvyn 105; *113*
Dovima 169
dress, pearl *25*
Dresser, Louise 26
Dressler, Marie 63, 108
Duff Gordon, Lady, costumes 62
Duke, Doris 108
Durante, Jimmy *114*
Dyer, Nina 138

E

Eagle, The (1925) 26–27
earrings 96; diamond and pearl *170;* drop *163;* floret *156;* girandole *18;* pearl button 144
Ecstasy (1933) 130
Edison, Thomas 7, 11
Edison Trust 11
Edward VII 14
Elizabeth, Princess 174
emeralds 46; *66*
Emery, John *108*
enamel 10
epics 175
Epstein, Rachelle 190; *189*
Erté (Romain de Tirtoff) 63; costumes 62; jewelry design 63
Esmerian, Raphael 91
Eternal Temptress, The (1917) 15; *17*
European jewelry industry, refugees 123–24
Evans, Bob 187
Evans, Ray 157
Expensive Women (1931) 45–47; *30*
Exposition des Arts Decoratifs (1925) *33; 35*
extravaganzas 151, 159
Eyes of a Mummy, The (1918) 16

F

Fairbanks, Douglas 12; *14*
Fairbanks, Douglas, Jr. 49, 51, *90*
Famous Players Film Company 11, 12
Famous Players-Lasky Studios 19–23, 139
fan magazines 12–13, *15*
Fantasia (1940) 124, 187, *136, 188*
Farrow, Mia 186; *185*
fashion, movies and 81
fashion magazines 169–70
Father of the Bride (1950) 171, 172
Father's Little Dividend (1951) 171
Father Takes a Wife (1941) 112; *120*
Fay, Frank 154
Faye, Alice 72, 98, 123, 125–29; *71, 132*
Ferrer, Jose *160*
Ferrer, Mel 170
15 Maiden Lane (1936) 52, 56; *56*
fifties jewelry 165–70
Fighting Caravans (1931) *39*
Fine Manners (1926) 20; *21*
First National 12
Fisher, Eddie 170, 175
Flame of Gold necklace 165; *166*
Flanner, Janet 81
Flash and Roll necklace-bracelet *165*
Flato, Paul 83, 92–96, 108–13, 118; *102, 106*; jewelry by 92–99, 135; *89, 90, 91, 98, 104, 107, 108, 109, 110, 111, 112, 113, 114, 115, 116, 117, 133, 135*
Flynn, Errol 75; *39, 79*
Folies Bergères 62–63
Folies-Bergères (1935) 92
Fool There Was, A (1915) 16
Forbes, Malcolm 182
Forbidden Fruit (1921) 20
Forbidden Paradise (1924) 16; *18*
Ford, Glenn 137
Forrestal, Josephine 98; *98*
Fortensky, Larry 182
For the First Time (1959) 161–62; *163*
For Whom the Bell Tolls (1943) 143
Fosse, Bob 186; *187*
Fouquet, Georges 10–11, 33; *7, 18*; jewelry by *6*
Four Horsemen of the Apocalypse, The (1921) 25, 26
Fox, William 16
Fox Studios 16, 135
Francis, Kay 47–49, 52, 53, 187; *50, 51, 52, 102*
Fredricks, John 87
Frisch, Edmond E. 96
Frohmen, Daniel 9
Funny Face (1957) 151, 168–70
Funny Girl (1968) 185, 186
Funny Lady (1975) 185, 186

G

Gable, Clark 49, 51, 79, 123, 124; *53, 78*
Gabor, Zsa Zsa 161–62; *163*; jewelry 162
Gang's All Here, The (1943) 125–29; *132, 133*
gangster movies 58–61
Garbo, Greta 54–56, 65, 72–75, 105–106; *73, 76, 117*
Garden, Mary 13
Gardiner, Reginald *103*
Gardner, Ava 138; *137*
Garland, Judy 130, 186
Garson, Greer 165; *65, 166*
Gautier, Marguerite 10, 72
gem-cutting 35, 39, 56–57, 65
Genn, Leo 155
Gentlemen Prefer Blondes (1953) 151, 159–61, 174; *159*
George White Scandals 61
Germany, refugees from 123
Gershgorn, John 152; *154*; jewelry by *95, 154*

Getaway (1972) 187
Ghost Breakers, The (1940) *97*
Giant (1956) 172
Gibbons, Cedric 51, 105; *90*
Gibson, Robert 91
Gilbert, John 63
Gilda (1946) 137; *123, 135*
Gilded Lily, The (1935) 81
Girls About Town (1931) 47; *50, 51*
Givenchy, Hubert 168, 170
Glick, Louis 182
Goddard, Paulette 62, 78; *116, 119, 126*; jewelry 83–87, 174; *96, 97, 100, 101, 104, 116, 119, 126*
gold 123, 167; box *141*; jewelry *123*; settings *137*
Goldwyn, Samuel 63, 92
Gone with the Wind (1939) 78–79, 86; *78, 116*
Goodman, Benny 129
Goodrich, Edna 7, 15–16; *17*
Goodwin, Nat C. 16
Gordon, Kitty 16
Gould, Florence 96
Grable, Betty 129
Grand Duchess Vladimir suite 177
Grand Hotel (1932) 52, 53–56, 134
Granger, Farley 144; *146, 147*
Grant, Cary 68, 99–104, 106, 120, 121, 142, 147, 155; *142, 147*
Great Depression 43–45, 86; jewelry during *58*
Great Dictator, The (1940) 86
Great Gatsby, The (1974) 186; *184, 185*
Great Ziegfeld, The (1936) 63; *60, 61*
Green Mansions (1959) 170
Greenstreet, Sidney 155
Griffith, D. W. 92
Guggenheim, Peggy 150
Gypsy Blood (1918) 16

H

Halston 186–87
Hamlet (1900) 7
Hand of God brooch *109*
Harlow, Jean 60–61; *40, 42, 59*; jewelry 60
Harper's Bazaar 12, 169
Harriman, Averill *60*
Harrison, Rex 175
Hays, Will 20
Hayward, Susan 167
Hayworth, Rita 123, 134–38; *123, 135*
Head, Edith 146
Headley, George 96–98, 112, 113
Hearst, William Randolph 63
Held, Anna 62–63
Helmore, Tom 149
Henie, Sonja, jewelry *54*
Henreid, Paul 125
Hepburn, Audrey 159, 168–70, 185; *170*
Hepburn, Katharine 87, 99–104, 105, 121, 175; *110, 111*
Heyward, Leland 99
High Society (1956) 149; *148*
Hilton, Conrad 162, 171, 172
His Girl Friday (1940) 155
historical films 65–79
Hitchcock, Alfred 139–50, 159
Hitting a New High (1937) 98
Hodiak, John 139
Hoeffer, William Howard 81, 153
Holden, William 156; *160*
Holiday (1938) 99–104; *110, 111*
Holliday, Judy *160*
Hollywood: exposes of 155–59; glamour of 81; and jewelry trends 185–90
Hollywood Canteen 123
Hollywood Canteen (1944) 123
Hollywood Revue, The (1929) 63; *62*
Holm, Celeste 149
Hope, Bob 123
Hope diamond 120
Hopkins, Miriam 52–53; *55, 80*; jewelry 53

Hopkins-Joyce, Peggy 39, 43, 47, 62; *46, 48*
Hopper, Hedda 157, 174, 175; *107*
House of Chanel 117–18, 176
Hoving, Walter 187
Howard, Jean 120; *119*
Howard, Leslie 79
Hubert, René 112
Hudson, Rock 166, 172
Hughes, Howard 99
Hugo, Victor 9
Hull, Henry 139
Hunter, Ian 131
Huntington, Arabella, estate 57
Hutton, Betty 165

I

Ideal Husband, An (1948) 86, 92
Idiot's Delight (1939) 124–25
I Dream Too Much (1935) 98
I. Magnin 112–13
I. Miller & Sons 87
Imitation of Life (1959) 158, 159; *164*
Independent Motion Picture Company of America 11–12
Indian-style jewelry 162, 168; *163*
Intolerance (1916) 92
Iribe, Paul 7, 23, 35; jewelry by *22*
Italy, refugees from 123
It Happened One Night (1934) 83
It's All Yours (1937) 87

J

Jaeckel (furs) 87
Jagger, Bianca 187
Jazz Age 185–86
Jazz Singer, The (1927) 31
jewelers: Academy Awards to 190; American 56–57, 81, 83; *49*; European refugees 123–24; screen credit for 73, 87, 112, 190
Jewel Robbery (1932) 52, 53
jewelry: artistic 9–11, 176–77; colors in 162–65, 190; daytime and evening, rules of 167; depicted as immoral 134; highlighted in movies 16; historical 65–79; in plot themes 78, 139–50; popular styles 152; from royal estates 65; in talking pictures, noisy 31; trends in 185–90
jewel thief movies 52–57, 147–48
Jezebel (1938) 78
jigsaw jewel 81
Jolson, Al 31
Jonker diamond 56, 57, 190; *57*
Joseff, Eugene (Joseff of Hollywood) 73; *79*
Joyce, Stanley 43
Juarez (1939) 75; *77, 78*
Judson, Edward 135
Julia Misbehaves (1948) 171

K

Kaplan, Lazare 57
Keaton, Buster 63, 157
Kelly, Gene 135
Kelly, Grace 146, 147–49, 180, 182; *147, 148*; jewelry 149; *148, 149*
Kennedy, Joseph 20
Kiam, Omar 87
Killers, The (1946) 138
King Kong (1976) 187
Kiss Me, Kate (1953) 120
Kitty (1945) 86
Klety, Adolph 96
kokoshnik 15
Korda, Alexander 86, 91–92
Kostelanetz, Andre 98; *114*
Krawly, Hans 27
Krim, Mathilde 183
Krupp diamond 178, 182–83; *176*

L

La Belle Otero 15
Lacloche Frères 33, 47, 49; *123*; jewelry by *44, 50, 51*
La Dame aux camélias (1911) 8
La Dame aux Camélias 37
Laemmle, Carl 11
Lake, Veronica *126*
Lalique, René 10, 23; *18*; pendant *11*
Lamarr, Hedy *130*; jewelry 130–31
Lancaster, Burt 138; *153*
Landis, Jessie Royce 147
Lang, Fritz 90
Lang, Jennings 90
Lang, June *82*
Lange, Jessica 187; *187*
Lanza, Mario 161; *163*
La Peregrina 179; *180, 181*
La Princesse Lointaine (play) 10; script 10
La Rocque, Rod 19
La Tosca (1908) 7–8
Laurel and Hardy 63
lavalliere 32
Lavalliere, Eve 32
Lawford, Peter 171
Lawrence, Florence 11
Laykin, Sol 108, 112–13
Laykin et Cie 106–16; jewelry by 158, 166, 167; *120, 163, 167*
Lee, Canada 140
Lee, Lila 25
Leigh, Vivien 78–79; *78, 121*
Leighton, Fred 186
Leisen, Mitchell 154
Letson, Neil 134
Le Marie (costumer) 31
Les Must de Cartier 187
Lifeboat (1944) 139–41; *140*
Lillian Russell (1940) 72; *70, 71*
lily brooch 112
Lindstrom, Peter 143
Linzeler, Robert 23
Little Caesar (1931) 61
Little Foxes, The (play) 141
Little Night Music, A (1977) 179; *180*
Little Women (1933) 99
Litvak, Anatole 86
Livingston, Jay 157
Lollobrigida, Gina 177
Lombard, Carole, jewelry *54*
Loos, Anita *107, 110*
Loos, Mary Anita *103*
Loren, Sophia 177
Love, Bessie 63
love bracelet 187
Lowe, Edmund 47
Loy, Myrna 167
Lubitsch, Ernst 16, 52–53
Luce, Claire *34, 35*; jewelry *36*
Lucky Baldwin Ruby 57

M

MacGraw, Ali 187
Machaty, Gustav 130
Machine style 81–83; *84, 85*
Mackay, Ellin *66*
Macready, George 137
Madame Satan (1930) 23
Madonna, jewelry 190; *189, 191*
Magnin, Grover 112–13
Mainbocher (designer) 167
Male and Female (1919) 20, 23; *25*
Mamoulian, Rouben 135
Man Hunt (1941) 90
Mann, J. Byrd 118, 121
Manon Lescaut (1914) 15
Man Who Came to Dinner, The (play) 118
Man Who Knew Too Much, The (1934) 139
Marcus, Stanley 153
Marcus & Co. 90–91
Margaret, Princess 162, 178
Marie Antoinette, Queen 75
Marie Antoinette (1938) 75, 121

Mark Cross 145
Marshall, Herbert 52; *52*
Marx, Mrs. Zeppo *123*
Mary of Scotland (1936) 99
Mary Pickford Company 12
Mauboussin, Pierre-Yves 33, 75; jewelry by *34, 35, 36, 37, 38, 44*
Mayer, Louis B. 105, 138
McAfee, Tom *107*
McCrea, Joel 47
McDowall, Roddy 175
McQueen, Steve 187
Melba, Nellie 13
Menjou, Adolphe 112; *120*
Meredith, Burgess 87, 105; *116*
Merrill, Dina 175
Metro-Goldwyn-Mayer (MGM) 49–51, 63, 138, 171
Midnight Lace (1960) 167
Midnight Sun, The (1925) *62*
Mildred Pierce (1945) 156
minaudière *126*
Minnelli, Liza 186–87; *187*
Minnelli, Vincente 178, 186
Miranda, Carmen 129; *132, 133*
models, professional 169–70
Modern Times (1936) 86
Mogambo (1953) 149
Monroe, Marilyn 159, 185; *159*
Monsieur Beaucaire (1924) 26
Monte Carlo Baby* (1951) 170
Moore, Gene 155
Moore, Grace 98; *64*
Moreau, Jeanne 150; *150*
Morell, Parker (jeweler) 69
Morley, Karen 61; *60*
Motion Picture Producers and Distributors of America 20
Mourning Becomes Electra (1947) 155
movies; adult themes 151–59; color 63, 151, 159, 185; distribution of 151–52; and fashion 81; plot themes, jewelry in 78, 139–50; silent era 157; sound 31–32; wide-screen 159. *See also specific types, e.g., gangster movies; jewel thief movies*
Mucha, Alphonse 11; jewelry by *6*
Mumtaz Mahal 182
Muni, Paul 61, 75; *60*
Muratore, Lucian 15
Murder on the Orient Express (1974) 143
Murray, Mae 62
musicals 61–63
Music Box Theatre 61
My Sister Eileen (1942) 155

N

Naldi, Nita 25; *27*
Napoleon III 14; *74*
National Velvet (1946) 171
naturalistic designs 98–99, 121; *22*
Nazimova, Alla 23–25; *25*
Nazli, Queen, jewelry 67
necklace *101*; bead *51*; cultured-pearl 141; diamond *135*; mixed-gem *164*; Napoleonic *74*; pearl *16, 21, 130*; vine *115*
Negri, Pola 7, 16–19, 29, 32; jewelry *19*
Neiman Marcus 124, 153, 173
Newman, Paul 171; *175*
New York, diamond district (Maiden Lane) *56*
New York, New York (1977) 186
New York Actors Studio 171
Nichols, Mike 178
Night After Night (1932) 65
Night and Day (1946) 120
Night of the Iguana, The (1964) 176; *173*
Night of the Iguana brooch 176–77
Nilsson, Anna Q. 157
Ninotchka (1939) 105
Nolan, Doris 104
Notorious (1946) 142–43; *142*
Novak, Kim 149
Nun's Story, The (1959) 170
Nype, Russell *157*

O

Oberon, Merle 91–92, 105; *74, 91, 93, 113, 116*; jewelry 91–92; *93*
O'Keeffe, Georgia 150
Oklahoma (1955) 173
Olivier, Laurence 92
Onassis, Aristotle 179–80
Onassis, Jacqueline Kennedy 180
one-jewel dressing 134
opera stars, jewelry 12–13
Orange, House of 83
Orry-Kelly (designer) 75–78
Oscar Heyman & Bros. *127*
Ostertag, Arnold, jewelry by *64*
Our Dancing Daughters (1928) 49
Our Modern Maidens (1929) 49
oversized jewelry *160*
Owsley, Monroe 39

P

Painted Woman (1932) *36*
Pallette, Eugene 47
Paramount Pictures 11, 26, 53
Paramount Studios 157
Parfums International 182
Paris Does Strange Things (1956) 143
parure 73; pearl and diamond 149
Pascaud of Paris, costume *61*
Pasteur Institute 183
Pastor, Tony 68
patriotic jewelry *126, 127*
pearls 14–15, 146, 152, 162, 179; choker 155; cultured 141; dress 23; necklaces *21, 130*
Peck, Gregory 142
pendants 152; *11*
Peretti, Elsa 187; jewelry by *187*
perfume 182–83
Perkins, Osgood *60*
Peyton Place (1957) 158
Philadelphia Story, The (1940) 121
Photoplay magazine 12
phrase jewelry *62*
Pickford, Mary 11–12, 20; *14, 15, 82*; jewelry 12, 86; *15, 54, 82*
Pillow Talk (1959) 151, 166–67; *164, 167*
Pin-Up Girl (1944) 129
pinup girls 129–38
Place in the Sun, A (1951) 172
platinum 123, 167
Poiret, Paul 8, 23; *62*
Pollyanna (1920) 12
Pons, Lily 98; jewelry *114, 115*
Porter, Cole 118–20; jewelry *119*
Porter, Linda 118–20
Portrait in Black (1960) 167
Possessed (1931) 49–51; *50*
Postman Always Rings Twice, The (1946) 134
Powell, Dick 158
Powell, William 53, 60, 63
Power, Tyrone 75, 123, 135; *118*
Pride and Prejudice (1940) 65
Prince, Hal 180
Printemps, Yvonne, jewelry *37*
Private Life of Henry VIII, The (1933) 91–92
Private Lives of Elizabeth and Essex, The (1939) 75–78; *79*
Prohibition Era 58
Public Enemy, The (1931) 60; *59*

Q

Queen Elizabeth (1912) 8–9, 11; *8*
Queen Kelly (1928) 20, 157
Queen of Outer Space (1958) 161

R

Rainer, Luise *61*
Rainier III, Prince 148–49; *148, 149*
Rains, Claude 143
Raintree County (1957) 173
Rambova, Natasha 7, 23–26
Ramsden, Dudley 153, 173
Randall, Tony 166
Rat Race, The (play) 176
Raye, Martha *82*
Raymond C. Yard Co. 90–91; jewelry by *94, 95, 129*
Rear Window (1954) 144–46
Redford, Robert 186; *185*
Reflection jewel 85
Remarque, Erich Maria 87
Remember the Night (1940) *154*
Renoir, Jean 143
Reputation (1917) 15–16
Restless Sex, The (1920) 63
Retro style 134, 137; *122*
Revson, Lyn 165
Reynolds, Debbie 175
Rhapsody (1954) 183
Rhodes, June Hamilton 65
Ricarde of Hollywood, jewelry by *78*
ring: citrine and gold *128*; crystal *84*; diamond 138, 149; *137, 148, 189*; engagement 149; *148, 171*; large *129*
Rivera, Diego 87
rivière 137, 152; *135, 156*
Road to Yesterday, The (1925) 23
Robinson, Edward G. 61
Robsjohn-Gibbings, Terance *133*
Rogers, Ginger 87, 98
Rogers, Millicent 98
Roland, Gilbert *69*
Roman, Ruth 144; *147*
Romance on the High Seas (1948) 165
Roman Holiday (1953) 170
Romero, Cesar 56; *102*
Rooney, Mickey 138; *137*
Rossellini, Roberto 143; *142*
Rostand, Edmond 9, 10
Rostand, Maurice 10
royal estates, jewelry from 65
Rubel, John (Jean) 124, 155; *123*; jewelry by 155, 187; *136, 155*
Rubel Frères (Jean and Robert) 124
rubies 190; bracelet *145*; slippers 190; *188*
Ruggles, Charles 52
Ruser, William 153; jewelry by 153, 165; *151, 152, 153, 156, 169*
Russell, Jane 161
Russell, Lillian 68–72; *69*; jewelry 68, 71
Russell, Rosalind 152, 155; *155*

S

Sabrina (1954) 170
Salome (1922) 23; *25*
Sanders, George 102
Sandpiper, The (1965) 178
Sarah Bernhardt at Home (1912) 9
Saratoga (1937) 60
sautoir *15, 50, 51, 184*
Scarface (1932) 61; *60*
Scarlet Street (1945) 90
Scheer, William, jewelry by *32, 33, 40, 51, 126*
Schiaparelli, Elsa 72, 92, 98, 176; *105*
Schlumberger, Jean 165; jewelry by 176–77; *173*
Scorsese, Martin 186
screwball comedy 99–121
Sea Beast, The (1926) 45
Seaman Schepps, jewelry by *133*
Secret Beyond the Door, The (1948) 90
Selznick, David O. 139
Selznick, Louis J. 71–72
settings, jewel 65; *137*
Seylor, Suzanne 11
Shadow of a Doubt (1943) 139

Shadow of Her Past (1916) 15
Shah Jahan 182
Sharaff, Irene 177, 178, 186
Sharif, Omar 186
Shaw, Artie 134, 138, 159
Shearer, Norma 32, 63, 75, 124; *31, 32, 127*
She Done Him Wrong (1933) 68, 72, 99
Sheik, The (1921) 25
Shelle Design 190; *189*
sign-language initials *110*
silver 187
Simpson, Wallace 125
Sinatra, Frank *119*
Sister Kenny (1946) 155
sixties fashions 177
skullcap *22*
Slezak, Walter 140; *140*
slippers, ruby 190; *188*
Smith, Maggie 176
smoking accessories *58, 119*
Snow, Carmel 169
Snow White and the Seven Dwarfs (1937) *137*
Société du Film d'Art 8
Song to Remember, A (1945) 92
Son of the Sheik, The (1926) 27–29; *28*
So Proudly We Hail (1943) *126*
Sorry, Wrong Number (1948) 151, 152–54; *151, 153*
Sothern, Ann *120*
souvenir jewels 77
Spellbound (1945) 141–42
Spy Who Came in from the Cold, The (1965) 178
Stage Door (1937) 87, 92, 99
Stage Fright (1950) 143–44; *144, 145*
Stanwyck, Barbara 62, 123, 152–54; *123, 151, 153, 154*; jewelry *153*
Star! (1968) 185
Star of Bombay *82*
Star of Burma 87; *87*
Star of India *82*
Starr, Ringo 182
star system 7, 12–13, 152; and fashion 81
Steele, Alfred *168*
steel jewelry 187
Steinbeck, John 139
Stella Dallas (1937) 154
Stevens, George 172
Stewart, James 121, 123, 131, 144, 149
Stoddard, Rebecca, estate 57
Stompanato, Johnny 159
Strangers on a Train (1951) 144; *146, 147*
Strasberg, Lee 171
Streets of Paris (musical) *133*
Streisand, Barbra, jewelry 185–86
studio system 12, 151–52, 171
Sturges, Howard *120*
Sturges, Preston 69
Suddenly Last Summer (1959) 175
Sullivan, Barry 158
Sunday's Child theme 165
Sunset Boulevard (1950) 151, 155–58; *160*
Surrealist jewelry 98, 142; *105, 141*
Swanson, Gloria 7, 19–23, 112, 156–58; *21, 24, 120, 157, 160*; jewelry 20, 158, 174

T

Tableau of Jewelry 63; *62*
Taming of the Shrew, The (1967) 178, 179
Tamis, Louis, & Sons *110*
Tashman, Lilyan 47, 62; *45, 51*
tassel *184*
Taylor, Elizabeth 170, 171–83, 187; *171, 177*; jewelry 172–74, 176–83; *173, 176, 179, 180*
Taylor, Robert 72, 154; *123*
Taylor-Burton diamond 179–80; *179*
Technicolor 185
television 151, 154, 159
Temple, Shirley 57, 190; *57*
Temptress, The (1927) 56

Ten Commandments, The (1923) 23
Texas 172–73
Thalberg, Irving *31*
That Girl from Paris (1937) 98
That Night in Rio (1941) 129
That Uncertain Feeling (1941) 105
Theodora (play) 10
Thirty-Nine Steps, The (1935) 139
Thompson, Kay 168
Thoroughly Modern Millie (1967) 185
Thru a Keyhole (1933) 47
tiaras 174
Tiffany & Co. 9, 98, 155, 170, 176, 190; *33;* jewelry by 131, 187; watches *29*
'Til We Meet Again (1940) 92; *91*
To Catch a Thief (1955) 147–48; *147*
Todd, Mike 172, 173–75; *177*
Todd, Richard 143
Todd-AO 173
toe ring 104–105; *111*
Tone, Franchot 95
Topper (1937) 106
Topping, Bob 159
Toussaint, Jeanne 158; *160*
Trabert, R. J. 81
Trabert & Hoeffer 75; jewelry by *75, 76*
Trabert & Hoeffer-Mauboussin 81–83, 87, 153; jewelry by *82, 85, 87, 88, 89, 90, 96, 97, 100, 101,* 141
Tracy, Spencer 99, 171
Trade Winds (1939) *109*
Trevor, Claire 56, 155
Tritt, Olga *80*
Trouble in Paradise (1932) 52–53; *52*
Truffaut, François 150; *150*
Trujillo, Rafael 162
Turner, Lana 78, 131–34, 158–59, 167; *123, 131, 163, 164;* jewelry 158–59
turquoise 162–65; *164*
twenties revivals 185–86
Twentieth Century-Fox 16, 123, 135
Two-Faced Woman (1941) 105–106; *117*

U

Ulric, Lenore *73*
United Artists Corporation 12, 26
United Service Organization (USO) 123

V

Valentino, Rudolph 19, 25–29; *27, 28*
Van Cleef & Arpels 33, 87, 96, 124, 162, 165, 190; *33;* jewelry by 125, 138, 149, 174, 179; *126, 137, 149*
vanities *21, 37, 55*
Vanity Fair (1919) *61*
Vanity Fair (magazine) 12
vaudeville 61–62
Velvet Touch, The (1948) 151, 155; *155*
Verdura, Duke of (Fulco) 98, 112, 117–21, 176; *102, 107, 108, 117;* jewelry by 121, 141; *118, 119, 121, 140, 141*
Vertigo (1958) 149–50
Victor, Sally 87
V.I.P.s, The (1963) 176
Vitaphone 31
Vogues of 1938, The (1937) 87; *87*
von Sternberg, Joseph 83
von Stroheim, Eric 20, 157; *160*
Vreeland, Diana 176

W

Wait Until Dark (1967) 170
Wales Plumes 183
Walker, Allen Breed 108
Walker, Robert 144; *146*
Wanger, Shelley 165
Wanger, Walter 87
Warhol, Andy 175, 186
Warner, H. B. 157
Warner, John 182
Warner, Mrs. Jack *141*
Warner Brothers 31
watches 25, 29; *28, 29, 122*
Waterston, Sam 186
Webb, David 165, 167–68
Weekend at the Waldorf (1945) 134
Week-End in Havana (1941) 129
Weidler, Virginia 121
Welles, Orson 137, 176
West, Mae 65–68, 72, 99, 108, 123; *69, 98;* jewelry 72; *124*
Westerns (cowboy movies) 58
Whalen, Michael *82*
White, George 61
White Peacock *61*
Whitney, Barbara 98
Whitney, Jock *116*
Whoopee! (1930) 63
Who's Afraid of Virginia Woolf? (1966) 178; *177*
Why Change Your Wife? (1920) 20
wiggly jewelry 98
Wilder, Billy 155
Wildfire 71–72
Wilding, Michael 172; *145, 171*
William, Warren 46; *30*
Williams, Tennessee 174
Wilson, Natasha (Mrs. John C.) 120
Windsor, Duchess of 167, 183
Windsor, Duke of 125
Winston, Harry 56–57, 172, 178, 190; *188;* jewelry by 143, 162, 179, 182, 190; *142, 191*
Winston, Ron 190; *188*
Winters, Shelley 187
Wizard of Oz, The (1939) 190; *188*
Woman in the Window, The (1944) 90
Woman of Affairs, A (1928) 56
Woman of the Year (1942) 105
Woo, Willie 190
Woods, Edward 60
working girl themes 43
World Film Corporation 72
World War II, jewelry in 123–24
World War II movies 123–38
Wright, Teresa 139
Wuthering Heights (1939) 92
Wyler, William 170
Wyman, Jane 123

Y

Yard, Raymond C. 90–91. *See also* Raymond C. Yard Co.
You'll Never Get Rich (1941) 135
Young, Loretta 159, 165; *112*
Young, Roland 106
Young Rajah, The (1922) 26; *27*
You Were Never Lovelier (1942) 135

Z

Zanuck, Virginia 112–13, 116
Zeffirelli, Franco 178
Ziegfeld, Florenz 61–63
Ziegfeld Follies 61–62, 185
Ziegfeld Follies (1946) *60*
Ziegfeld Girl (1941) 130, 131–34; *123, 131*
Zukor, Adolph 11, 12, 16, 23, 26

Illustration Credits

PHOTOGRAPHS AND ILLUSTRATIONS

The authors and publisher wish to thank the private collectors, jewelers, and auction houses named below or in the captions, for permitting reproduction of jewelry in their collections. We also thank the photographers, institutions, and film studios who provided us with material or gave us permission to print.

NYPL = General Research Division
The New York Public Library
Astor, Lenox and Tilden Foundations

BRTC = Billy Rose Theatre Collection
The New York Public Library for the Performing Arts
Astor, Lenox and Tilden Foundations

Abbe: 61 bottom right; Academy of Motion Picture Arts and Sciences: 131; AP/Wide World Photos: 177 left; David Behl: 6 (Courtesy Christie's, Geneva), 10, 11, 19 top right, 29, 37 left, 41, 42, 43 (Courtesy Turner Entertainment Co. All Rights Reserved), 44, 49, 50, 54 and 55 left (Courtesy Laykin et Cie at I. Magnin, Estate Collection and Private colls.), 58, 66, 67, 96 (Courtesy Sotheby's, New York), 101 bottom, 104 right, 105, 106 bottom (Courtesy Josie at Place, Inc.), 109 right (Courtesy Joan Bennett), 110 bottom right (Courtesy Verdura/Louis Tamis & Sons), 105, 122, 126 top (Courtesy Oscar Heyman & Bros., Inc.), 127 right, 129, 133 right (Courtesy Holly Solomon), 137 right, 141 left, 145 top left and right (Courtesy Sotheby's, New York), 150, 152, 156, 164, 165 (Courtesy Lyn Revson), 173 left (Courtesy Estate of Jean Schlumberger), 173 right, 176 (Courtesy Elizabeth Taylor), 180 right (BRTC), 181 (Courtesy Elizabeth Taylor), 184 (Courtesy Paramount Pictures/BRTC), 187 bottom (Courtesy Sandy Brandt, publisher. Artist, Richard Bernstein after photographs by Barry McKinley), 188 right (Courtesy Julius Cohen Jeweler), 189 top (Courtesy Jane Bovington Semel), 189 bottom; Black, Starr & Frost/NYPL: 47, 75 bottom; Gianni Bozzach/Forum (Courtesy Harry Winston Inc.): 179; Clarence Sinclair Bull/The Kobal Collection: 89; Anton Bruehl: 201 bottom (Courtesy *Vogue*. Copyright © 1940 (renewed 1961, 1964, 1968) by The Conde Nast Publications, Inc./NYPL); Cartier Inc.: 13; Christie's, Geneva: 6, 160 left center; Christie's, New York: 15 bottom, 36, 74, 93 bottom, 115 bottom left, 119 left, 141 right, 142 right, 160 center left; André Chervin: 115 top right; Julius Cohen Jeweler: 166 right; Louise Dahl-Wolfe: 65, 97 top and center (© 1940 Hearst Corporation. Courtesy *Harper's Bazaar*/NYPL); Paul Flato: 102 top and bottom right, 103 top and bottom left, 106, 107 left and bottom right, 112 left (NYPL), 115 top left, 111 bottom (NYPL); Courtesy Mrs. Greer Garson Fogelson: 166 left; Peter Freed/NYT Pictures: 25; Victor Georg: 17 right (Courtesy *Vanity Fair*. Copyright © 1918 (renewed 1942, 1946, 1949, 1959) by The Conde Nast Publications, Inc./NYPL); Courtesy John Gershgorn: 154; Sam Goldstein/BRTC: 100 bottom left; Horst: 80 (Courtesy *Vogue*. Copyright © 1936 (renewed 1961, 1964, 1968) by The Conde Nast Publications, Inc./NYPL), 119 top right (Courtesy *Vogue*. Copyright © 1941 (renewed 1969) by The Conde Nast Publications, Inc./NYPL); Hoyningen-Huene: 38 bottom (Courtesy *Vanity Fair*. Copyright © 1931 (renewed 1942, 1946, 1949, 1959) by The Conde Nast Publications, Inc./NYPL), 121 and 128 (© 1940 Hearst Corporation. Courtesy *Harper's Bazaar*/NYPL); International News Photos/BRTC: 168;

The Jewelers' Circular © Chilton Company/NYPL: 70 center and bottom; Laykin et Cie/NYPL: 120 left; © Lipnitzki-Viollet (Courtesy Verdura): 117; Frank Mastro/International News: 171; MoMA/Film Stills Archive: 7, 8, 14, 15 top, 17 left (Paramount Pictures), 18, 19 left and bottom right, 21 center (Paramount Pictures), 24, 27 bottom right, 30, 31, 32 right, 34, 35 right, 39 (Paramount Pictures), 40 top, 43, 46, 51 left, 52, 53 left, 55 right, 59, 60, 61 left, 62 right, 64, 69 left and right, 71, 73, 76, 77, 78 right, 79, 82 left and top right, 83 (© 1936 by Paramount Pictures Corporation. All Rights Reserved), 84 top, 90 top and center, 91, 93 top, 94 right, 95 top, 107 top right, 109 left (Courtesy Turner Entertainment Co. All Rights Reserved), 110 top right, 111 top, 113, 114 top right, 116 left, 117 left, 120 right, 123, 124, 125, 126 left, 127 left, 130, 132, 133 top left, 135 top, 137 left, 140 right, 142 right, 144, 145 bottom left, 146, 147 (Paramount Pictures), 148, 151 (Paramount Pictures), 153 left (Paramount Pictures), 153 right, 157, 155, 160 top and bottom right (Paramount Pictures), 163, 167, 170 (© 1953 by Paramount Pictures Corporation. All Rights Reserved), Mauboussin/*Vanity Fair*/NYPL: 38 top left and right; Movie Star News: 177 right; Munkacsi, copyright the Estate of Martin Munkacsi/NYPL: 104 left; Photofest, New York: 159; *Photoplay* (The MacFadden Group, Inc.)/NYPL: 62 left; Philip Pocock: 20 bottom left, 22 top left and right, 23, 27 left (BRTC), 27 top and bottom right (BRTC/Paramount Pictures), 32 left and 33 (Courtesy William Scheer, Inc. Archives), 35 left and 37 right (Courtesy Mauboussin), 40 bottom and 51 right (Courtesy William Scheer, Inc. Archives), 61 top right (NYPL/Courtesy *Vanity Fair*. Copyright © 1919 (renewed 1942, 1946, 1949, 1959) by The Conde Nast Publications, Inc.) 63, 75 top, *The Jewelers' Circular*, courtesy Trabert & Hoeffer-Mauboussin, 78 left BRTC, 90 bottom, 94 left and 95 bottom (Courtesy Raymond C. Yard), 97 right (Fawcett Publications/BRTC), 100 and 101 top © 1940 by Paramount Pictures Corporation. All Rights Reserved/BRTC, 114 left and bottom right (Courtesy Louis Tamis & Sons), 115 bottom right (Courtesy André Chervin), 116 right (BRTC), 118 (Courtesy Verdura), 126 top (Courtesy Liggett Group Inc.), 126 bottom center and right (Courtesy William Scheer, Inc. Archives), 136 left, top and middle right, (Courtesy John Rubel Co. Archives), 140 left International News Photo/BRTC, 180 left (Courtesy Cartier, Inc.); Sotheby's, New York: 88, 137 center; Edward Steichen, Reprinted with the permission of Joanna T. Steichen (Courtesy *Vanity Fair*/NYPL): 48; Trabert & Hoeffer, Inc.: 82 bottom left, 85 bottom (NYPL); Trabert & Hoeffer-Mauboussin/NYPL: 87; Pierre-Gilles Vidoli: 191; Verdura/NYPL: 119 bottom right; Van Cleef & Arpels: 149; Courtesy *Vogue*. Copyright © 1933 (renewed 1961, 1964, 1968) by The Conde Nast Publications, Inc./NYPL: 69 center; Harry Winston Inc.: 57, 188 left.

FILM COPYRIGHTS

8: *Queen Elizabeth* © 1912 by Famous Players-Lasky Corporation; 17 center: *Fine Manners* Copyright © 1926 by Famous Players-Lasky Corporation © 1953 by Paramount Pictures Corporation. All Rights Reserved; 24: *Male and Female* © 1919 by Famous Players-Lasky Corporation; 27 top right: *Blood and Sand* Copyright © 1922 by Famous Players-Lasky Corporation; 28: *The Son of the Sheik* © 1969 Killiam Shows, Inc.; 39: *Call Her Savage* © 1932 Paramount Pictures, Inc. Renewed Twentieth Century Fox Film Corporation. All rights reserved; 30: *Expensive Women* © 1931 Turner Entertainment Co. All Rights Reserved; 51 left: *Girls About Town* Copyright © by Universal Pictures, a Division of Universal City Studios, Inc. Courtesy of MCA Publish-

LYRIC COPYRIGHT